D0722815

Aspects of Consciousness

Aspects of Consciousness
Volume 2
Structural Issues

Edited by
Geoffrey Underwood and Robin Stevens

Department of Psychology
University of Nottingham
England

1981

ACADEMIC PRESS

A Subsidiary of Harcourt Brace Jovanovich, Publishers
London   New York   Toronto   Sydney   San Francisco

ACADEMIC PRESS INC. (LONDON) LTD.
24/28 Oval Road,
London NW1

United States Edition published by
ACADEMIC PRESS INC.
111 Fifth Avenue
New York, New York 10003

British Library Cataloguing in Publication Data

Aspects of consciousness.
Vol. 2: Structural issues
1. Consciousness
I. Underwood, G.   II. Stevens, R.
153   BF311
ISBN 0-12-708802-4

LCCCN 79-41233

Typeset by Oxford Publishing Services, Oxford
Printed in Great Britain by
John Wright & Sons, Ltd., at the Stonebridge Press, Bristol

Contributors

J. Graham Beaumont, *Department of Psychology, University of Leicester, Leicester LE1 7RH, England*

M. P. Bryden, *Department of Psychology, University of Waterloo, Waterloo, Ontario N2L 8G1, Canada*

Gordon Claridge, *Magdalen College, Oxford OX1 4AU, England*

James Crossland, *Department of Pharmacy, University of Nottingham, Nottingham NG7 2RD, England*

Christoper D. Frith, CRC *Division of Psychiatry, MRC Clinical Research Centre, Harrow, Middlesex HA1 3UJ, England*

Robert G. Ley, *Department of Psychology, University of Waterloo, Waterloo, Ontario N2L 3GI, Canada*

Andrew Mayes, *Department of Psychology, University of Manchester, Manchester M13 9PL, England*

Keith Oatley, *Laboratory of Experimental Psychology, University of Sussex, Brighton BN1 9QG, England*

Graham G. Shaw,[1] *Department of Pharmacy, University of Nottingham, Nottingham NG 7 2RD, England*

Robin Stevens, *Department of Psychology, University of Nottingham, Nottingham NG7 2RD, England*

[1]*Present address: Department of Pharmacology, School of Pharmacy, Trinity College, University of Dublin, 18 Shrewsbury Road, Dublin 4.*

Preface

A complete understanding of consciousness is clearly not yet within our grasp, but the pursuit of a satisfactory description of consciousness and the mechanisms supporting it are surely some of the most fascinating enterprises in contemporary science. One of the reasons why consciousness is of such interest is that its investigation makes demands on both the natural sciences and psychology, and moreover it raises many of the same philosophical questions as does the mind–brain problem since consciousness, like mind, is non physical yet the product of a physical system. What is clear at present is that no single discipline is adequate in studying the question of consciousness in its entirety, something which is evident in the selection of topics discussed in this volume.

Why should we regard the question of consciousness as being of such importance? The critic might argue that we can only know of consciousness by introspection and by assuming that it is common to all members of our species we are committing the error of taking a man-centred approach to the study of the life sciences. In rejoinder we might suggest that consciousness need not be unique to human beings since physiological correlates of the differing states of consciousness in ourselves, i.e. wakefulness, quiet sleep and dream sleep, are apparent in other mammals for instance. Moreover, aspects of our own consciousness such as remembering, attending, thinking (problem solving) and feeling are surely psychological functions that we have in common with other animals with highly developed nervous systems. Despite the importance of these issues they fail to answer why the study of consciousness is so important; although consciousness may simply be an epiphenomenon resulting from the functioning of a physico-chemical mechanism, the brain, in our opinion it has evolved as a psychological "tool" which furthers our survival. We may be mistaken in assuming this (and if this is so then most of the contributions in this volume are in serious error), but it is difficult to conceive why a complex biological system such as man should have a metaphysical characteristic such as consciousness without it having a purpose. Consciousness is not just the sum of the psychological processes contributing to it, but it guides and controls these processes. Thus consciousness has a similar relationship to psychological processes as do perceptual hypotheses in models of perception of the type proposed by Helmholtz and Gregory.

According to this view, consciousness has been honed by the forces of natural selection so that the advantages of possessing it are optimized. Although at present this, like other aspects of the theory of natural selection, is untestable, there is nothing to prevent us from using the tools of the natural sciences and especially biology to investigate consciousness.

This volume is devoted to discussions of consciousness from the standpoint of consciousness being the product of a biological mechanism. The first two chapters elucidate the physiological mechanisms underlying memory and attention; and both emphasize the essentially unconscious nature of most mnemonic and attentional phenomena. Following these is a chapter on the relationship between the representation of objects and perceptual processes from an artificial intelligence standpoint. The fourth chapter is on arousal and the maintenance of consciousness, in addition to describing the psychophysiological correlates of the state of wakefulness the interactions between arousal, emotion and psycho-pathological conditions are discussed. Disorders of consciousness are the subject of the following chapter; since the symptoms of schizophrenia include hallucinations, delusions and thought disorders it is possible that our understanding of "normal" consciousness may be furthered by studying the abnormal state as has happened in the case of amnesia and memory. Hallucinogenic drugs appear to have fascinated man since time immemorial and Chapter 6 provides a review of such substances. The final two chapters deal with hemispheric differences: one is concerned with cognition in split-brain patients, importantly emphasizing the distinction between consciousness and "conscious (self) awareness", while the other discusses right hemispheric functions, especially the question of whether the right hemisphere is specialized to deal with emotional stimuli and events.

Together with the previous volume the present contributions provide a comprehensive review on psychological and physiological aspects of consciousness. The breadth of topics covered indicates that a complete description of consciousness will be no simple task.

Nottingham
December 1980

Robin Stevens
Geoffrey Underwood

Contents

Contents of Volume 3

1 The Physiology of Memory

A. MAYES

*Department of Psychology,
University of Manchester*

1 Introduction

Psychologists have traditionally divided memory into the stages of registration, retention and retrieval. Within this trichotomy, although registration and retrieval have conscious aspects as well as physiological ones, retention is an essentially unconscious phenomenon. We have some conscious control over what we register in memory and what we retrieve from it. We can, also, consciously improve our memories through the use of mnemonics, rehearsal and systematic search strategies. We can perhaps even modulate our learning processes so as to retain information for as long as we need, but no longer, for intervals ranging from seconds to days. Generally, however, memory processes are unavailable to introspection. It is, therefore, the job of physiology to elucidate how the brain lays down, stores and subsequently retrieves different kinds of information.

There are three major classes of problem about the physiological basis of memory, which correspond to the traditional trichotomy. The first concerns how registration and learning lead to the storage of information. Within this general question, researchers have asked whether information is held in one or more short-term stores before gaining access to more permanent storage, and what consolidation processes need to occur following learning to bring this about. The second problem concerns the way information is represented in the brain when it is stored for long periods of time. Lashley's search for the location of the engram is a propaedeutic for the satisfactory formulation of this problem. In more recent years, this search has been pursued through the use of electrophysiological, rather than lesion techniques, by groups such as those of John and of Olds. The recording studies of these teams are also aimed at broaching the third major problem which is about how information is retrieved from storage. Some researchers believe that light is also thrown on this third problem by cases of organic amnesia and amnesia caused by post-learning treatments, such as

electroconvulsive shock. They believe that retrieval is disturbed in a
fairly selective fashion in these disorders. Other workers believe that
such amnesias are caused by a relatively selective disorder of registration and perhaps consolidation. This disagreement reflects the great
difficulty which exists in determining whether effects are caused by
registration/learning or retrieval variables. The two stages are strongly
interdependent. For example, it has been suggested that the memory
problems of old age are largely owing to poor encoding (see Eysenck,
1977). But this poor encoding could, in turn, be caused by inadequate
retrieval from long-term storage (Thomas *et al.*, 1977). Richness of
encoding requires the "interpretation" of new information in terms of
what we know already, and this "interpretation" is likely to be jejune if
there is difficulty in accessing stored information.

The term "memory" like "cancer" includes a multitude of phenomena which may share some features with each other, but may also
differ radically. Habituation, perceptual learning, classical and instrumental conditioning and the kinds of memory which represent persona-
lized or impersonal knowledge, are all likely to differ somewhat with
respect to their physiological bases. The differences may be in any or all
of the stages of memory. They may occur at the level where the brain
organizes and represents information, or at the microscopic level involving the kinds of changes shown by individual neurons, or both. We
know that primitive animals such as invertebrates show habituation,
instrumental and classical conditioning, and sensitization (for example,
see Davis, 1976). There is even evidence showing instrumental conditioning in spinal mammals (Spada and Buerger, 1976). It seems probable then that memory for these kinds of learning is represented
differently in the brain (at least, macroscopically) from the distinctively
human kinds of memory. Even with the latter, we have reason to
suppose that, in most people, verbal memories are stored primarily
within the left hemisphere whereas hard-to-verbalize information is
more likely to be stored in the right hemisphere (for example, see
Milner, 1971; Hardyck *et al.*, 1978). Whether this probable difference in
location of verbal and non-verbal engrams means that the information
is represented distinctively by the hemispheres is, however, a different
question.

This chapter will be mainly concerned with the physiology of distinctively human memory. Unfortunately, most of the available literature
involves animals! Great care must be taken, therefore, in extrapolating
any conclusions to the human system. As no one interpretation of the
data is compelling, even for the animal species studied, extrapolations
will be used merely to provide the general desiderata for the human
memory system.

2 Two influential approaches to how information gets into store

In the late 1960s there was a consensual view (often referred to as the modal model of memory) held by cognitive psychologists about how information comes to be stored in human memory. Differing versions of the viewpoint, were, for example, formulated by Waugh and Norman (1965) and Atkinson and Shiffrin (1968). A central distinction of the approach is between information processing, which is regarded as a very flexible activity, over which we exert considerable voluntary control, and structures (memory stores), which provide the constraints within which our processing capacities must operate. On arrival, it was claimed, information is held in large capacity, modality-specific stores from which it is rapidly lost unless the subject pays attention to it. If attended to, items are transferred into the short-term store or primary memory. This post-attentional store has limited capacity so that items can only be maintained in it by rehearsal (basically this means paying continued attention to them) or are displaced when new items gain access to the store. Rehearsal also enables information to be transferred to the very large capacity, long-term store of secondary memory, where some theorists believe items are forgotten mainly through interference. There was a further, generally believed characteristic of the model. This was that the pre-attentional stores hold information in a "crude", relatively unprocessed "sensory" form, whereas items in primary memory are encoded phonemically and those in secondary memory semantically.

Post-war research into the physiological development of durable memory has been greatly influenced by another broad model, the credit for which is usually given to Müller and Pilzecker (1900), who introduced it to help explain the results of an early verbal interference experiment. This model proposes that successful learning leads to the triggering of an interrelated sequence of physiological and biochemical events in the brain, whose occurrence is necessary for the formation of a functional long-term memory. These events are referred to as consolidation processes. The consolidation model is really a framework for a wide range of more specific physiological hypotheses, which make proposals about the time course of the processes as well as their exact nature. Regardless of their specific differences, all versions of the model posit one or more short-term memory stores, which hold information during the period (and for a while beyond) when the long-term store is not operational. The short-term store(s) is activated immediately by the learning experience. The major prediction of the model is that there will be a limited time following learning when memory will be labile, in the sense that physiological treatments which disrupt consolidation processes will cause amnesia.

Although the information-processing and consolidation models have guided research in radically different areas—the former mainly in human verbal memory, and the latter mainly in the physiology of animal instrumental and classical conditioning—they have many points of similarity and both postulate short- and long-term memory stores. Are these stores identical? The question is confusing for both models are Hydra-like because they are frameworks within which specific hypotheses can be formulated. Each model could be used, therefore, to postulate several different kinds of short-term store. Many workers have, however, argued that primary memory is verbal, containing only phonemically coded information, and even if they also allow a short-term store for visually coded verbal information, they often assert that non-verbal information is processed, during learning, straight into a long-term store (see, for example, Warrington and Taylor, 1973). This popular view conflicts with the spirit of the consolidation model, which is used to interpret the physiological data derived from animals so as to necessitate the existence of a short-term store(s) for clearly non-verbal information. There is no obvious reason, according to the consolidation model, why only verbal information should require short-term storage and yet this claim is made by cognitive psychologists, operating within the information processing model. Such a disagreement should not be brushed aside by asserting that different things are being referred to because the models *should* ultimately be talking about the same thing, viz. activities or states of the brain involved in information storage. The source of the conflict probably lies in the different kinds of evidence used by proponents of the two models.

Many of the data that were regarded as compelling evidence for the popular conception of primary memory were acquired from studies of the short-term retention of verbal material, following a single exposure and under conditions of high interference, with intact human subjects. The studies showed that memory in many of these situations could be divided into a stable component, identified with secondary memory, and a labile component, identified with primary memory. The two components were shown to be influenced differentially by variables such as the interval between presentation and recall. Particular emphasis was placed on the apparent discovery that the labile component (recency effect) comprised items which were encoded phonemically whereas items constituting the stable component were semantically encoded. More recent evidence, however, suggests that the recency effect consists of the last few "meaningful units" of a verbal input and these units may be coded semantically. Furthermore, the ability which underlies this short-term memory effect is independent of those which account for performance in immediate memory span tasks. Indeed Baddeley and Hitch (1974) have proposed that "working memory" should be viewed as a limited capacity general purpose processor to which are attached various buffers, holding information either about speech input or output, as well as visually coded input. It remains controversial whether these modifications of the modal model necessitate the postulation of separate stores because, independently, several workers have argued that the above kind of evidence is either irrelevant or unacceptably weak as support for the existence of a short-term verbal store (Wickelgren, 1973, 1974; Craik and Lockhart, 1972; Gruneberg, 1976). Wickelgren and Gruneberg contend that a single-store model is compatible with the data, whereas Craik and Lockhart have advanced a "depth of processing" approach, which is currently inspiring much research. This approach proposes that memory is a function of processing, such that material which is more "deeply", "widely" or "distinctively" encoded is better remembered. Thus semantically encoded material is remembered better than phonemically encoded material, not because it is held in a more durable kind of memory store, but within the same store, it is easier to distinguish from competing memories. Craik does accept that items may be retained in memory by continuing to pay attention to them, a process which he identifies with James' original concept of primary memory. This mode of storage is not, however, identified by the coding of information in it and he seems to accept that all information is held in a single store once the subject has ceased to attend to it.

Wickelgren (1973) proposed three types of evidence which he believed implied the existence of post-attentional short-term store for verbal material. These were (1) the operation of different retention functions in short- and long-term memory situations, (2) the occurrence of "fine grain" similarity effects with retroactive interference only over longer retention intervals, and (3) the existence of neurological disorders in which short- or long-term retention are apparently selectively disturbed. He (Wickelgren, 1974) subsequently rejected these three lines of evidence and gave unequivocal support to the single view. Short-term memory situations for obvious reasons, are associated with a great deal of interfering material, very similar to what has to be remembered. When allowance is made for this confounding variable, a single function can encompass both short- and long-term forgetting curves, and the undiscriminating nature of short-term interference effects can be seen as a result of the high degree of similarity of all interfering items in the short-term memory situation. The neurological evidence is dismissed in too cavalier a fashion and will be considered at greater length.

   Two kinds of neurological disorder have been interpreted as providing support for a separate short-term store. They are, respectively, conduction aphasia and organic amnesia. Conduction aphasia is a syndrome in which spontaneous speech and the comprehension of language are relatively preserved in the face of a severe difficulty in verbal repetition. It is possibly caused by damage to the left arcuate fasciculus, which disconnects Wermicke's area from Broca's area, or with more extensive left hemisphere damage which causes the release of right hemisphere language mechanisms (Geschwind, 1965). Shallice and Warrington (1977) have argued for some years that the repetition problem arises because conduction aphasics have a verbal short-term store which has a pathologically limited capacity and from which items are perhaps lost abnormally quickly. Conversely, it has been contended (see Warrington, 1971) that in organic amnesia short-term storage is within normal limits whereas long-term memory is grossly disturbed.

   Do conduction aphasics have deficient verbal–phonemic short-term stores or is their poor repetition caused by some other defect? Many repetition errors of these patients are associated with paraphasic responses, which suggests that the source of the problem may lie in a high-level speech defect, associated with normal underlying memory. Shallice and Warrington agree that this output failure is a contributory factor in the poor repetition of some patients, but they argue that other cases cannot be explained in these terms. This is because some "conduction" aphasics have near normal spontaneous speech with very few paraphasic errors (Shallice and Butterworth, 1977), and, also, appear to be worse than controls at recognizing recently spoken items (Shallice and Warrington, 1977). Although this argument would be more persuasive if some patients had been shown to make very few paraphasic errors in repetition, because the production deficit might be a selective one of imitation, as perhaps implied by Kinsbourne's (1972) disconnection hypothesis, nevertheless, subnormal recognition is clearly inconsistent with normal memory. Further, Shallice and Warrington (1977) have pointed out that most of their patients' errors in repetition are *omissions*, not paraphasic responses. Additionally, they have argued that their cases have normal immediate memory for visually presented verbal material, normal acoustic memory for non-verbal stimuli, and normal long-term memory for verbal material even when it is auditorally presented. These specific claims have been disputed by Tzortzis and Albert (1974) and clearly require further careful investigation. Even if all cases cannot be explained in terms of a subtle difficulty in speech generation, and forgetting of spoken verbal items is abnormally fast, it may be unnecesary to postulate a deficient short-term store. It is possible that disturbances in processing spoken language lead to the system getting overloaded so that items fail to achieve proper storage in the first place. Evidence suggests that aphasics have difficulty with the perception of complex non-verbal acoustic stimuli as well as of phonemes (Tallal and Newcombe, 1978; Blumstein *et al.*, 1977) and, by definition, nearly all have problems with the extraction of meaning from acoustic signals. Only if it proves feasible to unconfound such processing problems from the memory difficulties of conduction aphasics will this class of patient provide good evidence for the existence of a verbal–phonemic short-term store. Unfortunately, this is likely to be a difficult task because the predictions of the store defect and processing defect hypotheses will be very similar. Both will predict memory difficulties with sequences of items, especially if spoken close together, and normal performance if enough time is allowed for the processing of simple single items. Shallice and Warrington's demonstration of rapid forgetting of a single item in the Brown–Peterson task provides a difficult intermediate case. Would the extra burden and confusion associated with performing the interpolated task have caused patients to process even single items inadequately?

In Shallice and Warrington's patients both recency effects and immediate memory span are subnormal, and so it would seem, if Baddeley and Hitch (1974) are correct, the patients deal inadequately with both verbal input and output. If their storage interpretation of the syndrome is appropriate then we still only have evidence for a highly specialized short-term store (or stores), important for speech comprehension and perhaps production in some circumstances, and not for the global kind of short-term storage required by consolidation theory. Many researchers believe that support for this kind of store is provided by the existence of organic amnesics. This evidence is now considered.

It is well known that amnesic patients have normal immediate memory spans but are more or less incapable of learning supraspan sequences (Drachman and Arbit, 1966). Baddeley and Warrington (1970) reported that a group of amnesics, tested in a free–recall task, showed a normal recall of the last items presented (recency effect), but a defect in the recall of the first items presented (primacy effect). The former effect is labile and, according to some theorists, reflects the storage of items in the short-term store. Baddeley and Warrington also found their patients to have normal recall in the Brown–Peterson task over a 60-second period. Although this finding seems to conflict with observations of poor performance in this task in other groups of amnesics (for discussion, see Butters and Cermak, 1974), it serves to highlight a peculiarity of the amnesic data conceived as support for the existence of a short-term store. The Brown–Peterson tasks is supposed to reflect the activities of primary *and* secondary memory. This conclusion is based on the already discussed patterns of forgetting which occur with intact humans in short-term forgetting tasks. However, even if the form of memory breakdown found in amnesia cannot be mapped on to the short-term and long-term memory dichotomy, derived by some cognitive psychologists, it still does not explain how performance on some short-term tasks is normal. One possible answer is that in principle it is not, but the degree of preservation is a function of the overall severity of the amnesia. Severity of amnesia is a neglected dimension of the syndrome, so it is feasible to argue that performance in short-term memory tasks is normal only in milder cases of the disorders. This view is not, however, supported by the limited evidence available. The famous patient H.M., both of whose medial temporal lobes were surgically removed in 1954, is generally agreed to be a very densely amnesic subject and yet his performance on many short-term tasks is within normal limits. Wickelgren (1974) has argued that amnesics show this curious preservation of some short-term memory tasks because although they have a relatively unimpaired capacity to encode material at the phonemic level, their ability to encode semantically is markedly impaired. If it is accepted that good performance on the relevant short-term memory tasks can be achieved by processing phonemically encoding information into the single store, postulated by Wickelgren and Gruneberg, then there is no need to propose a short-term store which is normal to amnesics. In support of his position, Wickelgren cites evidence that amnesics are near normal in tasks such as perceptual and motor skill learning, which he presumes involve little semantic encoding. He could, more appositely, have referred to the Boston group of Butters, Cermak and Oscar-Berman (see Butters and Cermak, 1977), which has accumulated considerable evidence that, at least in some amnesics, there is a slowness in processing information, a deficiency in the spontaneous tendency to encode information semantically, and a tendency to adopt passive modes of rehearsing material.

Wickelgren's argument not only depends on the shaky claim that performance in short-term memory tasks is specially dependent on phonemic encoding of information, but also on the suggestion that amnesics are deficient at semantic encoding which has been found wanting. Thus, it has been shown that alcoholic amnesics' memory is affected identically to that of control subjects by orienting tasks which require semantic processing or make such processing more difficult (see Mayes *et al.*, 1978; Meudell *et al.*, 1979). It seems, therefore, that although there may be amnesics whose memory problem is compounded with secondary complications associated with inadequate semantic encoding (for example, possibly the Boston amnesics), others exist with good short-term memories and intact semantic processing. Thus, excluding the possibility of other impaired encoding or retrieval processes which are differentially involved in short-term memory tasks, amnesia provides evidence for the existence of an independent short-term store. Even so, although this store may hold non-verbal as well as verbal information, certain classes of input seem to by-pass it because amnesics have been reported to have abnormal immediate memory for faces (Warrington and Taylor, 1973) and there are many indications that conditioning and motor learning is relatively normal in these patients. Once more then data from humans do not relate directly to the consolidation model view of a global short-term memory store. The selective intactness of short-term and long-term memory in amnesics remains a puzzle. Perhaps the operation of a normal central processor, which can readily hold certain classes of input in consciousness even when that input is no longer present, can explain certain of their short-term memory abilities. Further, amnesia is unlikely to be caused by a failure of endogenous consolidation processes because of the apparent preservation of conditioning in amnesics. What does work within the consolidation model approach reveal about the time course of these endogenous processes and the need to postulate global short-term memory stores(s)?

3 Consolidation and the retrograde amnesia paradigm

The most popular means of investigating consolidation during the past thirty years has been the use of the retrograde amnesia paradigm. It involves the application of a disruptive physiological treatment within a limited period following learning and a subsequent assessment of the learner's memory for the relevant task. The use of appropriate control groups is essential to determine whether or not the effects are on memory rather than performance, and if they are on memory what aspect(s) of it they are disrupting. Researchers have hoped the technique will help decide not only what processes are required for consolidation but, also, what their time course is. To achieve this end many different treatments have been used, on many species, and in many different learning situations. The hermeneutical problems of the paradigm can, however, be illustrated by studies which use electroconvulsive shock (ECS) to disrupt memory. This treatment is also the one which has been most commonly used.

In a classic study, Chorover and Schiller (1955) demonstrated that ECS produced a steep gradient of retrograde amnesia lasting about 10 seconds, for rats learning a one-trial passive avoidance task. The animals were trained on one day and tested 24 hours later. This suggested that ECS disrupted processes which were important for consolidation only in the few seconds following memory. It soon became apparent, however, that the duration of the retrograde amnesia might be very much longer even in apparently similar situations. Thus, Kopp *et al.* (1966) found a retrograde amnesia gradient extending up to 6 hours in mice. Amongst the variables responsible for producing these very different retrograde amnesia durations was the intensity of the ECS. For example, Gold *et al.* (1973) showed that memory could be disrupted by ECS up to 4 hours following learning, provided its intensity was increased enough. The finding is clearly incompatible with the view that ECS is disrupting a process which is completed within a short period following learning.

Two further well-established effects make interpretation of the ECS literature even more difficult. The first is that the onset of amnesia is not immediate following ECS, and the second is that under a variety of ill-understood conditions, there may be recovery of memory following the onset of amnesia. The delayed onset of amnesia was not noticed in the early studies because they tested memory only after a 24 hour interval when forgetting had occurred. But subsequent studies (for example, see Geller and Jarvik, 1968), which tested with a number of shorter delays, revealed that retention declined over a 3–6 hour period following treatment. At first this interval of relatively good memory, following the disruptive treatment, was taken to be a reflection of the operation of one or more short-term stores unaffected by the disruption. In the normal animal these would subserve memory until the long-term store was operational. Unfortunately, it was shown that the forgetting rate was influenced by the training ECS interval and the intensity of the ECS (Hughes *et al.*, 1970). Such findings are inconsistent with the unmodified form of the above suggestion.

Zinkin and Miller (1967) provided the first clear experimental evidence that memory could recover following the induction of amnesia by ECS. They used rats in a one-trial task, in which the animals had to learn to stay on an elevated platform to avoid shocks on the grid floor below. Following a number of post-ECS exposures on the platform, without shock, the animals reacquired their previously learnt tendency not to step off on to the grid floor. This kind of "reminder effect" has been pursued at length by other workers. For example, Lewis *et al.* (1968) have shown that a "reminder" shock, given in a different apparatus from the one in which an animal was trained, can restore memory following ECS treatment. Without previous training, the "reminder" fails to produce any signs of apparent memory. It has been argued by Miller and Springer (1974) that the efficacy of non-contingent "reminders" in restoring memory indicates that ECS and other disruptive treatments do not block consolidation, but merely produce a disturbance of retrieval. In their view, some information is consolidated, about the one-trial task, in less than half a second (the interval at which ECS is given in such studies). This interpretation is disputed by Gold and King (1974) and McGaugh (1973) who make the contentious claim that although reminders cause recovery from "weak amnesia", animals with "complete amnesia" show no recovery.

Schneider (1975) has produced a more convincing explanation of the "reminder" phenomenon, which allows a modifed consolidation account of the data. He argues that, in one-trial aversive tasks, two kinds of learning occur. Animals learn not to make certain kinds of response in order to avoid punishment (instrumental conditioning) and, also, develop autonomic responses to the cues in the apparatus which are associated with shock (classical conditioning). ECS treatment blocks the consolidation of instrumental but not of classical conditioning—some evidence suggests that cortical mechanisms may be more important for the former kind of learning (Di Cara *et al.*, 1970). If on re-exposure to the apparatus the autonomic conditioning is still intact, then animals will experience unpleasant arousal and relearn to make the instrumental response to avoid this. When Schneider and his colleagues extinguished these arousal effects they prevented the occurrence of the "reminder" effect. Further evidence is, however, needed for this hypothesis. It should, also, be noted that it cannot explain spontaneous memory recovery without reminders, or recovery in tasks which involve no classically conditioned components.

Variable retrograde amnesia durations, different rates of forgetting following ECS, and recovery of memory after ECS-induced amnesia, are effects inconsistent with a simple consolidation model interpretation. More sophisticated formulations, in which ECS is held only to produce a partial block of consolidation, may be made compatible with the data, but are *ad hoc* speculation. Even so, the data reviewed so far all point to the existence of a labile period after learning during which memory is especially susceptible to disruption. Some researchers (see, for example, Lewis and Bregman, 1973) have argued that the special nature of the post-learning period is illusory. They claim that if a subject is re-exposed to the stimulus conditions of the learning situation just when ECS is given, then amnesia will be produced even when the memory is days old, and presumably well consolidated. A striking illustration of this effect is provided by a study of Robbins and Meyer (1970). They trained rats on a series of three discrimination tasks. Training took place over several days and acquisition of the last task was succeeded by an ECS treatment. The animals were then retrained on the two earlier problems. surprisingly, they showed impairment on these problems provided that they had been motivated for them in the same way as with the third task. If, however, the last task had been food-motivated and the second task motivated by shock, then the latter would be well remembered. Lewis and Bregman (1973) argued that ECS disrupts memories which are activated and has no effect on those not being actively evoked. They suggested that the idea of a labile period, special to the post-learning interval, is spurious, because ECS causes amnesia for any activated memory of whatever age. This is not a necessary interpretation of the cue-dependent amnesia phenomenon. Furthermore, empirical doubts have been raised about the generality or even the existence of the effect in animals (for example, see Dawson and McGaugh, 1969; and Squire *et al.*, 1976, have been unable to demonstrate a reactivation effect for ECS-induced amnesia in humans). Nevertheless, it is unarguable that, at least for animals and with ECS, the retrograde amnesia paradigm has failed to elucidate the processes of consolidation.

4 Pharmacological treatments and the biochemical basis of Memory

ECS has been a popular amnesia agent in animal studies because it is easy to administer, was known to cause amnesia in man, and was thought to block temporally organized forebrain electrical activitiy. Hebb (1949) had given vogue to the idea that reverberatory neural activity following learning is essential for developing a long-term store. There is little direct support for this view and as ECS causes a myriad of neural and biochemical changes (see Essman, 1972), it has proved very hard to establish which are responsible for its amnesic actions. Furthermore, Baldwin and Soltysik (1969) have shown that goats can remember the location of a reward, following one trial, for over an hour, despite showing isoelectric EEG's following the induction of cerebral ischaemia almost immediately after learning. This apparent independence of developing memory from continued neural activity is consistent with the argument of an excellent review by Squire (1975). Squire discusses habituation and dishabituation in simple systems such as Aplysia, and suggests that neural processes, like low-frequency depression and heterosynaptic facilitation seen in them, may be capable of retaining stimulus information for short-periods immediately on learning. Such processes would perhaps be resistant to ECS. This idea is compatible with the view that certain kinds of post-learning neural activity may play a modulatory role in the development of memory, as will be discussed later. The processes, postulated by Squire, are regarded as short-term stores subserving retention whilst biochemical changes are occurring, which will produce the synaptic changes under-lying long-term memory. This idea that enduring memory requires synaptic alterations, which in turn may require *de novo* synthesis of certain kinds of protein molecule in relevant brain regions, suggests that consolidation may be blocked more effectively by protein synthesis inhibitors than by agents like ECS.

Protein synthesis-blocking antibiotics have been used to produce amnesia since Flexner *et al.* (1963) made their pioneering observations. Although a massive body of data has now been accumulated it is clearly not amenable to a simple consolidation interpretation. Three major groups of antibiotics have been used. The first groups, the actinomycins inhibit protein synthesis by disturbing the synthesis of DNA-dependent RNA. These drugs are unfortunately highly toxic and although there is some evidence that intracerebral injections of Actinomycin D, given before or even up to a day following training, can cause amnesia in rodents and goldfish (see Squire and Barondes, 1970), other studies find no such effect (see Goldsmith, 1967). The second group of drugs, represented by puromycin, block RNA-dependent proteins synthesis, perhaps by acting as analogues for aminoacyl-transfer RNA, as well as causing the dissociation of polyribosomes to monoribosomes. Intra-cerebral puromycin injections, which inhibit 80–90% of brain protein synthesis, reliably cause amnesia in a wide range of species (see Barraco and Stettner, 1976, for a review). Permanent amnesia occurs when puromycin is injected up to 5 hours before training or a day afterwards. Indeed, Flexner *et al.* (1963) observed amnesia 43 days after training when puromycin injections were made in widely distributed cerebral sites. The third group of antibiotics are the glutarimides, mainly represented in this kind of work by acetoxycycloheximide and cycloheximide. These drugs act antagonistically to puromycin and are presumed to inhibit protein synthesis by interfering with the movement of the ribosome along the messenger RNA strand. The glutarimides have been found to produce amnesia reliably in a variety of species and training situations, provided they are injected before training so that protein synthesis inhibition is maximum during learning. Unlike puromycin, the glutarimides may be injected subcutaneously as well as intracranially (see Barondes and Cohen, 1968).

The amnesic effects of these drugs raise two kinds of methodological question. First, do they affect memory, and, if so, what aspects of memory do they effect? Second, are the amnesic effects caused by the inhibition of protein synthesis or some other action? Even though the effects of the actinomycins are both inconsistent and perhaps non-specific, control procedures suggest strongly that puromycin and the glutarimides disturb memory rather than merely performance. These drugs, however, produce very different retrograde amnesia gradients, a lack of uniformity reminiscent of the ECS data. The glutarimides, which are only reliably effective when injected before training, do not disturb initial learning and do not cause loss of memory until between 3 and 6 hours later (see Daniels, 1971). The rate of development of amnesia has been less studied with puromycin, but on the limited evidence, would seem broadly comparable to that found with the glutarimides (Squires and Barondes, 1973; Mark and Watts, 1971). Several features of this phenomenon should be noted. First, the rate of amnesic development is a functioning of initial training. Thus, Squire and Barondes (1972, 1973) found complete amnesia 3 hours post-training in mice, given subcutaneous cycloheximide injections 30 minutes prior to receiving 15 trials on a size discrimination habit. Those who received 21 trials, however, did not develop complete amnesia until 12 hours later. Second, in the same study, these experimenters showed that although cycloheximide does not impair initial learning, if it is continued beyond 21 trials, then a quick acting memory impairment becomes apparent. Third, ECS and cycloheximide seem to produce additive effects on memory. Andry and Luttges (1972) found that when ECS was given shortly after one-trial passive avoidance learing in cycloheximide-treated mice, amnesia developed at times when neither treatment alone caused amnesia.

Just as the antibiotics are similar to ECS, in that their use is associated with variable retrograde amnesia gradients and slowly developing memory loss, they are, also, similar because they provide reversible amnesias. There is frequently spontaneous recovery from glutarimide-induced amnesia, but in studies where this does not occur it has been shown that a variety of specific treatments can cause the return of memory (for a reivew, see Barraco and Stettner, 1976). These treatments can be behavioural, such as the application of "reminder" shocks, which also are believed to be effective in ECS-induced amnesia. They can also be pharmacological. Thus, Barondes and Cohen (for example, see Cohen and Barondes, 1968) have shown that when amphetamine is injected within 3 hours of training, there is recovery from cycloheximide-induced amnesia. There seems to be no spontaneous recovery from amnesia caused by puromycin. It has been shown, however, that intracranial injections of saline can restore memory following puromycin injections (se Flexner and Flexner, 1967). Although saline treatment can reverse amnesia when puromycin is injected one day after training, it has been claimed that it is ineffective when the antibiotic is injected before or immediately after training (Rosenbaum, *et al.*, 1968; Flexner and Flexner, 1970). A similar phenomenon has been noted with other kinds of physiological disruption such as hippocampal and cortical spreading depression, and serious concussion (Russell, 1959; Kapp and Schneider, 1971; Mayes, 1973). In all these cases, there is spontaneous memory recovery when the learning-disruption interval is of the order of hours or days, but little or none when the interval is only a few seconds. Even so, in none of these cases is the evidence strong that there is *no* recovery of memory when disruption occurs rapidly after learning (e.g. concussive retrograde amnesia in man may shrink so as to leave no blank period before the accident). Further, Deutsch (1969) has argued that Flexner and Flexner's differential effect was marginal, with saline producing some recovery even in the group which received puromycin injections immediately after training. He makes additional methodological criticisms which indicate that this important result should be interpreted cautiously.

The fact that the three kinds of antibiotic used in these studies have such different effects on memory suggests that their amnesic action is not simply related to their common action of disturbing cerebral protein synthesis. Indeed, Barraco and Stettner (1976) have proposed that antibiotics have three separate pharmacological modes of action on memory. First, they claim that puromycin, injected a day or more after training, disturbs the operation of a widely distributed network of adrenergic neurons required for longer term memory. Second, the glutarimides interfere with the transmitter processes of an adrenergic system, which is active during and shortly after learning. Third, puromycin, injected before or immediately following learning, interferes with a system of cholinergic neurons, involved in the consolidation of memory. Although these specific proposals are polemical, it is clear that the use of antibiotics in the retrograde amnesia paradigm has not provided critical evidence for the role of protein synthesis in consolidation, or even for the existence of a consolidation process which takes a few seconds to complete.

5 Are entities being multiplied beyond necessity?

Most, if not all, the data discussed so far are explicable in terms of a unitrace model which requires no short-term store and in which consolidation occurs at about the same rate as learning. The phenomenona of retrograde amnesia can be explained in a number of ways depending on which of its aspects are emphasized. If spontaneous recovery occurs, then a non-specific disturbance of retrieval may have dissipated so that remembering of recent and, therefore, weak memories becomes possible. If memory only returns with a reminder, then perhaps the physiological treatment has prevented the integration of the new memory into the organized retrieval system of established memories. In terms of the popular library analogy, this would mean that a book has got into the library (consolidation has occurred), but it has not been properly catalogued. The reminder somehow initiates this process.

Gold and McGaugh (1975) have advanced an ingenious hypothesis, similar to the examples above, in so far as they are offering a single trace, dual process explanation of the amnesia data. They suggest that a learning experience initiates a memory trace that will be transient unless the experience leads to non-specific physiological response, which will promote the strengthening of the trace. Amnesic agents do not necessarily affect the process which initiates the transient trace, but could interfere with the non-specific effects which are usually delayed. An implicit and attractive assumption of the hypothesis is that trial events will generate only mild non-specific responses and hence will be rapidly forgotten. If amnesia is caused by interference with learning's non-specific consequences, then not only should its onset be delayed but it should also be reversed provided replacement treatments are given soon enough. Further, ordinary memory should be improved, in many cases, by the artificial augmentation of non-specific physiological responses. Both these kinds of effect have frequently been observed. Some degree of arousal is an effect of learning, and it has been shown that direct electrical stimulation of the midbrain reticular formation can improve retention (see Bloch, 1970). Bloch *et al.* (1970) have shown that such stimulation compensates for the amnesic effects of fluothane anaesthesia. In both cases, the stimulation must be given shortly following learning. The hypothesis predicts that there will be an optimal level of non-specific responses so that very low or very high degrees of artificial effects may be ineffective. This effect will interact with the level non-specific responses produced by the learning task. In support of these expectations, Krivanek. (1971) showed that the amount of memory facilitation was smaller and the maximum effective does was lower when animals were trained on an aversive task using the higher of two levels of foot-shock.

Gold and McGaugh argue that the relevant non-specific effects of learning include not only general arousal, but also a range of hormonal actions such as the release of agents such as adrenocorticotropic hormone (ACTH), vasopressin, thyroid hormone, adrenaline and perhaps others. These hormones are certainly released following aversive experiences. They have shown that injections of adrenaline, ACTH or vasopressin, given shortly after learning an aversive task, can facilitate retention, with the effect depending on the level of foot-shock and dosage. Memory disruption results when both high doses and strong shocks are used. Barondes and Cohen (1968) have also shown that corticosteroids injected soon after training can prevent ECS- or cycoheximide-induced amnesia. Van Wimersma Greidanus and De Wied (1976) have found that intracerebroventricular injections of antivasopressin serum causes an amnesia at one day following passive avoidance learning, even when treatment was delayed until two hours after the single training trial. Also the antivasopressin serum caused retention deficits when administered one hour before the test trial. This result suggests that vasopressin may be non-specifically involved in retrieval processes as well as the strengthening of the memory trace.

It is tempting to extrapolate from the Gold–McGaugh hypothesis, which is focused on animal research, to the amnesic syndrome in man. This condition has a number of etiologies, but, of whatever origin, the damage critical to the memory disturbance seems to involve highly interconnected structures including the hippocampus, post-commissural fornix, mammillary bodies, anterior and dorsomedial nuclei of the thalamus, and possibly other thalamic nuclei such as the pulvinar (Brierley, 1977). With the exception of the hippocampus, and perhaps the fornix, it is controversial whether pathology of any individual one of these structures is sufficient to cause amnesia. It has recently been shown that whereas amygdala or center median nucleus lesions alone do not produce amnesia, if a left amygdala lesion is combined with a lesion of the left centre median nucleus then a verbal dysmnesia results (Jurko, 1978).

The limbic system, to which the structures implicated in amnesia either belong or with which they are strongly interconnected, acts as an interface between neocortex, which provides processed sensory information and more basal regions, such as the non-specific thalamus, which provide information concerning internal state and motivation (Powell and Hines, 1974). In a recent review, Rozin (1976) points out that many of these structures, damaged in organic amnesia, form part of a subcortical activation and arousal system. He likens damaging it to cutting the fuel pipe of a car but argues that the analogy must be wrong because amnesics do not show general cognitive disturbances. The defect may, however, be a more subtle one in which only certain aspects of the activation system are impaired. Rozin himself suggests that the fronto-temporal connections of the critical limbic-thalamic regions could indicate a memory-specific arousal function. Alternatively, memory processes are more susceptible than other cognitive processes to activational disturbances.

Independently, Ojemann and others (see Ojemann, 1975; Fedio and Van Buren, 1975) have argued that medial structures of the left thalamus perform an alerting function in verbal learning. They also hold that there is some degree of specialization of this function because anterior stimulation within the thalamic ventrolateral nucleus causes repetition errors whereas anomic errors are produced by more posteromedial stimulation. Preliminary evidence (see Lhermitte and Signoret, 1976) suggests that hippocampal, cingulate and mammillary body–dorsomedial thalamic lesions each cause a different kind of amnesic breakdown. Although the effects may well be caused by differential effects on non-mnemomic processes, it could be that each lesion leads to a specific type of disturbance of the interaction between memory processes and activation. For example, cingulectomy may result in disturbance of alerting which affects only retrieval. Such functional dissociation between registration and retrieval processes is indicated also by the work of Fedio and Van Buren (1974). These researchers have shown that stimulation of patients' posterior temporal lobes caused retrograde amnesia but no anterograde amnesia in a picture naming task, whereas anterior temporal lobe stimulation produced the reverse pattern of disturbance. At present, however, the proposal that a variety of activational deficits are causally implicated in amnesia is merely an informed speculation and requires more direct assessment with, for example, the use of electrophysiological measures of alerting. In intact humans, at least, EEG arousal measures have been shown to correlate with memory for sentences (Lehmann and Koukkau, 1974).

Another body of data is relevant in considering the Gold–McGaugh hypothesis. Although the area is controversial, there is now considerably more evidence that post-learning rapid-eye-movement (REM) sleep plays a role in the development of stable memories. Several studies have shown that REM deprivation can cause a retention deficit without impairing subsequent relearning (for example, see Pearlmann and Greenberg, 1973). More impressively, it has been shown that 2 days REM deprivation after learning can greatly extend the interval during which memory is susceptible to disruption by ECS (Fishbein et al., 1971; Wolfowitz and Holdstock, 1971). A similar prolongation to 40 hours for the period of memory susceptibility to ECS has been reported by Zornetzer and Gold (1976), following lesions of the locus coeruleus. In addition to being a major nuclear structure containing noradrenergic cells, this region has been implicated in the control of REM sleep and sends projections to many forebrain structures, including thalamus and hippocampus. Not only does REM disruption disturb retention, but learning is followed by selective augmentation of REM sleep in many situations (see Lucero, 1970). According to Bloch (1976) augmentation is related to the degree of learning achieved and is maximal whilst learning is actually progressing. Furthermore, the augmentation does not occur if training is followed by stimulation of the midbrain reticular formation. Controls indicated that this was a specific effect and not a general consequence of activation. Bloch contends that both REM sleep and midbrain stimulation produce general activation of the brain which is important for the stabilization of memory. It has been shown by using a variety of treatments that increases in the functional level of catecholamine activity in the brain can reverse REM deprivation-induced amnesia for passive and active avoidance tasks (Stern and Morgane, 1974). The catecholamine precursor, L-Dopa only seems to facilitate retention if animals are initially depleted of their central stores of the transmitter (see Hartmann and Stern, 1973). It is, therefore, of interest that REM deprivation causes catecholamine depletion (Stern and Morgane, 1974), especially, as catecholaminergic neurons are alleged to have a role in arousal.

Several sources of evidence, therefore, are compatible with the view that non-specific processes following learning help stabilize and strengthen a memory, which although "consolidated" would otherwise decay rapidly. If the phenomena observed in the retrograde amnesia paradigm can be explained as arising from disturbances of these non-specific responses, is there any need to postulate a relatively slow consolidation process and short-term store? Several points should be made in this connection. First, consolidation model interpretations can be made of the literature, which are just as plausible as "retrieval" explanations, provided one assumes that disruptive treatments do not totally stop the process or do so only temporally. This assumption is plausible. For example, unless lethal, antibiotics always leave some cerebral protein synthesis unblocked. Also, Mah *et al.* (1972) have shown that a second ECS one hour post-training, following one at 5 minutes, is more disruptive of retention than a single ECS at either interval alone, and have interpreted their results as showing that some consolidation continues following ECS. The second point relates to the general presumption that most workers accept, viz. long-term storage depends on stable synaptic changes in critical neurons which require further previous changes, generally involving protein synthesis. Squire (1975) has estimated that the *minimum* time between learning and the time when such synthesis can affect synaptic activity is around one minute. This calculation assumes special classes of protein might be synthesized at the synapse thus eliminating transport time. Interestingly, Cronly-Dillon *et al.* (1974) found they could produce amnesia for an active avoidance task in goldfish by giving intracranial injections of colchicine shortly following training. This drug impairs the function of microtubules, the organelles responsible for active transport in the neuron. The microtubules, however, also probably have a role at the post-synaptic membrane, stabilizing receptor changes, so colchicine might cause amnesia either by impairing molecular transport from the perikaryon or by destabilizing recent membrane changes (personal communication from Cronly-Dillon, 1978).

What evidence is there for the general presumption that memory requires protein-synthesis-dependent synaptic changes? Clearly, the antibiotic data are inadequate. There is, however, considerable evidence from several laboratories that learning is accompanied by changes in the synthesis of RNA polymerase, RNA and protein (for example, see Rose *et al.*, 1976). Rose and his colleagues, using the imprinting of chicks to a flashing light as their learning model, have shown that these changes occur selectively in the forebrain roof, and in the sequence given above, over a relatively long time period. There are unfortunately great problems over the interpretation of such studies. Some of their problems are biochemical, but, perhaps more intractably, their behavioural significance is unclear. Despite the use of ingenious control groups it is difficult to be confident that the observed biochemical changes are not caused by some concomitant attentional, motivational or motor activity, rather than learning *per se*. Finally, the changes could merely reflect increased metabolic activity in those cells directly involved in the memory trace, rather than the development of the trace itself.

Synaptic alterations certainly do take place in the adult brain under a range of conditions. Brain lesions have been shown to give rise to several kinds of regrowth. For example, Raisman (1969) has shown that severing the fimbria and hence the projections of the hippocampus to septum causes the medial forebrain bundle axons to sprout and form synaptic connections at the vacated sites. Medial forebrain bundle lesions causes a similar sprouting in fimbria fibres. Rozenzweig (1970), with his colleagues, has shown that rats, exposed to enriched environments, have cortical neurons with large numbers of dendritic spines, compared to rats exposed to impoverished conditions. This strongly suggests that the enriched environment animals had more synapses per neuron. No one, however, has yet demonstrated convincingly that synaptic changes are the direct consequence of a specific learning experience. At present then the presumption remains unproven.

Do any data compel us to use a consolidation interpretation? Squire cites the work of Deutsch (1971), in which cholinesterase inhibitors were used to produce amnesia in rats. These agents were injected at various intervals after learning and retention was tested 24 hours later. An inverted U-shaped retention function was obtained with no amnesia between 1–3 days, severe amnesia at 7 days, and under some conditions partial amnesia at 30 minutes post-training. A similar function has been found by Wiener (1970) using multiple ECS treatments. Deutsch's interpretation of this biphasic response claims that functional activity is high in cholinergic neurons immediately after learning, after which it drops to rise to a new peak about a week later. The first peak corresponds to the expression of a short-term store and the second to the slow growth of a long-term system. Squire himself (see Squire *et al.*, 1971) has, however, shown that the amnesia can be reversed by methylscopolamine, which has difficulty crossing the blood-brain barrier. It is possible therefore that the amnesia is related to performance variables. Even if it is not a performance effect, the cholinergic fluctuations could be affecting the expression of a steadily strengthening single trace. This view is supported by the fact that the amnesia does not seem to be permanent.

Another group of workers have recently argued that whereas protein synthesis inhibitors such as cycloheximide prevent the development of the long-term store they do not accelerate the decay of a separate short-term trace. In contrast, agents such as ouabain and lithium, which are thought to inhibit the sodium pump, not only disturb consolidation but accelerate the decay of the short-term trace (see Watts and Mark, 1971). They find that a relatively low pretraining injection dose of cycloheximide causes chicks to forget a normally learnt task over a 90-minute period, but increasing the dose tenfold does not accelerate the rate of forgetting. Sodium pump inhibitors caused forgetting over the same period, but this time the rate of forgetting was strongly dose-dependent and more rapid at high doses. Combined treatment with sodium pump and protein synthesis inhibitors did not produce faster forgetting than that found with sodium pump inhibitors. More recently, Gibbs and Nj (1976) have proposed a three-phase model, based on their observations that intracranial injections of potassium or lithium chloride cause more rapid forgetting in chicks than is found with ouabain. These results are certainly interesting. If it can be shown that agents with different actions cause *systematic* differences in the rate of forgetting in many tasks and across species, then a strong case will have been made for postulating short-term memory storage processes. This has not yet been done.

In the face of so much confusing material it is easy to slide into pyrrhonism. It is more heuristically advisable to offer some informed guesses about how memories are laid down and what lines of research should be pursued. Despite the lack of strong direct evidence the most likely bet is that enduring memories require synaptic changes, whatever kind of learning is involved. Current estimates indicate that such changes will be incapable of subserving memory in the first minute (and perhaps for much longer) after learning. Memory, in the meantime, will be served by physiological processes of the kind postulated by Squire (1975) which occur immediately on learning, have a shortish life-span and may be involved in triggering the sequence that results in synaptic changes (but need not be). Current disruptive agents show how resistant these processes are to complete, permanent inhibition. This could be a feature of the processes or reflect the inadequacy of the treatments. these consolidation activities will be best pursued in simple systems such as Aplysia where it is easier to locate neurons involved in plastic activity. Such work should help determine which *specific* agents will effectively disrupt memory in higher animals.

In higher animals it has been customary to regard long-term memory as permanent and biochemical hypotheses of such storage have been provided with feedback loops to fulfill this desideratum (see John, 1967). This assumption may be wrong and the durability of a memory may depend very much on the non-specific processes which accompany and follow learning. These secondary changes probably determine the extent and durability of the synaptic changes. Organic amnesia in man is likely to arise from a disturbance of these non-specific processes, rather than the basic triggering of the consolidation processes, because several kinds of learning and memory seem effectively intact in amnesia. The learning of complex material by humans is successful to the extent that the material is distinctively encoded. This involves the storage of many different attributes. The limbic structures, implicated in amnesia, are responsible for a variety of activational functions. These determine not only how many attributes an individual is able to encode, but also how well each of these is consolidated into the long-term store. Whether these two functions are dissociable can best be determined by comparing the effects of different limbic lesions, and through the combined use of physiological measures and pharmacological prostheses. Some limbic structures, such as the hippocampus, may continue to influence the evolution of the trace for much longer periods, perhaps even years. (The hippocampectomized patient H. M. has been shown to have a dense retrograde amnesia of two years, but his older memories seems relatively good—Marslen-Wilson and Teuber, 1975.) Such a process seems improbable, but if it occurs it must be determined whether such "boosts" are automatic and unconscious or whether they involve conscious activity.

6 Where and how are memories represented in the brain?

Knowledge of where engrams are stored is a necessary preliminary both to achieving better insight into the nature of the consolidation processes, which occur at neuronal levels, and into how the brain represents information. It seems probable that changes underlying memory occur in those regions concerned with processing the relevant information; consequently, different kinds of memory will be stored in different parts of the brain. Thus, Russell (1966) has argued, on the basis of cortical ablation and spreading depression studies in the rat, that classically conditioned information may be both stored and retrieved without the involvement of the cortex, whereas instrumental conditioning cannot occur without some intact cortex. The implication of this hypothesis is that instrumental conditioning requires more elaborate kinds of information processing. Even within a single learning paradigm, informational complexity may determine which brain sites are involved in storage. Thus, although habituation to simple stimuli can occur at spinal levels, with complex inputs it is likely that the cortex is required for storage (Soklov, 1960). Apropos of this phenomenon, it may be that Russell's hypothesis must be modified to allow for the possibility that "simpler" forms of instrumental conditioning can occur without cortical participation. This will be necessary if Spada and Buerger's (1976) claim for spinal conditioning is borne out.

Although it seems a reasonable assumption, the principle that storage occurs where processing occurs has little direct evidence in its favour. Whilst it is easy to use lesions to demonstrate that storage and retrieval can occur without a particular structure, methodological considerations make it impossible to infer confidently that a given structure is essential for storage and retrieval. This is because lesions must also prevent adequate processing of the information when they are inflicted in sensorimotor cortex. More generally, it is very hard to distinguish lesion effects on attentional, motivational and sensorimotor activities from those on storage and retrieval. Criticism of the classic work of Lashley (1950) has been grounded partly on these considerations. Lashley summarised his research about lesion effects on learning and retention in terms of two principles. Crudely, the principle of mass action asserts that it is the amount, not the location, of cortical damage which determines the degree of impairment in learning and retention. This is related to the principle of equipotentiality, which claims that various cortical regions are interchangeable with respect to memory function. Thus, memories were held by Lashley to be widely distributed in cortical tissue in such a way as to be degraded in proportion to the amount of critical tissue removed. These conclusions were drawn from two kinds of experimental procedure. The first involved studying the effects of bilateral lesions on learning and retention of complex multimodal maze problems. The second involved showing that striate cortex lesions plus peripheral blinding impaired maze learning more severely than peripheral blinding alone. Lashley never claimed that the whole cortex was equipotential for all functions. Clearly, visual cortex relative to other cortex is specialized for vision. He did, however, appear to think that all cortical regions had, in addition to their special functions, a superordinate computing function so that learning and retention of complex tasks, such as maze learning, was equally distributed over the entire cortex. Lashley's conclusions are not deemed to be supported by either of his experimental procedures. Maze learning and retention depends on multisensory cues, and as bilateral cortical lesions are extended these cues will be progressively eliminated. So the increasing performance deficit could be the result of the loss of more and more localized and specialized cortical functions. Secondly, Lashley's striate cortex lesions extended into non-striate regions so that maze learning could have been further disrupted by other sensory losses. Plotkin and Russell (1969a, b) have more recently defended Lashley's view that the whole cortex has an equipotential general computing function through the ingenious use of hemidecorticate rats. In these animals, the sensory losses are minimized and they, nevertheless, reveal large deficits in the acquisition of instrumental tasks. Prolonging the duration of the conditioned stimulus for the hemidecorticate animals was found to compensate for their learning disability.

In the light of Russell and Plotkin's findings with the rat, it is interesting that Zaidel and Sperry (1974) have reported that commissurotomized humans have memory difficulties. These are apparent in everyday life when patients forget appointments, telephone numbers and where they have put things, as well as repeating anecdotes may times to the same audience. Deficits are also apparent on more formal tests such as paired-associate learning, memory for stories and the Benton visual retention test. It seems possible that even for verbal material encoding is facilitated by the participation of the right hemisphere. Although suggestive, it would be unwise to argue from either the rat or the human data that the relevant memories are normally equipotentially distributed throughout both hemispheres. Both sets of data can be interpreted more plausibly in terms of a weaker version of the principle of equipotentiality, in which more limited cortical regions are equipotential for their specific functions. Thus, the visual cortex of both hemispheres may contribute in a "mass action" fashion to the encoding of visual material. On the present evidence there is no need to postulate a superordinate common function for the entire cortex. With some functions, even the weaker form of the principle may need modification because loss of function is not in proportion to quantity of tissue destruction in the relevant cortical region. Rather, the function remains practically intact until almost the whole of the area is eliminated. This kind of relative invulnerability seems of apply to the visual system and certain kinds of visual discrimination (see Chow, 1961).

The tradition of Lashley has been maintained in more recent years by Robert Thompson and his associates (for example, see Spiliotis and Thompson, 1973). These workers have explored what brain regions in that rat are essential for the expression of several kinds of memory by training rats on appropriate tasks and determining the effects on retention of a whole range of small lesions in cortex and subcortex. This approach entitles one to infer that only those sites where damage impairs retention can possibly be involved in memory storage. The hope (as yet unjustified) must be that more careful observation of the pattern of retention breakdown will enable one to discover which structures within the critical set comprise the engram. Thompson's group have examined the lesions which disturb retention of simple visual memories, kinaesthetic memory, avoidance memory and memory for manipulative responses. They draw several conclusions from their work. First, with all memory systems studied the integrity of retention depends on a limited number of cortical and subcortical regions, thus refuting extreme anti-localizationist ideas. Second, all the memory systems overlap within the posterior diencephalon, ventral mesencephalon and pontine reticular information—all structures intimately connected with the brainstem reticular formation. Their other conclusions are less general. Thus they contend that the frontal cortex and caudate constitute a functional unit because both are involved in all memory systems except the visual, where neither is significant. They also argue that the anterior–medial thalamic complex is only involved in memory systems motivated by fear because damage to it only disturbes retention of avoidance tasks. The existence of a "general" memory system for these four kinds of task is interesting and, in conjunction with some electrophysiological data, prompts Spiliotis and Thompson (1973) to speculate that the brainstem reticular formation is involved in memory storage. The alternative possibility is that the memories are stored largely in the cortical regions which process the information and that the brainstem regions are only important in activation for encoding and retrieval, regardless of the specific task. This second possibility seems even when plausible for varieties of human memory where it is hard to see how brainstem changes could represent the remembered material.

Before examining what bearing electrophyiological data have on the above alternatives, a particular vagueness of the second should be pointed out. This is perhaps best illustrated by a simple example. Suppose an individual learns to associate the sight of a chicken with clucking sounds. Although the integrity of the geniculostriate pathway is important the significance of "chicken stimuli" is only extracted at some later stage in the system—perhaps in the temporal lobes. Only when the meaning of the stimulus has been gleaned at this late stage can it be associated with clucking sounds. It therefore seems plausible that synaptic changes occur only at and beyond the stage where the system has extracted meaning. Yet to say that memory storage is coterminous with the processing structures could be taken to mean that the whole processing system is implicated in the engram. The former possibility is surely more parsimonious and can readily be extended to account for more complex multimodal memories. These could be mediated by changes in a number of "high-level" cortical processing sites, each intercommunicating via specific fibre bundles. This view is compatible with the occurrence of "disconnection" syndromes such as associative visual agnosia, in which a seen object can be accurately drawn and yet its significance remain unappreciated despite the fact that it can be identified by touch. This syndrome implies that cortically stored memories can be isolated from each other if linking fibre bundles are severed, with the result that complex memories disintegrate.

A different approach to the problem of disentangling the secondary consequences of conditioned responses from the primary changes, representing the engram, has been pioneered by Olds and his colleagues (see Olds *et al.*, 1972). They propose that learning causes rerouting of nerve impulses so that the new pathways become available to excitation. Following training, excitation might follow the old pathway for several stages before being rerouted into the new one, which would probably then involve many successive steps, all of them new. Olds proposes that "primary changes" will be those which occur very early in the sequence after the presentation of the conditioned stimulus at places in the brain where the old pretraining pathway could form a junction with the new pathway. Later changes may be primary but the technique does not allow their identification with any confidence. This group attempts to record single unit responses from a wide range of brain sites before and throughout classical conditioning of rats so as to gain a picture of the changing response of neurons throughout learning. If a changed pattern of response emerges with a very short latency after the presentation of the conditioned stimulus it is inferred that the change is one of the sites of the engram. Similarly, this conclusion is drawn if the change emerges very early in conditioning. If the altered firing pattern occurs at a plausible junction point these conclusions are strengthened.

The learning paradigm, adopted by Old's group, has been the differential classical conditioning of an auditory stimulus. With this kind of learning, short-latency learned unit-response changes were recorded from the medial geniculate and posterior nucleus of the thalamus, the cortex, hippocampus, pontine reticular formation and ventral tegmentum, but less clearly from the midbrain auditory system. It is striking that the particularly prominent changes in the posterior thalamus and ventral tegmentum have their counterpart in the lesion studies of Thompson. A more detailed examination of the changes in these structures has been made by Disterhoft and Olds (1972). They found that although the cortical changes to the conditioned stimulus occurred with about the same latency as the posterior thalamic ones the latter appeared earlier in the learning process. There was, however, a change in the background pattern of cortical activity which emerged at the same time as or even sooner in the course of conditioning. This reduced cortical tonic activity, and could have augmented the responsiveness of the posterior thalamic neurons by a corticofugal pathway. The responses of the thalamus were relatively non-specific as the neurons showed similar firing patterns to novel stimuli and revealed considerable generalization of responding to other auditory signals. One interpretation advanced by Disterhoft and Olds is that the posterior thalamus has an activating and motivating role in that its neurons can become attached to any interesting or significant stimuli, regardless of their specific sensory nature. Unfortunately, with this view, it remains unclear whether the posterior nucleus forms a part of the engram. The effects of electrical stimulation of this structure may have interesting effects on consolidation, as indeed the observations of Ojemann (1975) suggest. His work should be extended to animal studies.

The work of Olds and his colleagues faces considerable interpretative problems. The difficulty of chronic single unit recording in freely moving animals has led most subsequent workers to confine themselves to multiple unit recording (see, for example, Gabriel, 1976). Furthermore, their own data indicates that short-latency changes do not provide sufficient data for localizing engrams. The possibility that such changes are secondary consequences of primary tonic activity originating from a distant neural locus has already been mentioned, and has been developed by Gabriel (1976). He argues that if a biasing neural influence is present before, during and after the onset of a conditioned stimulus, then a structure may show altered responsivity to the stimulus at short-latencies, even though it does not itself store the memory. The engram may, in fact, reside in the system delivering the tonic selective biasing influence. Gabriel himself has recorded short-latency multiple-unit activity from the medial geniculate of the rabbit during differential conditioning and its reversal. He found abrupt loss and reversion to the neuronal response, appropriate to original learning, during the initial stages of reversal training. This rapid switching is compatible with the rapid alternation of a response set, which suggests that a biasing factor accounts for the short-latency changes in the medial geniculate.

Another kind of attempt to "map the engram" electrophysiologically has been epitomized by the work of John (1967, 1972). John and his associates have used the "tracer technique" to distinguish between electrical activity of the brain, which reflects information processing of the learned experience and that related to other ongoing types of brain activity. Cats are trained on instrumental conditioning tasks in which the conditioned stimulus is presented intermittently at a characteristic rate of repetition. Electrical rhythms which appear at the same frequency as the tracer stimulus in various parts of the brain are held to be "labelled responses", indicating the processing of learned information. The group, initially recorded EEG rhythms, but have more recently employed evoked potential measures, and even correlated these with single unit activity. Several general phenomena were noticed in the EEG research, which John claims are confirmed and extended by subsequent evoked potential studies.

First, the tracer technique revealed that learning produced changes in a widespread neural system. The extensive distribution of these changes persisted when differential conditioning was used, i.e. different stimuli had to be associated with different responses. With simple conditioning, however, prolonged training decreased the extent of the regions processing learned information. Second, many studies have show that in many brain structures which before learning showed radically different responses to the tracer stimulus, a striking increase in response similarity occurs as a result of learning. John argues that this suggests learning sets up a representational system in which many structures engage in a similar mode of activity. The third kind of effect noted is known as assimilation. This refers to the fact that during learning, the spontaneous EEG tends to assume the frequency of the tracer stimulus even when it is, in fact, absent (see John, 1976). John contends that these rhythms are absent in the home cage, appearing only when an animal enters the training compartment. Further, as they only appear in the trained hemisphere of a split-brain cat (Majkowski, 1967), this is taken as evidence that the rhythms reflect some kind of rehearsal of the learned information. Further evidence for such endogenous rhythms is provided by another phenomenon. When cats, highly overtrained to make differential responses to discriminated stimuli, were given generalization tests to a stimulus of intermediate frequency their induced electrical rhythms were appropriate to the response they made rather than to the test stimulus. On the basis of such observations John distinguishes between exogenous activity, which reflects the sensory input, and endogenous activity which reflects the release of stored information. The latter is most apparent in the generalization effect where the animal's misinterpretation of the tracer stimulus results in the brain rhythms mirroring retrieval from memory rather than reality.

Evoked potential measures have enabled the above observations to be extended. For example, a new "late" process with a 60-ms latency appears as conditioning proceeds but does not occur when the signal fails to elicit a conditioned response. John constructs an evoked potential measure of the information retrieval process by subtracting evoked potentials, elicited on trials in which generalization did not occur to an intermediate tracer stimulus, from evoked potentials occurring in association with generalization. The resulting difference waveshapes have a characteristic form which is specific to the information retrieval it reflects. The waveshape is similar across a wide range of brain sites but with striking latency differences from region to region. Changes appear first in a central corticoreticular system and then in a systematic sequence in other areas, emerging last in the lateral geniculate if the tracer stimulus is visual.

John's group have recently examined unit activity in discrimination learning through the use of chronically implanted microelectrodes (see Schwartz et al., 1976). Single evoked potentials were also recorded using computer-pattern-recognition techniques. These techniques were used to identify what information was being retrieved on a given trial. Two types of single unit response were found in the cortical and subcortical sites from which they recorded. The first type responded to specific stimuli in an invariant fashion, regardless of how these were perceived by the animals. The second type of unit showed one average temporal pattern of response when one kind of information was presumably being retrieved, and another when a different kind of information was being retrieved. These units showed great variability with each kind of information readout. It was only their average pattern of activity that was characteristic. There was a close correspondence between the peaks of the evoked potential and the probability of firing of neurons within the same region. The differences in such response patterns were, however, much smaller across different brain areas than across different readout modes.

Considerations of the above kind have led John to adopt the view that information is represented in a statistical fashion by the average behaviour of a widely distributed neural ensemble rather than by the specific behaviour of individual neuronal elements. Different spatiotemporal patterns of activity in such ensembles represent readout of specific kinds of information. The precise distinction between this statistical viewpoint and what John calls the switchboard theory is never made fully explicit. This could only be done if it was made clear how a given spatiotemporal pattern, widely distributed in the brain, does represent a specific kind of information retrieval. Without such elucidation, which must be a long way off, the distinction between the two viewpoints amounts to an emphasis either on the reliability of individual neuronal activity patterns, or on their variability. There is a serious need to extend this kind of work to learning situations which do not use intermittent conditioned stimuli. Until then the generality of these effects must be doubted. Furthermore, in the evoked potential studies, as John himself points out, although many brain regions show similar activity there are marked latency differences. If Olds' rationale is applied here, it is clear that we can only identify those regions which show the shortest latency responses with the site of the engram. If other regions are involved this needs to be shown by other means. Nevertheless, if the work of John's group can be extrapolated to a wider range of memory contexts, then it shows that retrieval at least is associated with the specific activation of a surprisingly large number of brain structures.

Phenomena such as state dependent memory (see John, 1967) also indicate that the patterned activity by which information is represented is partly determined by the background state of the brain during learning, and the efficiency of retrieval is related to the degree to which this whole pattern can subsequently be reinvoked.

Any conclusions about the locus and extent of engrams derived from the above techniques must be extremely tentative. Even so, the electrophysiological approaches are promising and further technical refinements may lead to confirmation of the impression that the storage of even simple memories involves many structures. The work of John, in particular, throws light on how memories are retrieved. Practically nothing is known about this process, although the classic studies of Penfield (1954) in which the cortex of conscious patients was stimulated suggest that parts of the temporal lobe play a paramount role in initiating the retrieval of complex experimental memories.

More recently, Fernandez Guardiola (1977) has found that periamydala stimulation elicited very old reminiscences linked with infantile experiences, rather than more recent memories. Although these results may be compounded by the patients' chronic epilepsy, they suggest that the medial temporal lobe's mediation of retrieval interacts in a complex way with the age of the memory. Despite the fact that many researchers believe temporal lobe amnesia to be a retrieval problem (see Iverson, 1977), the phenomena of transient global amnesia suggest that the anterograde and retrograde components have different origins. Thus, following recovery from this syndrome, there is typically complete recovery of memory for the retrograde period whereas knowledge of the affected anterograde period remains deficient (Frederiks, 1979). This putative distinction between retrieval and acquisitional mechanisms in memory is also supported by the electrical stimulation work of Fedio and Van Buren (1974), in which retrograde amnesia was produced by posterior temporal stimulation and anterograde amnesia by more anterior stimulation. Whether or not it is mediated by independent types of brain abnormality the consensual view of retrograde amnesia is that the older a memory is the less likely it is to be affected (for example, see Marslen-Wilson and Teuber, 1975). If the view is correct its explanation is a mystery. Perhaps as it ages the memory trace changes either spontaneously or as a result of repeated rehearsals. Alternatively temporal lobe retrieval mechanisms operate on the basis of time-tags associated with memories. Clearly these observations have only highlighted our ignorance of the basic physiological processes underlying complex memory. The fundamental problem of how information is represented and retrieved is still deeply perplexing. It is perhaps the central puzzle of neurobiology.

References

Andry, D. K. and Luttges, M. W. (1972). Memory traces: Experimental separation by cycloheximide and electro-convulsive shock. *Science*, **178**, 518–520.

Atkinson, R. C. and Shiffrin, R. M. (1968). Human memory: A proposed system and its control processes. *In* (Eds. K. W. Spence and J. T. Spence). "The Psychology of Learning and Motivation: Advances in Research and Theory, Vol. 2. Academic Press, London and New York.

Baddeley, A. D. and Hitch, G. (1974). Working memory. *In* (Ed. G. H. Bower), "Recent Advances in Learning and Motivation", vol. VIII, pp. 47–89. Academic Press, London and New York.

Baddeley, A. D. and Warrington, E. K. (1970). Amnesia and the distinction between long- and short-term memory. *Journal of Verbal Learning and Verbal Behaviour* **9**, 176–189.

Baldwin, B. A. and Soltysik, S. S. (1969). The effect of cerebral ischaemia or intracarotid injection of methohexitone on short-term memory in goats. *Brain Research*, **2**, 71–84.

Barondes, S. H. and Cohen H. D. (1968). Memory impairment after subcutaneous injection of acetoxycycloheximide. *Science*, **160**, 556–557.

Barraco, R. A. and Stettner, L. J. (1976). Antibiotics and memory. *Psychological Bulletin*, **83**, 242–302.

Bloch, V. (1970). Facts and hypotheses concerning memory consolidation processes. *Brain Research*, **24**, 561–575.

Bloch, V. (1976). Brain activation and memory consolidation. *In* "Neural Mechanisms of Learning and Memory", (Eds. M. R. Rozenzweig and E. L. Bennett), pp. 583–590. MIT Press, Cambridge, Massachusetts.

Bloch, V., Deweer, B. and Hennevin, E. (1970) Suppression de l'amnesie retrograde et consolidation d'un apprentissage à essai unique par stimulation reticulaire. *Physiology and Behaviour*, **5**, 1235–1241.

Blumstein, S. E., Baker, E. and Goodglass, H. (1977) Phonological factors in auditory comprehension in aphasia. *Neuropsychologia*, **15**, 19–30.

Brierley, J. B. (1977). Neuropathology of amnesic states. *In* "Amnesia" (Eds. C. W. M. Whitty and O. L. Zangwill), 2nd ed, pp. 199–223. Butterworths, London.

Butters, N. and Cermak, L. S. (1974). Some comments on Warrington and Baddeley's report of normal short-term memory in amnesic patients. *Neuropsychologia*, **12**, 283–285.

Butters, N. and Cermak, L. S. (1975). Some analyses of amnesic syndromes in brain-damaged patients. *In* "The Hippocampus" (Eds R. L. Isaacson and K. H. Pribram), vol. II, pp. 377–409. Plenum Press, New York.

Chorover, S. L. and Schiller, P. H. (1965). Short-term retrograde amnesia in rats. J. Comp. Physiol. Psychol. 59, 73–78.

Chow, K. L. (1961). Effects of local electrographic after discharge on visual learning and retention in monkey. *Journal of Neurophysiology*, **24**, 391–400.

Cohen, H. D. and Barondes, S. H. (1968). Cycloheximide impairs memory of an appetitive task. *Communications in Behavioural Biology*, **1**, 337–340.

Craik, F. I. M. and Lockhart, R. S. (1972). Levels of processing: A framework for memory research. *Journal of Verbal learning and Verbal Behaviour*, **11**, 671–684.

Cronly-Dillon J., Carden, D. and Birks, C. (1974). The possible involvement of microtubules in memory fixation. *Journal of Experimental Biology*, **61**, 443–454.

Davis, W. J. (1976). Plasticity in the invertebrates. *In* "Neural Mechanisms of Learning and Memory" (Eds M. R. Rozenzweig and E. L. Bennett),pp. 430–462. MIT Press, Cambridge, Massachusetts.

Dawson, R. G. and McGaugh, J. L. (1969). Electroconvulsive shock effects on a reactivated memory trace: further examination. *Science*, **166**, 525–527.

Deutsch, J. A. (1969). The physiological basis of memory. *Annual Review of Psychology*, 85–104.

Deutsch, J. A. (1971). The cholinergic synapse and the site of memory. *Science*, **174**, 788–794. •

Dicara, L., Braun, J. and Pappas. B. (1970). Classical conditioning and instrumental learning of cardiac and gastrointestinal responses following removal of neocortex in the rat. *Journal of Comparative and Physiological Psychology*, **73**, 208–216.

Disterhoft, J. F. and Olds, J. (1972). Differential development of conditioned unit changes in thalamus and cortex of rat. *Journal of Neurophysiology*, **35**, 665–679.

Drachman, D. A. and Arbit, J. (1966). Memory and the hippocampal complex. II. Is memory a multiple process? *Archives of Neurology and Psychiatry*, **15**, 52–61.

Essman, W. B. (1972). Neurochemical changes in ECS and ECT. *Seminars in Psychiatry*, **4**, 67–79.

Eysenck, M. W. (1977). "Human memory: Theory, Research and Individual Differences". Pergamon, Oxford.

Fedio, P. and Van Buren, J. M. (1974). Memory deficits during electrical stimulation of the speech cortex in conscious man. *Brain and Language*, **1**, 29–42.

Fedio, P. and Van Buren, J. M. (1975). Memory and perceptual deficits during electrical stimulation in left and right thalamus and parietal subcorted. *Brain and Language*, **2**, 78–100.

Fernandez-Guardiola, A. (1977). Reminiscences elicited by electrical stimulation of the temporal lobe in humans. *In* "Neurobiology of Sleep and Memory (Eds. R. R. Drucker-Colin and J. L. McGaugh), pp. 273–280. Academic Press, London and New York.

Fishbein, W., McGaugh, J. L. and Swarz, J. R. (1971). Retrograde amnesia; electroconvulsive shock effects after termination of rapid eye movement sleep deprivation. *Science*, **172**, 80–82.

Flexner, J. B. and Flexner, L. B. (1967). Restoration of expression of memory lost after treatment with puromycin. *Proceedings of the National Academy of Sciences of the United States of America*, **66**, 48–52.

Flexner, J. B. and Flexner, L. B. (1970). Further observations on restoration of memory lost after treatment with puromycin. *Yale Journal of Biology and Medicine*, **42**, 235–240.

Flexner, J. B., and Flexner, L. B. and Stellar, E. (1963). Memory in mice as affected intracerebral puromycin. *Science*, **141**, 57–59.

Frederiks, J. R. M. (1979). Transient Global Amnesia. *International Neuropsychological Society Bulletin*, Part II, 18.

Gabriel, M. (1976). Short-latency discriminative unit response: engram or bias? *Physiological Psychology*, **4**, 275–280.

Geller, A. and Jarvik, M. E. (1968). The time relations of ECS induced amnesia. *Psychonomic Science*, **12**, 169–170.

Geschwind, N. (1965). Disconnexion syndromes in animal and man. *Brain*, **88**, 237–294, and 585–644.

Gibbs, M. E. and Ng, K. T. (1976). Memory formation: A new three-phase model. *Neuroscience Letters*, **2**, 165–169.

Gold, P. E. and King, R. A. (1974). Retrograde amnesia: Storage failure versus retrieval failure. *Psychological Review*, **81**, 456–469.

Gold, P. E. and McGaugh, J. L. (1975). A single-trace, process view of memory storage processes. *In* "Short-term Memory (Eds. D. Deutsch and J. A. Deutsch), pp. 355–378. Academic Press, New York and London.

Gold, P. E. Macri, J. and McGaugh, J. L. (1973). Retrograde amnesic gradients: Effects of direct cortical stimulation. *Science*, **179**, 1343–1345.

Goldsmith, L. J. (1967). Effect of intracerebral actinomycin–D and of electroconvulsive shock on passive avoidance. *Journal of Comparative and Physiological Psychology*, **63**, 126–132.

Gruneberg, M. M. (1976). The distinction between short-term memory and long-term memory. *Bulletin of the British Psychological Society*, **29**, 327–333.

Hardyck, C., Tzeng, O. J. L. Wang, W, S-Y (1978). Cerebral lateralization of function and bilingual decision processes: Is thinking lateralized? *Brain and Language*, **5**, 56–71.

Hartmann, E. and Stern, W. C. (1972). Desynchronised sleep deprivation: Learning deficit and its reversal by increased catecholamines. *Physiology and Behaviour*, **8**, 585–587.

Hebb, D. O. (1949). "The Organization of Behaviour". Wiley, New York.

Hughes, R. A., Barrett, R. J. and Ray O. S. (1970). Retrograde amnesia in rats increases as a function of ECS-test interval and ECS intensity. *Physiology and Behaviour*, **5**, 27–30.

Iverson, S. D. (1977). Temporal lobe amnesia. *In* "Amnesia" (Eds. C. W. M. Whitty and O. L. Zangwill), 2nd ed, pp. 136–182. Butterworth, London.

John, E. R. (1967). "Mechanisms of Memory". Academic Press, New York.

John, E. R. (1972). Switchboard versus statistical theories of learning and memory. *Science*, **177**, 850–864.

John, E. R. (1976). A model of consciousness. *In* "Consciousness and Self-Regulation" (Eds. G. E. Schwartz and D. Shapiro), pp. 1–50. Wiley, London.

Jurko, M. F. (1978). Center median "alerting" and verbal learning dysfunction. *Brain and Language*, **5**, 98–102.

Kapp, B. S. and Schneider, A. M. (1971). Selective recovery from retrograde amnesia produced by hippocampal spreading depression. *Science*, **173**, 1149–1151.

Kinsbourne M. (1972). Behavioural analysis of the repetition deficit in conduction aphasia. *Neurology*, **22**, 1126–1132.

Kopp, R., Bohdanecky, Z. and Jarvik, M. E. (1966). Long temporal gradient of retrograde amnesia for a well-discriminated stimulus. *Science*, **153**, 1547–1549.

Krivanek, J. (1971). Facilitation of avoidance learning by pentylenetetrazol as a function of task difficulty, deprivation and shock level. *Psychopharmalogia*, **10**, 189–195.

Lashley, K. (1950). In search of the engram. Society of Experimental Biology, Symposium 4, pp. 454–482.

Lehmann, D. and Koukkau, M. (1974). Computer analysis of EEG wakefulness-sleep patterns during learning of novel and familiar sentences. *Electroencephalography and Clinical Neurophysiology* **37**, 73–84.

Lewis, D. J. and Bregman, N. J. (1973). Source of cues for cue-dependent amnesia in rats. *Journal of Comparative and Physiological Psychology*, **85**, 421–426.

Lewis, D. J., Miller, R. R. and Misdnin, J. R. (1968). Recovery of memory following amnesia. *Nature*, **220**, 704–705.

Lhermitte, F. and Signoret, J-L. (1976). The amnesic syndromes and the hippocampal–mammillary system. *In* "Neural Mechanisms of Learning and Memory", (Eds. M. R. Rozenzweig and E. L. Bennett), pp. 49–56. MIT Press, Cambridge, Massachusetts.

Lucero, M. (1970). Lengthening of REM sleep duration consecutive to learning in the rat. *Brain Research*, **20**, 319–322.

Mah, C. J. and Albert, D. J. (1973). Electroconvulsive shock-induced retrograde amnesia: An analysis of the variation in the length of the amnesia gradient. *Behavioural Biology*, **9**, 517–540.

Majkowski, J. (1967). Electrophysiological studies of learning in split-brain cats. *Electroencephalography and Clinical Neurophysiology*, **23**, 521–531.

Mark, R. F. and Watts, M. E. (1971). Drug inhibition of memory formation in chickens. Long-term memory. *Proceedings of the Royal Society London B*, **178**, 439–454.

Marslen-Wilson, W. D. and Teuber, H. L. (1975). Memory for remote events in anterograde amnesia; recognition of public figures from news photographs. *Neuropsychologia*, **13**, 353–364.

Mayes, A. R. (1973). Disruption of the interhemispheric transfer of active avoidance learnt during unilateral cortical spreading depression. *Behavioral Biology*, **8**, 207–212.

Mayes, A. R., Meudell, P. R. and Neary, D. (1978). Must amnesia be caused by either encoding or retrieval disorders? *In* "Practical Aspects of Memory" (Eds M. M. Gruneberg, P. E. Morris and R. N. Sykes), pp. 712–719. Academic Press, London and New York.

McGaugh, J. L. (1973). Drug facilitation of learning and memory. *Annual Reveiw of Pharmacology*, **13**, 229–241.

Meudell, P. R., Mayes, A. R. and Neary, D. (1979). Is amnesia caused by a consolidation impairment? *In* "Research in Psychology and Medicine" (Eds D. J. Oborne, M. M. Gruneberg and J. R. Eiser), pp. 323–330. Academic Press, London and New York.

Miller, R. R. and Springer, R. D. (1974). Implications of recovery from experimental amnesia. *Psychological Review*, **81**, 470–473.

Milner, B. (1971). Interhemispheric differences and psychological processes. *British Medical Bulletin*, **27**, 272–277.

Müller, G. E. and Pilzecker, A. (1900). Experimentelle Beltrage zur Lehre vom Gedachniss. Zeitschift fur Psychologie und Physiologie der suinesorgane, *Erganzungsband*, **1**, 1–288.

Ojemenn, G. A. (1975). Language and the thalamus: Object naming and recall during and after thalmic stimulation. *Brain and Language*, **2**, 101–120.

Olds, J. Disterhoft, J. F., Segal, M., Kornblith, C. L. and Hirsh, R. (1972). Learning centers of the rat mapped by measuring the latencies of conditioned unit responses. *Journal of Neurography Biology*, **35**, 202–219.

Pearlman, J. R. and Greenberg, R. (1973). Post-trial REM sleep: A critical period for consolidation of shuttlebox avoidance. *Animal Learning and Behaviour*, **1**, 49–51.

Penfield, W. (1954). The permanent record of the stream of consciousness. Proceedings of the 14th International Congress of Psychology, pp. 47–69.

Plotkin, H. C. and Russell, I. S. (1969). The hemidecorticate learning deficit: Evidence for a quantitative impairment. *Physiology of Behaviour*, **41**, 49–55.

Plotkin, H. C. and Russell, I. S., (1969). Quantitative adjustment in magnitude of the hemidecorticate learning deficit by CS duration manipulation. *Physiology of Behaviour* **4**, 709–721.

Powell, E. W. and Hines, G. (1974). The limbic system: An interface. *Behavioral Biology*, **12**, 149–164.

Raisman, G. (1969). Neuronal plasticity in the septal nuclei of the adult rat. *Brain Research*, **14**, 25–48.

Robbins, M. J. and Meyer, D. R. (1970). Motivation control of retrograde amnesia. *Journal of Experimental Psychology*, **84**, 220–225.

Rose, S. P. R., Hambley, J. and Haywood, J. (1976). Neurochemical approaches to developmental plasticity and learning. *In* "Neural Mechanisms of Learning amd Memory" (Eds. M. R. Rozenweig and E. L. Bennett), pp. 293–310. MIT Press, Cambridge, Massachusetts.

Rosenbaum, M. Cohen, H. D. and Barondes, S. H. (1968). Effect of intracerebral saline on amnesia produced by inhibitors of cerebral protein synthesis.

Rozenweig, M. R. (1970). Evidence for anatomical and chemical changes in the brain during primary learning. *In* "Biology of Memory" (Eds K. H. Pribram and D. E. Broadbent). Academic Press, New York and London.

Rozin, P. (1976). The psychological approach to human memory. *In* "Neural Mechanisms of Learning and Memory" (Eds M. R. Rozenweig and E. L. Bennett). MIT Press, Cambridge, Massachusetts.

Russell, I. S. (1966). The differential role of the cerebral cortex in classical and instrumental conditioning. *In* "Biological and Physiological Problems of Psychology XVIII International Congress of Psychology", Moscow. p. 115.

Russell, R. W. (1959). "Brain, Memory and Learning". Clarendon Press, Oxford.

Schneider, A. M. (1975). Two faces of memory consolidation: Storage of instrumental and classical conditioning. 340–355. *In* "Short-term Memory" (Eds D. D. Deutsch and J. A. Deutsch), pp. 340–355. Academic Press, London.

Schwartz, E., Ramos, A. and John, E. R. (1976). Single cell activity in chronic unit recording: A quantitative study of the unit amplitude spectrum. *Brain Research Bulletin*, **1**, 57–68.

Shallice, T. and Butterworth, B. B. (1977). Short-term memory and impairment and spontaneous speech. *Neuropsychologia*, **15**, 729–735.

Shallice, T. and Warrington, E. K. (1977). Auditory-verbal short-term memory impairment and conduction aphasia. *Brain and Language*, **4**, 479–491.

Sokolov, E. N., (1960). Neuronal models and the orienting reflex. *In* "The Central Nervous System and Behaviour: Transactions of Third Conference" (Ed. M. A. B. Blazin), Macy Foundation, New York.

Spada, F. and Buerger, A. A. (1976). Effect of stimulus location and response measure on an instrumental avoidance conditioning paradigm in spinal rat. *Physiological Psychology*, **4**, 219–223.

Spiliotis, P. H. and Thompson, R. (1973). The "Manipulative response memory system" in the white rat. *Physiological Psychology*, **1**, 102–114.

Squire, L. R. (1975). Short-term memory as a biological entity. *In* "Short-term Memory" (Eds D. Deutsch and J. A. Deutsch). Academic Press, London and New York.

Squire, L. R. and Barondes, S. H. (1970). Actinomycin–D: Effects on memory at different times after training. *Nature, London,* **225**, 649–650.

Squire, L. R. and Barondes, S. H. (1972). Variable decay of memory and its recovery in cycloheximide-treated mice. *Proceedings of the National Academy of Sciences, USA,* **69** 1416–1420.

Squire, L. R. and Barondes, S. H. (1973). Memory impairment during prolonged training in mice given inhibitors of protein synthesis. *Brain Research,* **56**, 215–225.

Squire, L. R., Glick, S. D. and Goldfarb, J. (1971). Relearning at different times after training as affected by centrally and peripherally acting cholinergic drugs in the mouse. *Journal of Comparative and Physiological Psychology,* **74**, 41–45.

Squire, L. R., Slater, P. C. and Chase, P. M. (1976). Reactivation of recent or remote memory before electroconvulsive therapy does not produce retrograde amnesia. *Behavioural Biology,* **18**, 335–344.

Stern, W. C. and Morgane, P. J. (1974). Theoretical view of REM sleep function: Maintenance of catecholamine systems in the central nervous system. *Behavioural Biology,* **11**, 1–32.

Tallal, P. and Newcombe, F. (1978). Impairment of auditory perception and language comprehension in dysphasia. *Brian and Language,* **5**, 13–24.

Thomas, J. C., Fozard, J. L. and Waugh, N. C. (1977). Age-related differences in naming latency. *American Journal of Psychiatry,* 90, 499–509.

Tzortzis, C. and Albert, M. L. (1974). Impairment of memory for sequences in conduction aphasia. *Neuropsychologia,* **12**, 355–366.

Van Wimersma, T. B. and De Wied, D. (1976). Modulation of passive-avoidance behaviour of rats by intracerebroventricular administration of anti vasopressin serum. *Behavioral Biology,* **18**, 325–333.

Warrington, E. K. (1971). Neurological disorders of memory. *British Medical Bulletin,* (Ed. A. Summerfield), **27**, pp. 243–247.

Warrington, E. K. and Taylor, A. M. (1973). Immediate memory for faces: long- or short-term memory. *Quarterly Journal of Experimental Psychology,* **25**, 316–322.
chickens. II. Short term memory. *Proceedings of the Royal Society (Series B: Biological Sciences),* 1971, 455–464.

Waugh, N. C. and Norman, D. A. (1965). Primary memory. *Psychological Revue,* **72**, 89–104.

Wickelgren, W. A. (1973). The long and short of memory. *Psychological Bulletin,* **80**, 425–438.

Wickelgren, W. A. (1974). Single trace fragility theory of memory dynamics. *Memory and Cognition,* **2**, 775–780.

Wiener, N. I. (1970). Electroconvulsive shock induced impairment and enchantment of a learned escape response. *Physiology and Behaviour,* **5**, 971–974.

Wolfowitz, B. E. and Holdstock, T. L. (1971). Paradoxical sleep deprivation and memory in rats. *Communications in Behavioural Biology,* **6**, 281–284.

Zaidel, D. and Sperry, R. W. (1974). Memory impairment after commissurotomy in man. *Brain,* **97**, 263–272.

Zinkin, S. and Miller, A. J. (1967). Recovery of memory after amnesia induced by electroconvulsive shock. *Science,* **155**, 102–104.

Zornetzer, S. F. and Gold, M. S. (1976). The locus coeruleus: Its possible role in memory consolidation. *Physiology and Behaviour,* **16**, 331–336.

2 Changing Focus: Brain Mechanism and Selective Attention

R. STEVENS
Department of Psychology,
University of Nottingham

1 Introduction

Contemporary approaches to the study of attention have been strongly influenced by two historically important figures. One is William James whose writings, after many years of neglect during which psychology was dominated by a strong behaviouristic approach, are once more acknowledged for the clear insight they show into cognitive processes. Thus in 1890 James wrote:

> Everyone knows what attention is. It is the taking possession of the mind in clear and vivid form, of one out of what seem several simultaneous possible objects or trains of thought. Focalization, concentration of consciousness are of its essence. It implies withdrawal from somethings in order to deal effectively with others . . .

It would be difficult to find a recent definition of attention which would receive a similar consensus of agreement on the meaning of attention. Two aspects of attention seem implicit in the above quotation. One is that the mind can concentrate preferentially on some rather than other current sensory inputs, and second that attention is a process controlling the direction of a person's stream of thoughts. However, nearly all studies on attention deal with stimulus selection and not surprisingly the majority of this chapter is devoted to a discussion of some brain mechanisms involved in selective attention.

The second historically influential figure is Sir Charles Sherrington whose major contribution to physiological psychology was his demonstration of the importance of inhibitory processes in the central nervous system. In relation to attention he suggested (Sherrington, 1906) that inhibitory processes may be the means by which the brain *ignores* some of the impulses ascending the sensory pathways. What is probably the best known contemporary physiological model of selective attention is based on inhibitory processes. Hernandez-Peon (1969) argues that sensory input is controlled by a "variable-gain system" involving corticofugal efferent inhibitory fibres which reduce the transmission of inpulses in afferent nerve fibres. This is exemplified by studies by Horn (1960) who found that cortical evoked responses to a light flash were attentuated when a cat looked actively at a mouse outside the flash zone, and Hernandez-Peon *et al.* (1965) who discovered that somatosensory evoked responses were diminished when a cat investigated a tin of sardines. Although the mechanism by which sensory gating is implemented may well involve inhibition of sensory input, there are aspects of selective attention such as the shift of attention to a novel or previously ignored stimulus which must involve complex processes which can not be treated as being just excitatory or inhibitory.

Hernandez-Peon's theory of sensory gating provides an explanation for selective attention which is not restricted to a single sensory modality. Therefore it is surprising that this theory has not come to dominate physiological studies of attention. Instead, there are at present a number of different and relatively independent lines of investigation into the brain mechanisms involved in attention. Indeed many areas of the brain have been purported as being involved in selective attention. For instance, the following structures have all been implicated: the hippocampus (Grastyan *et al.*, 1959; Douglas, 1967; Stevens and Cowey, 1973, 1974; Bennett, 1975), the foveal prestriate region of circumstriate cortex (Cowey and Gross, 1970; Mishkin, 1972; Gross, 1972, 1973), inferotemporal cortex (Pribram, 1974) and superior colliculus. This list is not complete, merely indicative of the broad approach taken in investigating brain mechanisms and attention. Clearly it would require several chapters or even several volumes to adequately discuss the full range of studies on the physiology of attention. Therefore the bulk of this chapter will be restricted to a discussion of the role of the superior colliculus in attention. One of the reasons for this choice is that the superior colliculus has been implicated in saccadic eye movement control and since directed visual attention in human beings requires strategical visual search patterns, the issues raised are of particular interest in trying to understand attentional processes in ourselves.

2 Problems and pontifications

Some of the theoretical and technical problems confronting anyone interested in investigating brain mechanisms and attention are different from those arising in other areas of physiological psychology, and therefore they merit a brief discussion. One frequently used technique in studies of attention involves single unit recordings of the activity of feature detecting neurons in awake–active animals. If in the course of such a study the animal starts to attend to a specific environmental event, there is almost certainly going to be the same short-lived alteration in its neural activity. But since a phasic response is to be expected when a feature detector is activated because the animal has been exposed to the appropriate trigger stimulus, how can an attentional response be distinguished from a feature detection response? Although we might on *a priori* grounds argue that cessation of a phasic response correlates with the animal ceasing to attend to a stimulus, there is still no obvious rule that can be used to distinguish between feature detection responsiveness and an attentional response. The enhancement response shown by neurons in the superior colliculus (Goldberg and Wurtz, 1972b; see section 7) exemplify this problem.

Attention, by definition, is a control function which ensures that cognitive processing is directed towards significant features of the environment. Therefore mechanisms of attention must utilize information pertinent to the animal's past experience, and its motivational and emotional states. In consequence, an alteration in the animal's motivational state or some new experience may cause it to ignore a previously significant stimulus or alternatively it may respond to a previously disregarded stimulus. Once again, this problem can cause difficulties in interpreting the data from studies using electrophysiological recording techniques. For instance, if the response charateristics of a neuron change during the course of an experiment, does this reflect the operation of an attentional mechanism or has it been caused by habituation, dishabituation or sensitization? Although it could be argued that habituation corresponds with learned inattention and dishabituation or sensitization are alternative ways of viewing a selective attentional response (see for instance, Sokolov's (1963) discussion of the orienting response), they are also characteristics of basic learning processes. One solution to this problem which was proposed by Buser (1976) is to treat long-term changes in the response characteristics of neurons as reflecting learning processes, and only short term changes as correlates of attention. However useful such a distinction may be in interpreting the findings from single neuron recording studies, it would be dangerous to generalize the rule to the interpretation of behavioural studies involving attention and learning.

2.1 Attention and action

The actions of an animal which is attending are not invariant across different behavioural situations. For instance, when an animal is confronted with a relatively novel stimulus, it makes an orienting response towards the stimulus. This includes a number of components such as pupillary dilation, erection of pinnae, shifts in eye gaze, changes in posture to orient the head towards the stimulus, a reduction in galvanic skin response, slowing of the heart rate and so on (see Sokolov, 1963). But the orienting response involves some different actions from those exhibited, for example, in a discrimination task which also requires the animal to attend. Behavioural arrest is a marked characteristic of an animal which is orienting towards a novel stimulus, whereas in visual discrimination tasks animals display a lot of active searching or sampling of the stimuli, commonly known as vicarious trial-and-error behaviour.

But visual sampling behaviour can also differ qualitatively in that in some situations it is directed and in others it appears to be random. One instance of directed visual attention was graphically named the "visual grasp reflex" by Adamuk (1872). This involves a saccadic eye movement which brings macular vision to bear on a visual target originally present more peripherally in the visual field. Such directed eye movements are characteristic of the orienting response. But random or non-directed visual sampling behaviour can also involve saccadic eye movements, as is found when a person explores a visual field such as a photograph or painting (Yarbus, 1967). In this instance, the choice of visual target for each saccade is interoceptive, and the pattern of selected visual targets is fairly random. However, if the person is asked a question about the picture prior to visual exploration his eye movements became very selective. Thus the same action can be involved in very different aspects of attentional behaviour.

Discussions on attention frequently disregard response-selection, concentrating instead on stimulus-selection. But as William James pointed out, attention is a control function acting either on sensory input, by focalizing on some stimuli at the expense of others, or it can direct which way our thoughts will turn, or even determine what responses will be made. The latter two aspects of attention are emphasized by non-continuity learning theorists such as Krechevsky (1935) who propose that in problem solving situations animals select and reject hypotheses or strategies of responding in order to maximize their rewards. Since hypotheses are thoughts, the selection of hypotheses can obviously, according to James' definition, be considered an aspect of attention. One way of studying hypothesis selection is to work through a protocol of an animal's responses in a problem solving task (see for instance, Kimble, 1975) to determine what hypotheses it has been using and therefore infer something about the attentional processes involved in hypothesis selection. Using such an approach it has been found that animals with hippocampal lesions tend to perseverate hypotheses in learning tasks (Silveira and Kimble, 1968; Kimble and Kimble, 1970; Stevens 1973; Kimble, 1975).

2.2 Aspects of attention

Neuropsychological investigations into attention have concentrated either on non-specific arousal effects or on selectional processes. But a clear distinction between arousal and selectional aspects of atention is by no means generally accepted, and arousal and selection become merged in theories such as Sokolov's (1963) model of the orienting responses. One explanation for this could be that the reticular formation is implicated in both arousal and in the modulation of sensory relay nuclei like the lateral geniculate nucleus and sensory areas of neocortex (see Buser, 1976, for a recent review). Moreover, it has several times been pointed out that one reflection of attentional processes in the central nervous system may be selective arousal.

The selectional aspect of attention is not, however, an undifferentiated process. As has already been proposed, there is a distinction between stimulus selection and the selection of hypotheses. But even such a two-staged selectional system is not adequate. For instance, if a raisin is moved into the peripheral visual field of a monkey it will move its eyes to bring the object into foveal vision. If the same monkey is being trained on a simultaneous visual discrimination task it will direct its gaze first at one stimulus and then at the other. Arguably, the same focalization aspect of attention could occur in both situations, but in the second the monkey may be selectively attending to specific aspects of the information available in its macular field of vision. This latter level of selective attention corresponds with the type of control process which must direct the selection of particular stimulus analysers in Sutherland and Mackintosh's (1971) two-stage theory of discrimination learning.

Attention is too often treated by psychologists as an undifferentiated process, but it should by now be clear that it can not be viewed as such. If any serious progress is to be made in exploring the brain mechanisms underlying selective attentional processes, it will be necessary to individually explore some of these aspects of attention. Already there are indications that different brain areas are involved in different aspects of selective attention. As previously noted the hippocampus has been implicated in hypothesis selection (see review by Kimble, 1975) and the part of the circumstriate belt which is anterior to the foveal region of area 17 appears important for the selection of appropriate visual stimulus analyzers (see reviews by Gross, 1972, 1973). But for the remainder of this chapter we will consider the structure and functions of the superior colliculus, another brain region which has been regarded as essential in selective attention.

3 Two visual systems?

Sensory physiologists and neuroanatomists have tended to concentrate on the retinal–geniculate nucleus–visual cortical system, but recently a phylogenetically more primitive part of the visual system, the retinal–tectal pathway, has gained more interest. One result of this was the publication in the late 1960s of two papers in which similar views were proposed that there was evidence for two interrelated visual systems.

Schneider (1967) based his suggestions on experiments in which he compared the behaviour of golden hamsters which had visual cortex ablated or had intact visual cortices but with undercut superior colliculi. Animals with superior colliculus damage showed quite remarkable visual neglect in contrast to visually decorticate hamsters. For example they ignored visual stimuli such as a sunflower seed which was moved around in front of them beyond whisker distance whereas cortically damaged hamsters showed visual following behaviour. Schneider trained his hamsters on a light–dark and a horizontal–vertical simultaneous discrimination task using a testing procedure that allowed two types of errors to be scored: in one an error was an approach to the incorrect stimulus (approach error) and the other was if the hamster actually touched or pushed the incorrect panel (door push error). Cortically lesioned hamsters learned the brightness discrimination according to both error criteria but as expected they could not learn the pattern discrimination. Those with collicular damage failed to learn according to the approach error score, but did so if errors were measured in terms or door pushes. Their strategy in this task was different from the hamsters with visual cortex lesions which ran fairly directly to one or other of the stimuli. Animals with tectal damage approached one door and if it were correct they pushed through it; if not they passed in front of the door (without necessarily touching it) and moved to the adjacent correct panel. Schneider suggests that the geniculo–visual cortex system provides an animal with information about *what* it is seeing, whereas the retinal–tectal system gives it information about *where* an object is in visual space.

Trevarthen (1968) also argued that there were different functions performed by the cortical and the midbrain visual mechanisms. The geniculate–cortical component is necessary for what he terms *focal* vision and the midbrain section provides for *ambient* vision. The focal system is primary in animals like monkeys and man, in which macular vision predominates and in which there is a highly magnified representation of the central parts of the visual field in primary visual cortex (Allman, 1977; Cowey, 1979). In contrast with the focal system which provides a detailed analysis on the features of an object, the ambient system has the function of locating objects in visual space without providing detailed information as to the object's characteristics. Thus the ambient system tells the animal something is present in its visual world and where it is, but the focal system tells it what the object is. Trevarthen suggests that the two systems operate conjointly when an object enters the peripheral field of view. The ambient system responds by directing eye movements (and possibly body and head movements) to "capture" the object for the focal system which then analyses its details. Trevarthen's ambient visual system appears synonymous with the "visual grasp reflex" proposed by Adamuk (1872) on the basis of his findings that electrical stimulation of superior colliculus generated conjugate eye movements.

Since the publication of Schneider's and Trevarthen's papers an increasing interest has been shown in the role of midbrain visual structures. Many studies have now been published on the superior colliculus, the midbrain structure which receives the largest proportion of fibres from the retina and visual areas of neocortex.

4 Superior colliculus, structural considerations

In the roof of the midbrain of mammals there are four humps which together form the. corpora quadrigemina. The two which are most caudal are the inferior colliculi while the rostral pair are the superior colliculi, also called the optic tectum. Bordering the superior colliculi rostrally is the pretectum, and the mesencephalic central grey and reticular formation lie below it.

The mammalian superior colliculus is less obviously stratified than is the optic tectum in other vertebrates but nevertheless, as can be seen in Fig. 1, there are seven generally agreed strata (Szekely, 1973; Kanaseki and Sprague, 1974; Sprague, 1975). These strata are usually grouped into superficial, intermediate and deep layers which are probably functionally distinct.

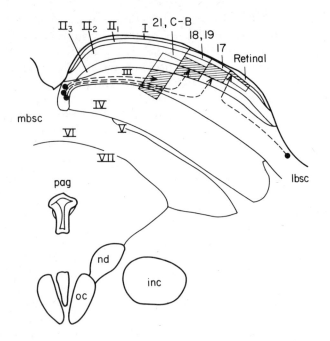

FIG. 1. A schematic drawing of cat superior colliculus showing the layers and visual inputs to superficial laminae. Terminal fields from optic tract (retinal) and visual corticotectal projections from areas 17, 18, 19, 21 and C-B (Clare–Bishop) are boxed with major focus of termination being hatched. lbsc, lateral brachium of superior colliculus; mbsc, medial brachium of superior colliculus; oc, oculomotor nuclei; pag, periaqueductal gray; inc, interstitial nucleus of Cajal and adjacent reticular formation; nd, nucleus of Darkschewtsch; oc, oculomotor nucleus. (After Sprague, 1975.)

It is difficult to distinguish between the outermost laminae, stratum zonale (lamina I) and stratum griseum superficiale (lamina II) which receive projections from the optic tract. At the boundary of the second layer (superficial grey) and the deeper stratum opticum (lamina III), there are terminals of cortico–collicular projections. The optic layer consists of myelinated fibres with a few small cell bodies. Optic fibres entering this layer turn 90 degrees towards the surface and terminate in the overlying layer. Afferents of non-optic cortical origin on entering this layer turn 90 degrees inward and terminate in deeper laminae. These outer three strata are grouped into the superficial layer.

More ventrally lies the relatively wide stratum griseum mediale (lamina IV), an area of large multipolar neurons whose axons form an important efferent projection from superior colliculus. These myeli-nated fibres leave colliculus in the stratum album medium (lamina V).

The intermediate grey layer receives fibres from the superficial grey layer.

The deep layers of superior colliculus consist of the poorly defined stratum griseum profundum (lamina VI) and stratum album profundum (lamina VII) which delimits colliculus from central grey matter. Neurons in the deep grey layer are, like those in intermediate grey, large and multipolar. They project their myelinated axons via the deep white lamina around central grey to enter the crossed predorsal bundle (Kanaseki and Sprague, 1974). Axons of the commissural fibres which interconnect the superior colliculi pass within the seventh layer. Kanaseki and Sprague (1974) among others have proposed that in the cat the lateral nucleus of periaqueductal grey should be considered an eighth lamina of the colliculus since dendrites from its neurons project into the deep layers and its axons project to intermediate layers of colliculus (Hamilton, 1973).

4.1 Afferents to colliculus

The superficial layers of superior colliculus receive visual connexions whereas deeper layers receive multimodal afferents including visual, auditory and somesthetic fibres. There are two distinct visual inputs, one from the retinae directly and the other from cortical areas 17, 18 and 19 (and also in the cat from areas 21 and Clare–Bishop). Each retina projects both ipsilaterally and contralaterally to each colliculus with fibres entering stratum opticum from the lateral brachium to terminate in stratum zonale and to a lesser extent in superficial grey. Fibres from occipital cortex like those from the retina enter the optic layer, but from the medial brachium of superior colliculus. A few of the more dorsal fibres turn dorsally to terminate in stratum zonale, and most of the rest also turn dorsally to end in the adjacent superfical grey layer. The remainder of visual-cortical fibres turn ventrally to terminate more diffusely in deep laminae IV, V and VI. In general the retinal fibres end more superficially than do the fibres from visual cortex, and the deep layers have a visual input independent of that sent to layer II. It has been shown using anatomical and electrophysiological techniques that both the retinal and the visual cortical inputs to colliculus are topographically organized, and, moreover, the retinotopic and visuotopic maps coincide.

There is a difference in the way that the visual field is represented on the colliculus in primates compared with other mammals (Allman, 1977) even those with frontally directed eyes such as cats. In both primates and non-primates, the projection of the visual field on to the

R. Stevens

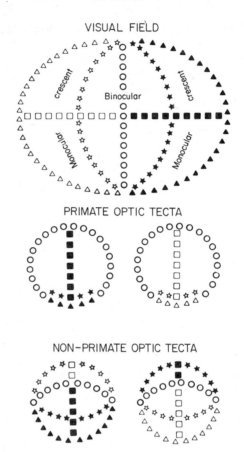

FIG. 2. Visual field plans showing how the visual field is represented in the superior colliculus of primates and non-primates. Vertical meridian dividing the two halves of the visual field shown by circles; squares, the horizontal meridian; triangles, the periphery of the visual field; stars show the division between the binocular and monocular portions of the visual field. (After Allman, 1977.)

colliculi is rotated through 90 degrees, so the horizontal meridian bisects colliculus in an antero-posterior direction. Homonymous halves of the retina and hence of the visual field are represented on the contralateral colliculus in primates with the upper visual field being projected on the medial half of the colliculus and the lower visual field in the lateral half. The centre of the visual field is disproportionately represented in the primate superior colliculus. Wilson and Toyne (1970) found that the central 30 degrees of the visual field occupies approximately three quarters of the colliculus whereas the remaining 60 degrees is crammed into the caudal quarter. Notably they also found that the magnification is greater along the horizontal than the vertical meridian. In addition Wilson and Toyne found that the foveal representation in rostral superior colliculus comes almost entirely from a cortical projection. Enucleation produced remarkably little terminal degeneration in the rostral superior colliculus of monkeys. However, Hubel *et al.* (1975) found that radioactively labelled amino acids when injected into the foveal part of the retina were transported to rostral superior colliculus.

In non-primates, the superior colliculus receives an almost completely crossed retinal projection, with few fibres from the ipsilateral retina. Thus even in cats which have frontally directed eyes there is only a 5–10% projection from the ipsilateral retina (Kanaseki and Sprague, 1974), and this apparently goes to posterior tectum (Graybiel, 1975). Since the ipsilateral part of the visual field is represented on the anterior surface of colliculus, Powell (1976) suggests that an ipsilateral eye input to the anterior tectum comes via a projection from contralateral visual cortex. Some non-primates such as cats have a disproportionately large area of superior colliculus devoted to the centre of the visual field whereas in the rat, for instance, no region of the retina has a magnified representation on the colliculus. Perhaps surprisingly, since they are usually classed as primates, tree shrews (Tupaia) conform to the non-primate tectal visuotopic organization (Lane *et al.*, 1971).

Intermediate and deep layers of colliculus receive afferents from a considerable variety of sources. Apart from visual cortex, other cerebral cortical areas including auditory, sensory-motor regions (but not in rhesus monkeys according to Kuypers and Lawrence, 1967), and the frontal eye fields (area 8) contribute fibres to superior colliculus. Subcortical afferents to colliculus come from both visual structures and non-visual ones although the former predominate. The ventral lateral geniculate nucleus projects to superficial and intermediate layers (Graybiel, 1974) and the pulvinar projects profusely to superficial layers.

Inputs to the intermediate and/or deep layers arise from substantia nigra, the central grey matter, cerebellar fastigial nucleus, medullary and pontine reticular nuclei, the spinal trigeminal nucleus and the spinal cord (for references see Sprague *et al.*, 1973; Sprague, 1975; Hashikawa and Kawamura, 1977). In two species, the mouse (Drager and Hubel, 1975a, 1975b) and the cat (Stein, *et al.*, 1976), there is evidence for a remarkable conguence between the visual field map in superficial superior colliculus and the somatotype plan in deeper layers. For instance Drager and Hubel (1975b) found that the somatosensory representation of the mouse's vibrissae lies in an area of the colliculus with a visual representiation that includes the area of space traversed by the whiskers. In the intermediate and deep layers of colliculus many cells are bimodal or trimodal responding to auditory, tactile or visual stimulation.

Astruc (1971) reports a projection from the frontal eye field region of cortex (area 8) to several layers of superior colliculus in the rhesus monkey. The superficial layers receive some fibres but the main projection is to the intermediate and deep laminae. Since there are no direct projections from frontal eye fields to oculomotor nuclei, eye movements generated by electrical stimulations of area 8 may be mediated in part by the projection to superior colliculus.

In the cat, all layers of superior colliculus receive a profuse afferent projection from extraocular and neck miscles (Abrahams and Rose, 1975). These inputs converge on visually responsive cells, thereby possibly providing the necessary feedback for goal-directed eye and head movements which have been demonstrated with electrical stimulation in the superior colliculus of the cat (Straschill and Rieger, 1973; Roucoux and Crommelinck, 1976).

4.2 Efferents from superior colliculus

There are ascending and descending projections from superior colliculus and it appears that whereas the former arise in both superficial and deep layers of colliculus, the latter originate primarily in deeper laminae. The cat has probably been the species most extensively investigated but similar results have been found in the tree shrew and rhesus monkey. Ascending efferent fibres predominantly terminate in regions commonly considered to be visual: pretectum, lateral posterior nucleus of thalamus (or the pulvinar, which is its prosimian and simian homologue) and dorsal and ventral lateral geniculate nuclei (cat: Altman and Carpenter, 1961; Graybiel, 1972; tree shrew: Harting et al., 1973; rhesus monkey: Benevento and Fallon, 1975). In the rhesus monkey the projections from superficial colliculus terminate in inferior pulvinar, centro-intermediate nucleus, magnocellular dorsomedial nucleus and intralaminar nucleus.

Deep layers of superior colliculus project to the magnocellular portion of the medial geniculate nucleus, suprageniculate nucleus, limitans nucleus and various posterior thalamic nuclei. In the rhesus monkey the deep superior colliculus has efferents to medial and oral pulvinar, dorsomedial nucleus and the intralaminar nuclei plus a variety of midbrain areas such as inferior colliculus, parabigeminal nucleus, and the olivary nucleus. The strong ascending projections to the lateral posterior nucleus of thalamus (or pulvinar) should be particularly noted since it appears to be a major route by which colliculus can communicate with prestriate visual areas. Also of possible theoretical importance is the projection from the deep layers to visual and other areas which shows a correspondence with the multimodal afferent projection to deep superior colliculus.

Decending efferent fibres from colliculus terminate in a variety of regions in the pons, reticular formation and spinal cord (cat: Altman and Carpenter, 1961; Kawamura and Brodal, 1973; Kawamura *et al.*, 1974; Hashikawa and Kawamura, 1977; Kawamura and Hashikawa, 1978; tree shrew: Harting, *et al.*, 1973; monkey: Myers, 1963). The major descending projection travels to the dorsolateral and lateral pontine nuclei. A. tecto-reticular projection terminates on both sides in nucleus reticularis pontis oralis, nucleus reticularis pontis caudalis and nucleus reticularis gigantocellularis. In addition, arising from cells in laminas IV and VI is a tectal projection that forms the predorsal bundle which travels to the interstitial nucleus of Cajal, the nucleus of Dark-schewitsch, the reticulo-tegmental nuclei, the inferior olivary nucleus and a diffuse termination in the upper cervical cord. In tree shrews Harting *et al.* (1973) found there was also a projection to the motor facial nucleus. Although there are no direct connexions with oculo-motor nuclei there are considerable possibilities for disynaptic connexions via the interstitial nucleus of Cajal, the nucleus of Darkschewitsch and the pontine reticular formation. Also head and neck movements could be controlled by colliculus since fibres from the predorsal system reach neck motorneurons via interneurons in medullary reticular formation and upper cervical segments (Sprague (1975).

5 Electrical stimulation of superior colliculus

In early studies on eye movements evoked by electrical stimulation of superior colliculus either encéphale isolé or lightly anaesthetized animals were used. The eye movements spontaneously generated in the former preparation were infrequent and in the latter evoked eye movements were slow and abnormal. Nevertheless, Adamuk's (1872) observation that stimulation of superior colliculus produced movements of both eyes to the contralateral side (conjugate contraversive movements) has been replicated by Apter (1946) and Hess *et al.* (1946).

Recent stimulation studies have used awake animals whose heads have been held firmly to some framework by bolts implanted in the skull in a previous operation. Using this technique, Robinson (1972) found that in the rhesus monkey the eye movements elicited by unilateral collicular stimulation were always contralateral conjugate saccades. The direction of the saccade depended on where on colliculus the stimulation was applied. In effect, there was a motor map on the surface of the colliculus. Eye movement were made in an upward direction with medial stimulation but in a downward direction with lateral collicular stimulation. Stimulation of rostral sites in colliculus produced small saccades whereas sites in caudal colliculus elicited large saccades with amplitudes up to 50 degrees of visual arc. Stimulus parameters had no effect on eye movements which had an all-or-nothing character, providing stimulation was above the threshold level. Thus the amplitude and direction of an evoked saccade depended entirely on which site on the collicular surface the electrode tip had been placed. Long trains of stimulation caused two or more saccades of identical amplitude and duration with an inter-saccade interval of 100 ms.

It has consistently been reported that the stimulus intensity required to elicit a saccade decreases with electrode penetrations from surface layers of superior colliculus to deep laminae. Thus Robinson found that the stimulus threshold near the surface was 800 μA, it dropped to 200 μA as the electrode tip entered the deep fibre layer. The latency between the onset of stimulation and the start of a saccade was found by Robinson to be about 20 ms, but other studies (see Schiller and Stryker, 1972) report latencies as short as 10 ms.

As can be seen in Fig. 3, initial eye position did not systematically affect the evoked saccade in Robinson's study nor in other reports of similar experiments on rhesus monkeys (Schiller and Stryker, 1972; Schiller, 1972). This is strong support for a foveation theory, since one would expect on *a priori* grounds that collicular evoked eye movements would be independent of initial eye position if as will be discussed later the eye movement motor map and the visual map are coincident and retinotopic.

However, studies on the cat report what has been termed goal directed eye movements in response to collicular stimulation (Straschill and Rieger, 1973; Roucoux and Crommelinck, 1976) as well as "foveation" as found in monkeys. If eye movements are goal directed then stimulation of a specific site in the visuomotor map in superior colliculus will elicit a saccade, but the direction of the eye movement will depend on the initial position of the eye. That is, the evoked saccade will bring the eye to a point fixed in space rather than one having a fixed relation to the initial position of the eye. The study by Roucoux and Crommelinck helps to resolve the discrepancy between the reports of Schiller, Stryker and Robinson on the one hand, who, working with monkeys, found only foveation with collicular stimulation, and

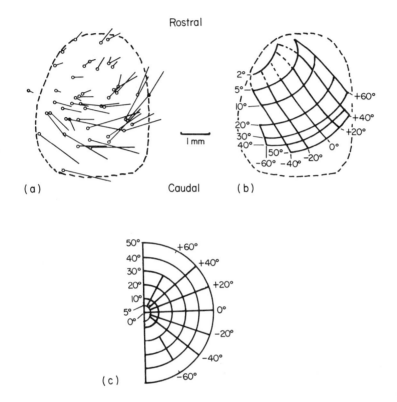

FIG. 3. Oculomotor map of monkey's (left) superior colliculus. (a) Dorsal view of colliculus showing points of stimulation (by a circle) and the resultant eye movement as a vector of amplitude and direction of movement. (b) An approximate oculomotor map plotted on the same left colliculus from observations like that shown in (a); contour lines of saccades of equal amplitude (2° to 50°) and direction (−60° to +60°) are represented. It can be seen by comparing (b) and (c), which shows the contralateral visual field, how visual space is represented on the superior colliculus. (After Robinson, 1972.)

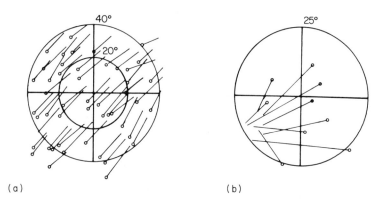

FIG. 4. Comparison of position independent with goal-directed eye movements. In both figures the circle represents the position of the eye when a point in the colliculus would be stimulated, plotted with respect to a primary position; the direction and length of the line correspond with the direction and size of the induced saccade. (a) Direction and size of position independent saccades are not affected by where the eye is looking when stimulation is applied (after Robinson, 1972). (b) Goal-directed eye movements are dependent on eye position at time of stimulation (after Roucoux and Crommelinck, 1976). (Figure 4(a) redrawn from Robinson (1972) and Figure 4(b) from Roucoux and Crommelinck (1976)).

Straschill and Rieger on the other hand, who found goal directed eye movements with similar stimulation in cats. Collicular stimulation in the cat, as in the monkey, generates conjugate contraversive saccades and current level over threshold has no effect on the characteristics of the saccades. However, there is a distinction between what happens when stimulation is applied to the anterior half of the colliculus, which in the cat corresponds to the central 12–15 degrees of visual space as opposed to the posterior part. Roucoux and Crommelinck found that anterior stimulation evoked saccades which had amplitudes and directions determined entirely by the site of stimulation. That is upward saccades were elicited near the midline, downward saccades in lateral colliculus, while horizontal saccades occurred with stimulation on an anterior–posterior line approximately in the middle of colliculus.

In the posterior half of superior colliculus, for a particular stimulation site, direction and amplitude of evoked saccades varied as a function of the initial eye fixation but the eyes always ended gazing in a particular direction. These goal-directed saccades were contralateral and contraversive. Repeated stimulation of the same site caused a goal directed saccade followed by fixation or a series of small movements within the goal area. Goals stimulated above the horizontal meridian were observed with medial stimulation whereas lateral posterior collicular stimulation produced goals below the horizontal meridian. The foveation motor map found in anterior colliculus of the cat appears to be continuous with the visual goal motor map in posterior superior colliculus.

Why should cats and monkeys differ in the types of eye movements elicited by collicular stimulations? One reason could be that the mechanical limits on the cat's ocular motility is much less than the monkey's. In cats, the mechanical limit is about 25 degrees from the centre of gaze (Roucoux and Crommelinck, 1976) whereas in monkeys the largest saccades can exceed 50 degrees (Robinson, 1972). For the cat, peripheral goals would not be in oculomotor range and therefore movements of the head and trunk might be necessary to allow a visual goal to be fixated. Roucoux and Crommelinck found in fact that some electrode placements in posterior colliculus caused contraction in muscles in the contralateral side of the neck.

6 Response characteristics of collicular cells

In addition to the motor properties discussed in the preceding section, neurons in superior colliculus also have sensory responses. As would be expected on the basis of the afferent connexions to superior colliculus visual responses predominate in colliculus especially in the superficial and intermediate layers although the latter and deep collicular cells respond to stimulation in other modalities. A great deal has been discovered in recent years about the response characteristics of collicular cells in a variety of species. No attempt is to be made to catalogue this extensive literature; instead we shall concentrate on studies which have used primate subjects.

Cells in the superior colliculus of rhesus monkeys which are responsive to visual stimulation are found predominantly in the superficial and intermediate layers (Humphrey, 1968; Cynader and Berman, 1972; Goldberg and Wurtz, 1972a). But, Cynader and Berman also report that in the deep grey and white layers there are cells which respond when large dark objects enter extensive receptive fields. Rather interestingly, these deep collicular cells are multimodal, responding to auditory and visual stimuli; in addition they could be subliminally facilitated by auditory stimulation occurring simultaneously with the visual stimulus.

The receptive fields of superior colliculus cells are far larger than those found in visual cortex when comparing cells responding to stimulation in the same area of the retina. In the superficial layers of the monkey's superior colliculus single units are binocularly driven and have receptive fields consisting of a circular or ellipsoid-activating region surrounded by suppressive areas (Schiller and Koerner, 1971; Cynader and Berman, 1972), although Goldberg and Wurtz (1972a) report that 20–30% of cells have no inhibitory surrounds. In accordance with what would be expected on the basis of the direct and indirect (via visual cortex) retinotopic projections to superior colliculus, the visual receptive fields are topographically arranged on the surface of colliculus. The size of the receptive fields generally increases as they become located more eccentrically. Thus Schiller and Stryker (1972) found that receptive fields near the fovea could be as small as 8 min in diameter, but field size increased rapidly as a function of eccentricity so that at 20–30 degrees from the fovea field sizes were 10 degrees in diameter.

It is also apparent that the size of the receptive fields in the superficial layers of colliculus increases with depth (Humphrey, 1968; Goldberg and Wurtz, 1972a). This is also characteristic of other species (rat: Humphrey, 1968; cat: McIlwain, 1975). A comprehensive study of this phenomenon in the cat by McIlwain indicated that the receptive fields of the more superficial cells are nested within the fields of the underlying cells for electrode penetrations which are normal to the collicular surface.

The optimal stimulus in the receptive field appears to be relatively formless, thus a small spot of light is as effective as a shaped stimulus and a moving spot is more effective than a stationary one (Cynader and Berman, 1972; Goldberg and Wurtz, 1972a). Increasing the size of the stimulus has relatively little effect until stimulus size approaches the size of the receptive field when a reduced response is likely. In the majority of species which have been studied most collicular cells which respond to moving stimuli show directional sensitivity (see, for example, for the mouse: Drager and Hubel, 1975a; ground squirrel: Michael, 1972; cat: Sterling and Wickelgren, 1969; squirrel monkey: Kadoya et al., 1971; cebus monkeys: Updyke, 1974). The macaque, however, is an exception, 90–95% of its movement-sensitive cells have no preferred direction. Even in those species which have strongly directionally sensitive cells there is a lack of consistency in the distribution of preferred directions, so it is not clear whether directional selectivity is relevant to understanding collicular function. But Ingle, (1973) has related preferred directional selectivity of collicular units in various species to the types of movements generated in the visual fields of members of the species during natural behaviour.

The visual receptive fields of neurons in the intermediate and deep layers of superior colliculus in rhesus monkey have also been explored (Cynader and Berman, 1972). These cells had larger receptive fields than the superficial cells but they were activated by similar stimuli. Schiller and Koerner (1971) and Cynader and Berman (1972) refer to the cells in superficial layers as "event detectors". Such cells responded strongly on the first presentation of a stimulus but gave a weakened response with repeated presentation. Schiller and Stryker (1972) and Cynader and Berman also found a class of intermediate layer neurons which respond to short jerky movements, but Wurtz and Goldberg (1972a) failed to do so. However, this may have been because of technical differences in experimental procedure. Cynader and Berman used lightly barbituate anaesthetized monkeys and Schiller and Stryker's animals were awake but with a paralised eye, whereas Goldberg and Wurtz used awake monkeys with intact ocular mobility.

Questions about the relative roles of the retinal and visual cortical inputs in producing the response properties of superior collicular cells have been posed. One answer to such questions lies in a comparison of the anatomical and physiological characteristics of the two projections to colliculus. It is now accepted that in the cat there is a retino–tectal projection consisting of collaterals from fibres that terminate in lateral geniculate nucleus as well as a separate retinal midbrain projection (Fukuda and Stone, 1974). The bifurcating fibres originate in the Y-type of retinal ganglion cells[1] and collicular cells receiving this input are responsive to fast moving stimuli but without being directionally sensitive (Hoffman, 1973). According to Hoffman and Sherman, (1974) the visual cortical projection to superior colliculus also originate from the retinal ganglion Y-cells since some movement-sensitive collicular cells can be driven with a shorter latency by cortical stimulation. It is argued that X-cells do not project to colliculus and indeed their characteristics appear adapted to provide precise spatial resolution, a property more characteristic of foveal vision. On the other hand the Y-type with their high speed directionally selective property are an obvious

[1]Recently it has been proposed that the retinal ganglion cells should be classified into three functional groups, termed X, Y and W. This followed the distinction which Enroth-Cugell and Robson (1966) first suggested for the X- and Y- cells which was based on the linear and non-linear spatial summation properties of ganglion cells. The properties of these three types of cell are as follows. Y-cells have fast conducting axons $(35–45 \text{ ms}^{-1})$, transient responses to visual stimuli and they respond to fast (faster than 200 degrees per second) stimuli moving in any directions in their large receptive fields. Few Y-cells occur in area centralis (1%) but they are more abundant (10%) at the periphery. X-cells have moderate conduction velocities $(20–25 \text{ ms}^{-1})$, tonic responses and the smallest receptive fields. W-cells are the most recently discovered type, and have slow conduction velocities $(3–15 \text{ ms}^{-1})$ large unstructured receptive fields and a small majority are directionally sensitive to slow-moving stimuli (less than 100 degrees per second). (Based on studies using cats by Fukuda, 1971; Hoffman, 1973; Fukuda and Stone, 1974; and Stone and Fukuda, 1974).

prerequisite for movement-sensitive collicular cells (Fukuda and Stone, 1974).

Until recently it was though that the W-type retinal ganglion cells projected only to superior colliculus and the pretectal region (Fukuda and Stone, 1974), but Wilson and Stone (1975) have evidence that these cells also project to the lateral geniculate nucleus. Hoffman (1973) suggests that collicular cells receiving W-type afferents are directionally sensitive to low velocity movements. It is quite probable that Wilson and Toyne's (1970) failure to detect any direct retino-tectal projection from the central 7 degrees of retina in rhesus monkeys is because this consists of slender W-type fibres.

The major cortical connexion to superficial colliculus in the cat comes from area 17, with another strong projection arising in the Clare–Bishop area, and more sparse afferents arising in areas 18 and 19 (Kawamura *et al.*, 1974; Hollander, 1974). Not surprisingly, the cells which project from visual cortex to colliculus have complex receptive fields and respond to movement in a directionally selective fashion; in addition they are binocularly driven (Palmer and Rosenquist, 1974). Many of the visually responsive cells in colliculus receive both retinal and visual cortical inputs (Hoffman, 1973), which helps explain why the retinotopic and visual cortical visual field maps in colliculus are superimposed.

6.1 Movement fields

Stimulation studies have demonstrated that a visuomotor map can be topographically represented on the surface of superior colliculus, with neurons capable of driving saccadic eye movements lying in both superficial and intermediate layers (Robinson, 1972; Schiller and Stryker, 1972). As neurons in these regions are also visually responsive the superior colliculus is ideally situated to provide for sensori-motor integration. But even more convincing are the studies which demonstrate that there is a remarkable correlation between the characteristics of *voluntary* saccades and single cell activity in superior colliculus. For example, Straschill and Hoffman (1970) found that in the superior colliculus of the cat there are cells which increased or decreased their discharge rate with eye movements in the dark. Moreover, the motor characteristics of cells in the intermediate layers of colliculus have been mapped by using chronic microelectrode recording techniques in rhesus monkeys which were free to make eye but not head movements (Schiller and Koerner, 1971; Schiller and Stryker, 1972; Wurtz and Goldberg, 1972a; Sparks, 1975; Mohler and Wurtz, 1976; Sparks *et al.*, 1976). Neurons in the intermediate grey and white layers discharge between 20 and 100 ms *before* rapid eye movements of specific distance and direction. The cells discribed by Wurtz and Goldberg (1972a) made the same response whether the eye movement was a visually guided saccade, a spontaneous saccade in total darkness, or the fast phase of caloric nystagmus. Each cell had a "movement field", an area in the contralateral visual field to which the associated saccade would bring fixation. The retinotopic organization of movement fields across the surface of colliculus coincides with that of the receptive fields of visually responsive cells in both superficial and intermediate layers.

Some cells are not just responsive to movement, they also have visual receptive fields without these necessarily being superimposable (Schiller and Koerner, 1971; Wurtz and Goldberg, 1972a; Mohler and Wurtz, 1976). The movement response tends to be more vigorous than the visual response. Sparks (1975) and Sparks *et al.* (1976) performed a computer analysis of movement fields which showed their size is a function of the amplitude of the ocular movement. Thus neurons discharging before small saccades have relatively small and sharply tuned fields whereas those discharging prior to large saccades have large and coarsely tuned fields. Neurons in rostral superior colliculus (representing the centre of the visual field) discharge before small saccades whereas cells firing prior to large saccades are found more caudally. In a really decisive demonstration, Schiller and Stryker (1972) showed that saccadic eye movements produced by stimulation of intermediate layer cells using a microelectrode were made to the movement fields of the same neuron as determined by recording from the electrode while the monkey made eye movements.

The traditional view of collicular organization supposes that oculomotor integration in colliculus proceeds in a "downward" direction (Fig. 5). Visual information enters via the cells in the superficial layers, proceeds via eye movement cells in intermediate layer and output to the oculomotor nuclei leaves from the deeper intermediate layers and the deep layers. However, there are reasons for doubting this widely, if only implicitly, held view. The movement fields of cells in intermediate layers quite probably increase in size with depth of cell (Sparks, 1975; Mohler and Wurtz, 1976; Sparks, *et al.*, 1976). But Sparks *et al.* argue that this may be an artifact produced by the electrode penetration being non-normal to the surface of colliculus resulting in more caudal cells being recorded from as the electrode is advanced. However, Mohler and Wurtz (1976) found similar effects when the deeper cells were rostral to the superficial cells. If oculmotor integration in colliculus proceeds in a "downward" direction then it is to be expected that the movement fields of deeper cells should be smaller and more finely tuned than are those of the superficial cells.

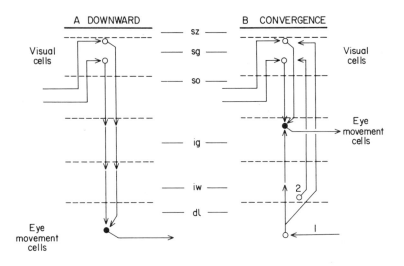

FIG. 5. Two hypothetical models of superior colliculus organization. A. The traditional "downward" flow model in which visual input to cells in superficial laminae is fed to eye movement cells in intermediate and deep layers. B. A "convergence" model in which "motor" signals arriving in deeper layers (1) pass "upwards" to meet "downward" travelling visual signals from superficial laminae at intermediate layer cells which provide eye movement or attentional output. Also shown in B are the pathways which may be involved in producing the phasic enhancement effect in visually responsive cells in superficial layers. These pathways may arise from either intermediate layer cells (2) or afferents to intermediate layer cells. sz, stratum zonale; sg, stratum griseum; so, stratum opticum; ig, intermediate grey; iw, intermediate white; dl, deep layers; (after Mohler and Wurtz, 1976, and Wurtz and Mohler, 1976.)

A further reason for doubting the traditional "downward" processing theory is the finding that the deeper cells of the intermediate layers of colliculus start discharging *before* the more superficial ones (Mohler and Wurtz, 1976). If the traditional view were correct the converse should be true. An alternative organization of colliculus which fits the data better is the visual-motor "convergence" model proposed by Mohler and Wurtz. According to this theory visual information passing downwards through the superficial layers combines with eye movement information ascending through the intermediate layers. The cells at the boundary of the optic and intermediate grey layers are visually triggered movement cells which combine sensory and motor information serving as an important collicular efferent. Although Mohler and Wurtz can readily identify the retina and visual cortex as the source of the sensory information they have no suggestion as to the origin of the motor input to the intermediate layer cells. This is not going to be from brain stem eye movement neurons since the response of these cells is not tied to a retinal map, but instead varies with the position of the eye in its orbit, whereas the collicular eye movement cells are arranged on a retinal map. Input of motor information is therefore likely to be from cortex which projects extensively to the intermediate layers.

7 Behavioural enhancement

This discussion of the role of the superior colliculus in attention has quite properly concentrated on "foveation" since bringing a potentially significant peripheral visual (and possibly tactile or auditory) stimulus into that part of the visual field where detailed visula processing can occur is a central issue in attention. But as Goldberg and Wurtz (1972b) suggest:

> The awake animal does not treat objects in the visual world uniformly: it responds to some and ignores others. At some point in the brain neurons must reflect not only the external parameters relating to the physical properties of the stimulus, but also the internal parameters relating to whether or not the animal will respond to the stimulus.

This cogently sums up what is possibly the crucial issue in the neuro-biology of attention. What is the nature of the process which causes the animal to select one out of several possible stimuli to be the focus of its attention?

Goldberg and Wurtz explored this problem in awake rhesus monkeys which were trained to fixate a point of light and when the fixation light went off to make a saccade to a second light which came on. Recordings were made of single cell activity in the superficial layers of superior colliculus during the task. Approximately half the cells showed en-hanced response when the visual target stimulus lay within their recep-tive field. The saccade normally occurred at approximately 250 ms after the target switched on, long after the enhanced response had occurred. Two types of enhancement were found; in one the on-response became brisker and more regular (an "early" effect) and in the other it was more persistent (a "late" effect). Sometimes this "late" response accom-panied an enhanced "early" response. The "late" response terminated when the eye started moving so removing the stimulus from the cell's receptive field. If the target stimulus was present while the fixation light was on, i.e. while the animal maintains fixation, no enhancement occurred. But, when the fixation light went off the enhancement res-ponse occurred. Enhancement does not happen when eye movements are made in darkness indicating that it does not represent a pre-movement discharge.

The characteristics of the receptive field of cells displaying the enhancement effect were investigated further by Wurtz and Mohler (1976a). Enhancement occurs when the visual stimulus is anywhere within the receptive field of a cell. Also enhancement of response occurs when the visual target is close to the boundaries of the visual field but not when the target is at a distance from the field's perimeter.

Wurtz and Mohler additionally demonstrated that the enhanced visual response is restricted to the behavioural response of making eye movements. Thus if the monkey has to make a manual response and not a saccadic eye movement when the target visual stimulus changed no enhancement occurred. This indicates that the enhancement does not simply reflect arousal but is related specifically to eye movements. There are a number of possible sources for the enhancement effect. Since it is not found in cells in the most dorsal 0·25 mm of the superficial layers, which Hubel et al. (1975) found to receive afferents from only the retina, the effect may originate from visual cortex which projects to the ventral regions of the superficial layers. However, since the selected enhancement response in collicular cells occurs in both colliculi after unilateral striate cortex lesions (Mohler and Wurtz, 1976b) and the type of enhancement seen in visual cortical cells was non-selective (Wurtz and Mohler, 1976b) this is unlikely. The frontal eye fields are a potential source of the visual enhancement effect since Wurtz and Mohler (1976b) found that cells there have visual receptive fields, and 40% of their sample showed selective enhancement effects like the collicular cells. However, since the latency of the visual response is longer in the cells in the frontal eye fields (50–120 ms, Mohler et al., 1973) than in the superior colliculus (35–60 ms, Wurtz and Mohler, 1976a) the former cells probably follow rather than drive the collicular cells if there is any sequential relationship between the two structures.

According to the convergence model of collicular organization proposed by Mohler and Wurtz (1976), the oculomotor cells in the ventral strata of the intermediate layers send their axons dorsally to the visually receptive movement cells at the boundary of the superficial and intermediate layers. Wurtz and Mohler (1976a) consider that the enhanced visual response of the superficial cells may arise either from these axons or the afferents to the intermediate layer oculomotor cells. In support of this suggestion they cite two principle arguments. First, the time course of the enhancement closely matches the activity of the deeper movement cells which start firing as early as 300 ms before a saccade which would account for the early component of the enhancement effect. Also the late component of the enhancement effect corresponds with the increased excitability of the movement cells at 140–165 ms before an eye movement. Second, the "enhancement field" is greater in area than is the visual receptive field of the superficial cells. Since the movement fields of the intermediate layer oculomotor cells is larger than the visual receptive fields of the overlying cells, clearly the enhancement field could reflect the influence of movement cells. If, as has been outlined earlier, the afferents to the movement cells in the ventral regions of the intermediate layers originate in neocortex then the enhancement effect also presumably originates there. The oculomotor cells of the intermediate layers of colliculus act as a relay and not as the originator for the enhancement response.

7.1 Theoretical implications

The work of Goldberg, Mohler and Wurtz has major implications for theories of collicular function. They do not rule out a role for superior colliculus in "foveation" (see Wurtz and Mohler, 1976a) but favour the view that the enhancement phenomenon is a neural correlate of selective attention (Goldberg and Wurtz, 1972b). This is primarily because enhancement reflects a modification of the central representation of the stimulus although the sensory stimulation is unchanged, and the effect is selectively related to eye movements to that part of the visual field containing the stimulus. The fact that the enhancement effect is specifically related to an eye response and fails to occur when the subject makes a hand response to the visual target does not rule out the consideration that superior colliculus is involved in selective attention. Although attention has often been used in a way that implies response independence there is no reason why at a neural level there should not be several mechanisms for what, at a behavioural level, is called selective attention.

The role the superior colliculus plays in the selective process according to Wurtz and Mohler (1976a) is one of "facilitation" of eye movements or alternatively what can be regarded as a refining of a "readiness to respond". It does not initiate stimulus selection but is the agent of the response readying process. Thus inputs to the intermediate layer oculomotor cells carry information about the approximate area in the visual field for the target of an eye movement. This eye movement related activity then leads to an enhanced response in the visual receptive cells which have salient targets in the appropriate part of the visual field. The convergence of activity from the excited visually responsive cells in the superficial layers with the oculomotor activity arising from the intermediate layer cells determines the actual target for the eye movement.

Small lesions in superior colliculus do not grossly disrupt eye movements in monkeys (Wurtz and Goldberg, 1972b; Mohler and Wurtz, 1977) but large lesions prevent them making accurate eye movements and also lead to visual neglect (Denny-Brown, 1962). Thus Wurtz and Goldberg found that focal lesions in superior colliculus led to an increase in latency in making a saccade to a visual target which lay in the field of the focal lesion, and Mohler and Wurtz report that in addition such partial lesions result in an increase in the frequency of small corrective saccades, since the initial saccades were consistently short. It appears that the metrics of a saccadic eye movement can be computed, although less accurately, elsewhere in the oculomotor system, and this lesion data is consistent with the view that superior colliculus "facilitates" but does not initiate eye movement.

Although the minimal effects of small collicular lesions on eye-movements is damaging for a "foveation" model of superior collicular functioning, is such a model still viable? According to this view, superior colliculus is instrumental in initiating eye movements as well as in computing the metrics for a saccade which will bring a target visual stimulus into focal vision (Schiller, 1972; Robinson, 1972; Sparks, 1975; Sparks et al., 1976). Most of the evidence which is supportive of Wurtz, Goldberg and Mohler's position also sustains the "foveation" hypothesis, i.e. the congruence of the visual and motor maps in superior colliculus and the reliability with which eye movements can be generated when intermediate layer cells are electrically stimulated. Moreover, the decrease in threshold currents required to stimulate the oculomotor cells in the ventral regions of superior colliculus is consistent with the descending sensory-motor integration model. But a major difficulty with the "foveation" hypothesis is the finding that the size of the movement fields of oculomotor cells is larger in ventral than in dorsal regions of the intermediate layers. However, Sparks et al. (1976) contend that precise saccadic movements are not made by the discharge of a small population of finely tuned neurons in colliculus. Instead they result from the weighted sum of the simultaneous movement tendencies produced by the activity of a large set of less finely tuned neurons. Because of the strong correspondence between the sensory and oculomotor maps in superior colliculus, which in the monkey are plotted entirely with retinotopic coordinates, the saccadic parameters could be readily computed. A visual target by activating a specific locus in the sensory map could in turn stimulate corresponding motor cells. The "error-signal" for the saccade is then the difference between the focus of activity and the centre of the retina and the ensuing eye movement annuls the "error-signal". It is not crucial to this "foveation" model whether the motor signal is the weighted sum of a few finely tuned neurons or of many coarsely tuned neurons.

8 Behavioural effects of collicular lesions

The effects of lesions in superior colliculus have been studied in several species by means of a variety of behavioural techniques. Although early findings that collicular lesions do not produce gross deficits in visual discrimination ability *per se* (Layman, 1936) can be accepted with some reservations, more recent studies have indicated that collicular lesions can sometimes produce subtle and at other times quite striking alterations in cognitive behaviour. The main theoretical influence underlying contemporary studies has been the two-visual system hypothesis proposed by Schneider (1967) and Trevarthen (1968). Not surprisingly doubts have now been raised about the details of this two-system view of visual functioning as well as a more fundamental worry voiced by Berlucchi *et al.* (1972) about the concept of there being two visual systems rather than a single integrated mechanism.

8:1 Visual neglect

A number of discrepancies have appeared in the literature on the effects of collicular ablations. As is often the case in physiological psychology, some of these arise from the comparison of different species which have been tested in tasks which are only superficially or nominally comparable. Another source of problems in comparing different studies arises from variations in the exact placement and extent of the collicular lesions, and the amount of additional damage in structures such as pretectum or periaqueductal grey. However, one of the most reliable effects of ablating superior colliculus is that subjects develop a sensory neglect. The extent of the neglect varies in different species and it seems likely that the lesions have to encroach on the deeper layers of colliculus for the effect to be demonstrated. But since deep lesions are frequently larger than superficial lesions it is possible that such sensory neglect may arise from a combination of deep superior colliculus plus pretectal damage. Sensory neglect has now been demonstrated in the following species: rhesus monkeys (Denny-Brown, 1962; Anderson and Symmes, 1969), tree shrews (Casagrande and Diamond, 1974), cats (Blake, 1959; Sprague and Meikle, 1965; Berlucchi *et al.*, 1972), rats (Goodale and Murison, 1975; Kirvel, 1975; Goodale *et al.*, 1978) and hamsters (Schneider, 1967). Although Vetter (1974) failed to find any effect of collicular lesions on visual location and following behaviour in squirrel monkeys, the lesions only damaged between 10 and 25% of superior colliculus and it is not clear whether this extended into deep collicular layers.

However, there is some doubt about the causation of the sensory neglect reported in colliculectomized rhesus monkeys by Denny-Brown (1962). These animals displayed a dramatic sensory deficit appearing blind and ignoring many kinds of sensory stimulation, but the lesions in these monkeys were very large and included damage to pretectum as well as other midbrain areas. In contrast to Denny-Brown, Pasik *et al.* (1966) found that large ablations restricted to superior colliculus only transiently impaired visual localization in one monkey and it is also possible that the monkeys that failed to regain visual following responses as reported by Anderson and Symmes (1968) had pretectal damage in the course of ablating superior colliculus. There was no reported visual neglect in the colliculectomized rhesus monkeys tested by Butter (1974), but since he considered the lesions to be of small to moderate size, usually sparing the more ventral layers of colliculus, this is not surprising.

The pretectal region also appears to be of possible importance in producing sensory neglect in cats. Berlucchi *et al.* (1972) carried out an elegant series of experiments in which split brain cats were given unilateral collicular and/or pretectal lesions. During testing the eye contralateral to the lesion was covered. They found as did Sprague and Meikle (1965) that lesions restricted mainly to superior colliculus produced a temporary visual neglect plus deficits in orienting to tactile or auditory stimulation presented on the side contralateral to the lesion. Considerable recovery occurred with time following this lesion. However, cats with lesions to large parts of pretectum as well as superior colliculus showed much less recovery in visual localization ability and virtually no improvement in tactile localization over a three-year period.

Tree shrews which have large collicular lesions extending as far as central grey display a marked visual inattentiveness (Casagrande and Diamond, 1974), failing to visually follow a moving food object or to avoid what an intact animal would regard as a visual threat. However, tree shrews which had lesions restricted to superficial layers of colliculus did not demonstrate visual neglect. Such sensory neglect appears to be a failure in the orienting response to novel or significant stimuli, and Goodale and Murison (1975) and Goodale *et al.* (1978) found colliculectomized rats to be deficient in making orienting responses. The rats were first trained to "shuttle" between two illuminated visual targets where they were reinforced. Control animals and those with visual cortex ablations stopped, while running between goals, and oriented to flashing lights presented at various points around the perimeter of the apparatus, but colliculectomized rats did so only if the light was no further than 40 degrees either side of their midline.

A failure to make an orienting response could result from an animal not noticing a novel stimulus or it could arise from a deficit in the action component of the orienting response. There are reasons for assuming that the latter deficit is at least a plausible explanation for the sensory deficit in animals with collicular damage. Raczkowski *et al.* (1976) found that the visual neglect characteristic of tree shrews suffering from deep collicular lesions could be replicated by transecting the fibres from deep superior colliculus which cross and descend in the predorsal bundle. Although these descending collicular efferents may indirectly influence neocortex via synapses in pontine and reticular nuclei it is also possible that colliculus affects attentional processes at a non-cognitive level by acting on the brain stem motor components of the orienting response.

In support of this suggestion can be cited some recent reports which demonstrate that colliculectomized rats are much more active in an open field exploratory situation than are controls (Smith and Weldon, 1976; Foreman *et al.*, 1978; Pope and Dean, 1979; Weldon and Smith, 1979). This hyperactivity in the open field in colliculectomized rats should be contrasted with the hypoactivity in other species (monkey: Denny-Brown 1962; cats: Myers 1964; tree shrews: Casagrade *et al.*, 1972), but since these species have been observed mainly in their home cages it is not clear whether there are fundamental species differences in activity after colliculectomy. The collicular damaged rats in Foreman *et al.*'s study showed more walking and running behaviour but were not otherwise more exploratory since they had decreased head raising, rearing and sniffing scores. Previously Goodale and Lister (1974) failed to demonstrate hyperactivity in rats with lesions restricted to superficial laminae of superior colliculus, whereas the collicular lesions made by Foreman *et al.* extended into deep colliculus. Also it is apparent from the histology published by Smith and Weldon that their lesions invaded not just deep laminae of superior colliculus but also central grey. It has previously been proposed that the deep layers of colliculus project to reticular formation via an ipsilateral pathway terminating in dorsal midbrain reticular nuclei, and a contralateral projection ending in rostral nucleus reticularis gigantocellularis, nucleus reticularis pontis caudalis and the caudal part of nucleus pontis oralis. Circumstantial evidence from electrophysiological (Anderson *et al.*, 1972) and lesion studies (Lynch and Crain, 1972) indicate that these latter pontomedullary reticular formation nuclei are predominantly inhibitory in nature exerting an influence on reticulo–spinal systems. Thus deep collicular lesions may reduce the inhibitory influence of these nuclei producing hyperactivity and a loss of response inhibition.

Reduced distractibility was also found in colliculectomized stumptail macaques by Milner *et al.* (1978). The subjects were preoperatively trained to respond to the left or right of a central panel depending on whether a press on the latter panel caused it to turn red or green. Animals with collicular damage were unimpaired on post-operative reacquisition of the task but they were less distractible than controls while making an "observe" response when an irrelevant white light was flashed peripherally. Colliculectomized monkeys were less distractible than controls on the basis of trials on which the distracting stimulus was noticed at all as well as having a shorter response latency, but a group of animals with lesions to the frontal eye fields showed reduced distractibility only as measured by duration of distraction. It is possible that the colliculectomized monkeys were less distractible because they were less sensitive to visual stimuli since Lepore *et al.* (1976) and Latto (1977) found increases in brightness threshold in lesioned monkeys, although in Latto's study the decrease in sensitivity was transient, occurring up to two weeks postoperatively and disappearing six weeks later.

It is possible that lack of distractibility in colliculectomized monkeys could be explained by impaired saccadic eye movement control as demonstrated by Wurtz and Goldberg (1972b) and Mohler and Wurtz (1977). But these deficits were inaccurate and slow saccades rather than failures to make a saccade to a visual target. In Milner *et al.*'s experiment, colliculectomized monkeys often failed to respond at all to a distracting stimulus which is indicative of a failure in the orienting response mechanism rather than just a deficit in eye movement control.

8.2 Visually guided behaviour

In addition to showing visual neglect, the hamsters with undercut superior colliculi, which Schneider (1967) tested, were impaired in visually guided locomotor behaviour. When animals with collicular damage were forced to choose a short distance away from the stimulus panels in a simultaneous discrimination task, their performance was at chance level using an approach error criterion, but they did learn the discrimination according to a door push error criterion since they learned not to press the incorrect door even if they approached it first. A similar visual locomotor guidance impairment was reported by Barnes *et al.* (1970) in colliculectomized rats which failed to learn to jump to the one unilluminated box out of six in a jumping stand apparatus. However, when a continuous floor replaced the jumping stand the experimental animals were able to solve the problem by moving around the perimeter and examining each box individually. Barnes *et al.* suggested that the animals with collicular lesions could discriminate brightness cues at a distance but could not orient to the correct stimulus.

There are, however, a number of studies which throw doubt on the hypothesis that the superior colliculus is necessary for organizing accurate locomotor responses under visual stimulus control in rats or in cats. Weinberg and Stein (1978) used a similar task and apparatus to that used by Barnes *et al.* and found that rats given one-stage or two-stage bilateral collicular lesions were able to learn a brightness discrimination when jumping a distance of 10 cm, although both groups were impaired. The two-stage lesion groups also learned a harder brightness discrimination which involved jumping 15·7 cm. Collicular lesioned rats often used a strategy of leaning over the gap to visually explore the boxes, but two-stage lesioned animals could respond correctly without such stretching, sampling the cues from the centre of the jumping platform.

In the experiment reported by Barnes *et al.* colliculectomized rats were reported as being able to learn a brightness discrimination provided they could approach each stimulus in turn. But Goodale and Murison (1975) and Goodale *et al.* (1978), using a task comparable with that of Barnes *et al.* in which a continuous floor led up to the boxes, found that colliculectomized rats were able to localize and discriminate a lighted door from four dark ones. Moreover, observational data showed that colliculectomized animals made their choice some distance from the goal doors. Nigel Foreman, working in this laboratory, has obtained similar observational evidence that rats with collicular lesions are in fact more and not less accurate in running to an illuminated target.

Also there is evidence from Dyer *et al.* (1976) on rats and Winterkorn (1975) on cats that colliculectomized animals are able to learn visual discriminations involving horizontal versus vertical stripes to either a door-push or an approach error criterion. In fact there was no impairment in learning ability on either criterion for the rats with collicular lesions in Dyer *et al.*'s experiment. But cats with collicular plus pretectal damage made a larger number of approach errors during learning than did unoperated animals in Winterkorn's study.

Although it is tempting to argue away the differences between the above studies on the basis that hamsters with collicular damage behave unlike other animals with similar damage, some additional explanation is required for the failure of colliculectomized rats to orient to distant visual stimuli in the study by Barnes *et al.* However, the findings of this latter experiment must remain equivocal since Weinberg and Stein (1978) failed to replicate it. Moreover, an alternative explanation of Schneider's (1976) finding that hamsters with undercut superior colliculi fail to learn a visual discrimination according to an approach error criterion can be given. Original training was provided on the task using the door push error criterion, and the animals were able to correct themselves by walking past the incorrect stimulus to the adjacent correct door. "Alleys" leading to the two stimulus panels were then produced by inserting a perpendicular barrier between the doors. Hamsters with collicular damage contined to respond as before but control animals changed their strategy so that their choice was made at a more distant point from the stimulus panels. Thus an alternative explanation for the findings is that hamsters with undercut superior colliculi have difficulty in shifting response strategies or alternatively they fail to notice the novel stimulus, the partition, until they are forced to walk around it. An impairment in shifting response strategy may be a side effect of visual neglect or it could be an additional impairment in colliculectomized animals. There is little evidence pertinent to this issue but Smith and Weldon (1976) and Weldon and Smith (1979) did find that colliculectomized rats were impaired in performance on the Hebb–Williams closed field test. This task involved learning a new maze problem each day for twelve days. Although the closed field test obviously involves many psychological processes, an important requirement is for the animal to shift strategies from one day to the next.

There are a number of studies on the ability of colliculectomized monkeys on visual localization tasks which test a comparable visual guidance ability to the above studies on hamsters, rats and cats. Butter (1974) found that rhesus monkeys with collicular lesions were impaired in learning a visual discrimination response in which the response site was at a distance from the visual stimulus, but they were not impaired when the cue and the response were contiguous. The impaired performance in the former condition could be explained as follows. Meyer *et al.* (1965) have suggested that monkeys monitor their hands in visual learning situations, presumably attending to those visual stimuli which they touch. When a visual discrimination task involves cue-response separation, a monkey looking at his hand at the response site will not have the stimulus in foveal vision. Thus colliculectomized monkeys, which may have impaired abilities in reorienting their eyes, would be at a strong disadvantage in visually sampling cues displaced from the response site.

Three other studies (Keating, 1974, 1976; Mackinnon *et al.* 1976) on the effects of superior colliculus lesions on visual orientation and localization tasks confirm the findings of Butter, but all imposed a time constraint on the animal's response. The task used by Keating required the monkey to respond to the dimmer of two lights which came on for 200 ms in two out of twenty-four possible locations. With such a brief stimulus duration even intact monkeys could not make saccades to capture each stimulus successively in order to compare the intensities using focal vision. Thus in this task the monkey had to compare the stimulus intensities using peripheral vision alone, or occasionally using foveal plus peripheral vision depending on where the animal was fixating when the stimuli came on. Since the monkey had to make a saccade to the "dimmer" of the lights before reaching towards it, two types of mistake would be expected. One would be the choice of a location close to the dimmer stimulus because the saccade was inaccurate. But only fifty per cent of the errors in the colliculectomized group were of this variety; the remainder were reaches towards the vicinity of the *unrewarded* light. Thus it appears that the superior colliculus may play different roles in this task, selectively guiding the animal's attention towards the relevant stimulus *and* in guiding its response to the appropriate point in space.

Similar inaccurate reaching towards a visual target at one of six locations was found in colliculectomized monkeys by MacKinnon *et al.* (1976) but only when the target light remained on for 1 s as opposed to 5 s (the animal could only respond when the light went off). This study, by including a separation of stimulus and response sites together with a time variable helps clarify some of the issues arising from these studies. In Butter's (1974) study there was no time constraint on the animals, so they could spend as long as they wished examining their hands, the stimuli or the response sites. Therefore the deficit in that study could be indicative of a loss in attention in the sense that the monkeys had difficulty in discriminating the "complex" stimuli. But the discrimination task in the experiment of MacKinnon *et al.* was trivial and therefore in the long exposure condition the colliculectomized animals could easily target the stimulus light and attend to the response site in front of it. In the short exposure condition the colliculectomized animals were presumably impaired because there was insufficient time to visually capture the light *and* seek out the response site.

A recent study by Milner *et al.* (1979) also shows that colliculectomized rats are more impaired than controls when stimulus-response site separation is introduced in a horizontal–vertical visual discrimination task. A second experiment by these authors, however, produced a nice dissociation effect which can help clarify our understanding of the collicular deficit. In the relevant phase of this experiment it was found that colliculectomized rats were *less* impaired than controls when contradictory distracting stimuli were placed at various heights above the base of the discriminative cues. Thus it appears that the colliculus may act to allow orientation *towards* potentially relevant stimuli, but in order also to provide for flexible scanning of alternative stimuli which could

be important the colliculus causes orientation *away* from stimuli which
may be guiding responses.

9 Comments and reflections

The wealth of recent evidence on the anatomical organization and
physiology of the superior colliculus has not, unfortunately, been
accompanied by an incontrovertible theory as to its function. However,
it is clear that the midbrain visual system is important in vision even in
the highly encephalized primates. Animals of these species may not
suffer from the severe visual neglect apparent in colliculectomized
rodents, cats or prosimians such as tree shrews, but nevertheless they
are disturbed in visually guided behaviour.

One possible interpretation of the differing degrees of deficit which
occur after colliculectomy in different species is that there have been
modifications in collicular function through evolution and this has been
especially marked at the primate level because of the development of
macular vision. But it is also possible that the colliculus is an organ of
attention in all mammals and because of the differing actions required
of an attentional mechanism in different species its mode of operation
differs. Thus in primates the behavioural response characteristic of an
animal switching its attention to a novel stimulus, whether visual,
auditory or tactile in origin, is almost always going to require directed
eye movements which capture the locus of the stimulus for the fovea.
This may be accompanied by head or upper body movements. In
animals with less well-developed macular vision or even retinas without
foveas the maximum amplitude of an eye movement is restricted and
therefore changes in attention necessitating redirection of gaze are
almost always going to require head and upper body movements or
even gross changes in body posture. In view of the differences between
non-primate mammals and primates, the two groups will be discussed
separately.

The two-visual system hypothesis of Schneider and Trevarthen has
proved a useful but now apparently limited model of visual system
functioning. Although Schneider's interpretation of the behaviour of
hamsters with undercut colliculi as being a result of an inability to
visually locate objects in space was realistic, there are alternative
explanations for the apparent inability of these animals to locate a goal
door at a distance as previously discussed. Since rats with collicular
lesions are able to accurately locate objects in visual space we either
have to accept that the hamsters in Schneider's study suffered from a
loss in behavioural flexibility (changing response strategies) and/or

suffered from visual neglect, or accept the rather implausible possibility that there is a marked difference in collicular function between hamsters and rats. However, Schneider's demonstration of visual neglect in collicular damaged hamsters has been supported by similar findings in colliculectomized rats, cats and tree shrews. The suggestion of Goodale and Murison (1975) and Goodale *et al.* (1978) that such neglect occurs because of some disruption with the mechanism of the orienting response is convincing and appropriate. Additionally it is surely not just fortuitous that the cells in deep layers of colliculus are multimodal and have response fields which coincide with the spatially mapped visual cells in the overlying superficial layers. The colliculus may use this sensory information to reorient the animal's body so that its eyes and ears are directed towards the source of a novel stimulus in any sensory modality. Its precise role in the control of orienting is not, however, completely clear although anatomical and lesion studies point to the strong probability that the behavioural arrest which is characteristic of the orienting reflex is generated within the deeper layers of superior colliculus which project caudally to nuclei in pontine reticular formation and ultimately the reticulospinal tract. It is not yet known why damage to this descending projection at the level of the predorsal bundle in tree shrews causes a severe sensory neglect (Raczkowski *et al.*, 1976); possibly this pathway carries commands for active search behaviour involving head, neck and body movements.

The ascending projection of superior colliculus travels via the lateral posterior nucleus of the thalamus to various parts of neocortex in non-primate mammals. Lesions in the lateral posterior nucleus in rats (Thompson, 1969; Legg and Cowey, 1977) impairs some visual discrimination learning tasks and in tree shrews lesions of temporal cortex have been found to cause severe deficits in the reversal of a visual discrimination. (Killackey *et al.*, 1972). The latter result is especially interesting since failure in reversal learning may reflect a disability in shifting attention. Since the superficial layers of superior colliculus are the source of the thalamic projection, the visual discrimination learning deficits in tree shrews with superficial collicular lesions probably also arise from disrupted attention.

The most intriguing possibility arising from studies on the non-primate superior colliculus is the apparent functional division between superficial and deep layers. Thus the role played by the deep colliculus in attention is most probably through control of components of the orienting response, but the exact function in attention of superficial superior colliculus has still to be resolved. However, a number of technical problems need to be answered before we finally accept the accuracy of this dual function model. For instance, deep collicular lesions are almost always bigger than superficial ones. Moreover, lesions of superficial layers will disrupt a major source of visual input to the deep layers although there are alternative visual inputs to deep layer cells from the frontal eye fields. Also, since the ascending and descending efferents from colliculus arise primarily in superficial and deep layers respectively, what are apparently different functions in the two regions of colliculus may be a result of blocking one rather than the other output of an integrated attentional mechanism.

In primates, and in cats, the electrophysiological studies clearly implicate superior colliculus in eye movement control. Schiller (1972) and Robinson (1972) have taken up the position that the superior colliculus calculates the parameters for a saccadic eye movement which will centre the fovea on a visual target. But, strong as the evidence from single cell recording and stimulation studies is, this theory is gravely weakened by the finding that monkeys with collicular lesions are only slightly impaired in ability to make accurate saccades. Unless we resort to the argument that the superior colliculus is part of a parallel, and therefore highly redundant mechanism for eye movement control, it does not appear that the colliculus plays any critical role in the control of eye movements.

The attention hypothesis proposed by Wurtz and Goldberg (1972a) also implicates superior colliculus in saccadic eye movements but not in calculating their metrics or in their generation. They argue that the superior colliculus either itself selects a visual object to be attended to or does so in conjunction with other visual areas in the brain. Those cells in superficial layers of colliculus which have visual fields in which the target for a forthcoming eye movement lie show an enhanced response prior to the eye movement with concomitant inhibition of responsiveness in cells with receptive fields outside the target area. The implication of this theory is that "exploration" of the stationary visual field occurs in superior colliculus, and when an appropriate target for attention occurs there is an enchanced response which in effect informs some other brain region that something interesting exists at a particular locus in the visual field.

The ascending fibres which travel to the rostral pulvinar could therefore inform extravisual areas in the circumstriate belt and inferotemporal cortex which have also been implicated in attention (see review by Gross, 1972, 1973) as to the existence of the object of interest. These areas could then in turn cause selective analysis of the appropriate visual region, with an eye movement being generated if necessary. The descending projection from colliculus to the oculomotor nuclei could then short circuit the calculations of the parameters for the eye movement providing the cortical mechanisms have determined that an eye movement is necessary because the target is significant. Wurtz and Goldberg's attentional theory of superior colliculus function need not be restricted to primates and those animals which use saccadic eye movements for visual exploration. However, the characteristics of the attentional response will differ between species which make few or small eye movements, relying more on postural changes to orient themselves towards a target, and species capable of making large amplitude accurate eye movements.

Clearly there is still much to be learned about the function of superior colliculus, but few would now deny that it plays an important role in attention. Its contribution to the attentional process may not be the same in different species, but a resolution of this problem is confounded by the differing responses which animals make when attending to objects in their world. Before concluding this chapter on consciousness and attention, it seems appropriate to remark on the phenomena of "blindsight". Weiskrantz *et al.* (1974) report the case history of a patient who had a restricted lesion in the right occipital lobe following a large occipital arteriovenous malformation. Eight months after receiving this lesion, the patient was extensively tested to assess his visual capacities. Although he denied awareness of "seeing" in his blind field, a variety of tests showed that when visual stimuli were present in his scotomatic region, he could accurately reach for visual stimuli, he could differentiate the orientation of vertical, horizontal and diagonal lines and he could differentiate the letters X and O. The clinical importance of "blindsight" is clear but theoretically it provides us with an intriguing question as to how a person's behaviour can be controlled by the information provided by the visual mechanisms of the midbrain, but without this information being available to conscious reflection.

References

Abrahams, V. C. and Rose, P. K. (1975). Projection to extraocular, neck muscle, and retinal afferents to superior colliculus in the cat: their connection to cells of origin of tectospinal tract. *Journal of Neurophysiology*, **38**, 10–18.

Adamuk, E. (1872). Uber augeborene und erworbene Association von F. C. Donders. *Albrecht v. Graefes Archiv für Opthalmologie*, **18**, 153–164.

Allman, J. (1977). Evolution of the visual system in the early primates. *In* "Progress in Psychobiology and Physiological Psychology" (Eds J. M. Sprague and A. N. Epstein), vol. 7. pp. 1–58. Academic Press, London and New York.

Altman, J. and Carpenter, M. B. (1961). Fiber projections of the superior colliculus in the cat, *Journal of Comparative Neurology*, **116**, 157–177.

Anderson, K. V. and Symmes, D. (1969). The superior colliculus and higher visual functions in the monkey. *Brain Research,* **13,** 37–52.

Anderson, M. E, Yoshida, M. and Wilson, V. J. (1972). Tectal and tegmental influences on cat forelimb and hindlimb motorneurons. *Journal of Neurophysiology,* **35,** 462–470.

Apter, J. T. (1946). Eye movements following strychninization of the superior colliculus of cats. *Journal of Neurophysiology,* **9,** 73–86.

Astruc, J. (1971). Corticofugal connections of area 8 (frontal eye field) in macaca mulatta. *Brain Research,* **33,** 241–256.

Barnes, P. J, Smith, L. M. and Latto, R. H. (1970). Orientation to visual stimuli and the superior colliculus in the rat. *Quarterly Journal of Experimental Psychology,* **22,** 239–247.

Benevento, L. A. and Fallon, J. H. (1975). The ascending projections of the superior colliculus in the rhesus monkey (macaca mulatta). *Journal of Comparative Neurology,* **160,** 339–361.

Bennett, T. L. (1975). The electrical activity of the hippocampus and process of attention. "The Hippocampus vol. 2: Neurophysiology and Behaviour" *In* (Eds R. L. Isaacson and K. H. Pribam), pp. 71–100 Plenum Press, New York.

Berlucchi, G, Sprague, J. M, Levy, J. and Diberardino, A. C. (1972). Pretectum and superior colliculus in visually guided behaviour and in flux and form discrimination in the cat. *Journal of Comparative and Physiological Psychology, Monograph,* **78,** 123–172.

Blake, L. (1959). The effect of lesions of the superior colliculus on brightness and pattern discrimination in the cat. *Journal of Comparative and Physiological Psychology,* **52,** 272–278.

Buser, P. (1976). Higher functions of the nervous system, *Annual Review of Physiology,* **38,** 217–245.

Butter, C. M. (1974). Effect of superior colliculus, striate and prestriate lesions on visual sampling in rhesus monkeys. *Journal of Comparative and Physiological Psychology,* **87,** 905–917.

Cardu, B, Ptito, M., Dumont, M. and Lepore, F. (1975). Effects of ablations of the superior colliculi on spectral sensitivity in monkeys. *Neuropsychologia,* **13,** 297–306.

Casagrande, V. A. and Diamond, I. T. (1974). Ablation study of the superior colliculus in the tree shrew (Tupaia glis). *Journal of Comparative Neurology,* **156,** 207–238.

Casagrande, V. A., Harting, J. K., Hall, W. C., Diamond, I. T. and Martin, G. F. (1972). Superior colliculus of the tree shrew: a structural and functional subdivision into superficial and deep layers. *Science,* **177,** 444–447.

Cowey, A. (1979). Cortical maps and visual perception. The Grindley Memorial Lecture. *Quarterly Journal of Experimental Psychology,* **31,** 1–18.

Cowey, A. and Gross, C. G. (1970). Effects of foveal prestriate and inferotemporal lesions on visual discrimination by rhesus monkeys. *Experimental Brain Research,* **11,** 128–144.

Cynader, M. and Berman, N. (1972). Receptive field organization of monkey superior colliculus. *Journal of Neurophysiology,* **35,** 187–201.

Denny–Brown, D. (1962). The midbrain and motor integration. *Proceedings of the Royal Society for Medicine,* **55**, 527–538.

Douglas, R. J. (1967). The hippocampus and behaviour. *Psychological Bulletin,* **67**, 416–442.

Drager, H. C. and Hubel, D. H. (1975a). Physiology of visual cells in mouse superior colliculus and correlation with somatosensory and auditory input. *Nature,* **253**, 203–204.

Drager, U. C. and Hubel, D. H. (1975b). Topography of visual and somatosensory projections to mouse superior colliculus. *Journal of Neurophysiology,* **39**, 91–101.

Dyer, R. S., Marino, M. F., Johnson, C. and Kruggel, T. (1976). Superior colliculus lesions do not impair orientation to pattern. *Brain Research,* **112**, 176–179.

Enroth-Cugell, C. and Robson, J. G. (1966). The contrast sensitivity of retinal ganglion cells of the cat. *Journal of Physiology,* **187**, 517–552.

Foreman, N. P., Goodale, M. A. and Milner, A. D. (1978). Nature of postoperative hyperactivity following lesions of the superior colliculus in the rat. *Physiology and Behaviours,* **21**, 157–160.

Fukuda, Y. (1971). Receptive field organiztion of cat optic nerve fibers with special reference to conduction velocity. *Vision Research,* **11**, 209–226.

Fukuda, Y. and Stone, J. (1974). Retinal distribution and central projection of Y-, X- and W-cells of the cat's retina. *Journal of neurophysiology,* **37**, 749–772.

Goldberg, M. E. and Wurtz, R. H. (1972a). Activity of superior colliculus in behaving monkey. I. Visual receptive fields of single neurons. *Journal of Neurophysiology,* **35**, 542–559.

Goldberg, M. E. and Wurtz, R. H. (1972b). Activity of superior colliculus in behaving monkey. II. Effect of attention on neuronal response. *Journal of Neurophysiology,* **35**, 560–574.

Goodale, M. A. and Lister, T. M. (1974). Attention to novel stimuli in rats with lesions of the superior colliculus. *Brain Research,* **66**, 361–362.

Goodale, M. A. and Murison, R. C. (1975). The effects of lesions of the superior colliculus on motor orientation and the orienting reflex in the rat. *Brain Research,* **88**, 243–261.

Goodale, M. A., Foreman, N. P. and Milner, A. D. (1978). Visual orientation in the rat: a dissociation of deficits following cortical and collicular lesions. *Experimental Brain Research,* **31**, 445–457.

Grastyan, E., Lissak, K., Madarasz, I. and Donhoffer, M. (1959). Hippocampal electrical activity during the development of conditioned reflexes, *Electroencephalography and Clinical Neurophysiology,* **11**, 409–430.

Graybiel, A. M. (1972). Some extrageniculate visual pathways in the cat. *Investigations in Opthalmology,* **11**, 322–332.

Graybiel, A. M. (1974). Visual–cerebellar and cerebello–visual connections involving the ventral lateral geniculate nucleus. *Experimental Brain Research,* **20**, 303–306.

Graybiel, A. M. (1975). Anatomical organization of retinotectal afferents in the cat: An autoradiographic study. *Brain Research,* **96**, 1–23.

Graybiel, A. M. (1976). Evidence for banding of the cat's ipsilateral retino-tectal connections. *Brain Research*, **114**, 318–327.

Gross, C. G. (1972). Visual functions of inferotemporal cortex. "Handbook of Sensory Physiology" *In* (Ed. R. Jung), vol. 7, part 3, pp. 451–482. Springer–Verlag, Berlin.

Gross, C. G. (1973). Inferotemporal cortex and vision. *In* "Progress in Physio-logical Psychology" (Eds. E. Stellar and J. M. Sprague), vol. 5, pp. 77–123. Academic Press, New York and London.

Hamilton, B. L. (1973). Projections of the nuclei of the periaqueductal gray matter in the cat. *Journal of Comparative Neurology*, **152**, 45–48.

Harting, J. K., Hall, W. C., Diamond, I. T. and Martin, G. F. (1973). Anterograde degeneration study of the superior colliculus in *Tupaia glis*. Evidence for a subdivision between superficial and deep layers, *Journal of Comparative Neurology*, **148**, 361–386.

Hashikawa, T. and Kawamura, K. (1977). Identification of cells of origin of tectopontine fibres in the cat superior colliculus: an experimental study with the horseradish peroxidase method, *Brain Research*, **130**, 65–80.

Hernandez-Peon, R. (1969). Neurophysiologic aspects of attention, *In* "Hand-book of Clinical Neurology" (Eds P. J. Vinken and G. W. Bruyn). North Holland, Amsterdam.

Hernandez-Peon, R., O'Flaherty, J. J. and Mazzuchelli-O'Flaherty, A. C. (1965). Modifications of tactile evoked potentials at the spinal trigeminal sensory nucleus during wakefulness and sleep. *Experimental Neurlogy*, **13**, 40–57.

Hess, W. R., Burgi, S. and Bucher, V. (1946). Motorische funktion des tectal-und Tegmentalgebietes. *Psychiatrie, Neurologie and Medizinische Psycho-logie*, **112**, 1–52.

Hoffman, K.-P. (1973). Conduction velocity in pathways from retina to superior colliculus in the cat: a correlation with receptive field properties. *Journal of Neurophysiology*, **36**, 409–424.

Hoffman, K.-P. and Sherman, S. M. (1974). Effects of early binocular depri-vation on visual input to cat superior colliculus. *Journal of Neurophysiology*, **37**, 1276–1286.

Hollander, H. (1974). On the origin of the corticotectal projection in the cat. *Experimental Brain Research*, **21**, 433–439.

Horn, G. (1960). Electrical activity of the cerebral cortex of the unanesthetized cat during attentive behaviour. *Brain*, **83**, 57–76.

Hubel, D. H., Levay, S. and Wiesel, T. N. (1975). Mode of termination of retinotectal fibres in the macaque monkey: an autoradiographic study. *Brain Research*, **96**, 25–40.

Humphrey, N. K. (1968). Responses to visual stimuli of units in the superior colliculus of rats and monkeys. *Experimental Neurology*, **20**, 312–340.

Ingle, D. (1973). Evolutionary perspectives on the function of the optic tectum, *Brain Behav. Evol.*, **8**, 211–237.

James, W. (1980). "The Principles of Psychology". Holt, New York. Reprinted Dover, New York, 1950.

Kadoya, S., Wolin, L. R. and Massopust, L. C. (1971). Photically evoked unit activity in the tectum opticum of the squirrel monkey. *Journal of Comparative Neurology*, **142**, 495–508.

Kanaseki, T. and Sprague, J. M. (1974). Anatomical organization of pretectal nuclei and tectal laminae in the cat. *Journal of Comparative Neurology*, **158**, 319–338.

Kawamura, K. and Brodal, A. (1973). The tectopontine projection in the cat: an experimental anatomical study with comments on pathways for teleceptive impulses to the cerebellum. *Journal of Comparative Neurology*, **149**, 371–390.

Kawamura, K. and Hashikawa, T. (1978). Cell bodies of origin of reticular projections from the superior colliculus in the cat: an experimental study with the use of horseradish peroxidase as a tracer. *Journal of Comparative Neurology*, **182**, 1–16.

Kawamura, S., Sprague, J. M. and Nimi, K. (1974). Corticofugal projections from the visual cortices to the thalamus, pretectum and superior colliculus in the cat. *Journal of Comparative Neurology*, **158**, 339–362.

Keating, E. G. (1974). Impaired orientation after primate tectal lesions. *Brain Research*, **67**, 538–541.

Keating, E. G. (1976). Effects of tectal lesions on peripheral field vision in the monkey. *Brain Research*, **104**, 316–320.

Killackey, H., Wilson, M. and Diamond, I. T. (1972). Further studies of the striate and extrastriate visual cortex in the tree shrew. *Journal of Comparative Neurology*, **81**, 45–63.

Kimble, D. P. (1975). Choice behaviour in rats with hippocampal lesions. *In* "The Hippocampus Vol. 2: Neurophysiology and Behaviour" (Eds R. L. Isaacson and K. H. Pribram), Plenum Press, New York.

Kimble, D. P. and Kimble, R. J. (1970). The effect of hippocampal lesions on extinction and "hypothesis" behaviour in rats. *Physiology* and *Behaviour*, **5**, 735–738.

Kirvel, R. D. (1975). Sensorimotor responsiveness in rats with unilateral superior collicular and amygdaloid lesions. *Journal of Comparative and Physiological Psychology*, **89**, 882–891.

Krechevsky, I. (1935). Brain Mechanisms and "hypotheses". *Journal of Comparative Psychology*, **19**, 25–462.

Kuypers, H. G. J. M. and Lawrence, D. G. (1967). Cortical projections to the red nucleus and the brain stem in the rhesus monkey. *Brain Research*, **4**, 151–188.

Lane, R. H., Allman, J. M. and Kaas, J. H. (1971). Representation of the visual field in the superior colliculus of the grey squirrel (*Sciurus carolinensis*) and the tree shrew (*Tupaia glis*). *Brain Research*, **26**, 277–292.

Latto, R. (1977). The effects of bilateral frontal eye-field, posterior parietal or superior colliculus lesions on brightness thresholds in the rhesus monkey. *Neuropsychologia*, **15**, 507–516.

Layman, J. D. (1936). Functions of the superior colliculus in vision. *Journal of Genetic Psychology*, **49**, 33–47.

Legg, C. R. and Cowey, A. (1977). The role of ventral lateral geniculate nucleus and posterior thalamus in intensity discrimination in rats. *Brain Research*, **123**, 261–273.

Lynch, G. and Crain, B. (1972). Increased generalized activity following lesions in the caudal reticular formation. *Physiology and Behaviour*, **8**, 747–750.

Lepore, F., Ptito, M., Cardu, B. and Dumont, M. (1976). Effects of striatectomy and colliculectomy on achromatic thresholds in the monkey. *Physiology and Behaviour*, **16**, 285–291.

Mcilwain, J. T. (1975). Visual receptive fields and their images in superior colliculus of the cat. *Journal of Neurophysiology*, **38**, 219–230.

Mackinnon, D. A., Gross, C. G. and Bender, D. B. (1976). A visual deficit after superior colliculus lesions in monkeys. *Acta Neurobiologiae Experimentalis*, **36**, 169–180.

Martin, G. F. and Harting, J. K. (1972). Efferent projections of the superior colliculus in the tree shrew (*Tupaia glis*): An analysis of the projections of individual strata. *Anatomical Research*, **172**, 364.

Meyer, D., Treichler, F. and Meyer, P. (1965). Discrete trial training techniques and stimulus variables. *In* "Behaviour of Non Human Primates" (Eds A. Schrier, H. Harlow and F. Stollnitz), vol. 1. Academic Press, New York and London.

Michael, C. R. (1972). Visual receptive fields of single neurons in superior colliculus of the ground squirrel. *Journal of Neurophysiology*, **35**, 815–832.

Milner, A. D., Foreman, N. P. and Goodale, M. A. (1978). Go-left go-right discrimination performace and distractibility following lesions of prefrontal cortex or superior colliculus in stumptail macaques. *Neuropsychologia*, **16**, 381–390.

Milner, A. D., Goodale, M. A. and Morton, M. C. (1979). Visual sampling following lesions of the superior colliculus in rats. *Journal of Comparative and Physiological Psychology*, **93**, 1015–1023.

Mishkin, M. (1972). Cortical visual areas and their interactions. *In* "Brain and Human Behaviour" (Eds A. G. Karczmar and J. C. Eccles), pp. 187–208. Springer-Verlag, New York.

Mohler, C. W. and Wurtz, R. H. (1976). Organization of monkey superior colliculus: intermediate layer cells discharging before eye movements. *Journal of Neurophysiology*, **39**, 722–744.

Mohler, C. W. and Wurtz, R. H. (1977). Role of striate cortex and superior colliculus in visual guidance of saccadic eye movements in monkeys. *Journal of neurophysiology*, **40**, 74–94.

Myers, R. E. (1963). Projections of superior colliculus in monkey. *Anatomical Record*, **145**, 264.

Myers, R. E. (1964). Visual deficits after lesions of brainstem tegmentum in cats. *Archives of Neurology*, **13**, 73–90.

Palmer, L. A. and Rosenquist, A. C. (1974). Visual receptive fields of single striate cortical units projecting to the superior colliculus in the cat. *Brain Research*, **67**, 27–42.

Pasik, P., Pasik, T. and Bender, M. B. (1966). The superior colliculus and eye movements. *Archives of Neurology*, **15**, 420–436.

Pope, S. G. and Dean, P. (1979). Hyperactivity, aphagia and motor disturbance following lesions of superior colliculus and underlying tegmentum in rats. *Behavioural and Neural Biology*, **27**, 433–453.

Powell T. P. S. (1976). Bilateral cortico-tectal projection from the visual cortex in the cat. *Nature London*, **260**, 526–527.

Pribram, K. H. (1974). How is it that sensing so much we can see so little? *In* "The Neurosciences: Third Study Program" (Eds F. O. Schmitt and F. G. Worden). MIT Press, Cambridge, Massachusetts.

Raczkowski, D., Casagrande, V. A. and Diamond, J. T. (1976). Visual neglect in the tree shrew after interruption of the descending projections of the deep superior colliculus. *Experimental Neurology*, **50**, 14–29.

Robinson, D. A. (1972). Eye movements evoked by collicular stimulation in the alert monkey. *Vision Research*, **12**, 1795–1808.

Roucoux, A. and Crommelinck, M. (1976). Eye movements evoked by superior colliculus stimulation in the alert cat. *Brain Research*, **106**, 349–363.

Schiller, P. H. (1972). The role of the monkey superior colliculus in eye movement and vision. *Investigations in Opthalmology*, **11**, 451–460.

Schiller, P. H. and Koerner, F. (1971). Discharge characteristics of single units in superior colliculus of the alert rhesus monkey. *Journal of Neurophysiology*, **34**, 920–936.

Schiller, P. H. and Stryker, M. (1972). Single unit recording and stimulation in superior colliculus of the alert rhesus monkey. *Journal of Neurophysiology*, **35**, 915–924.

Schneider, G. E. (1967). Contrasting visuomotor functions of tectum and cortex in the golden hamster. *Psychologische Forschung*, **31**, 52–62.

Sherrington, C. (1906). "The Integrative Action of the Nervous System". Charles Scribner's Sons, New York.

Silveira, J. M. and Kimble, D. P. (1968). Brightness discrimination and reversal in hippocampally-lesioned rats. *Physiology and Behaviour*, **3**, 625–630.

Smith, C. J. and Weldon, D. A. (1976). Hyperactivity and deficits in problem solving following superior colliculus lesons in the rat. *Physiology and Behaviour*, **16**, 381–385.

Sokolov, Ye N. (1963). Higher nervous function: the orienting reflex. *Annual Review of Physiology*, **25**, 545–580.

Sparks, D. L. (1975). Response properties of eye-movement-related neurons in the monkey superior colliculus. *Brain Research*, **90**, 147–152.

Sparks, D. C., Holland, R. and Guthrie, B. C. (1976). Size and distribution of movement fields in the monkey superior colliculus. *Brain Research*, **113**, 21–34.

Sprague, J. M. (1975). Mammalian tectum: intrinsic organization, afferent inputs and integrative mechanisms. *Neurosciences Research Program Bulletin*, **13**, 204–213.

Sprague, J. M. and Meikle, T. H. (1965). The role of the superior colliculus in visually guided behaviour, *Experimental Neurology*, **11**, 115–146.

Sprague, J. M., Berlucchi, G. and Rizzolatti, G. (1973). The role of the superior colliculus and pretectum in vision and visually guided behaviour, *In* "Handbook of Sensory Physiology" (Ed. R. Jung), vol. 7, part 3, pp. 27–101. Springer-Verlag, Berlin.

Stein, B. E., Magalhaes-Castro, B. and Kruger, L. (1976). Relationship between visual and tactile representations in cat superior colliculus. *Journal of Neurophysiology*, **39**, 401–419.

Sterling, P. and Wickelgren, B. G. (1969). Visual receptive fields in the superior colliculus of the cat. *Journal of Neurophysiology*, **32**, 1–15.

Stevens, R. (1973). Probability discrimination learning in hippocampectomized rats. *Physiology and Behaviour*, **10**, 1023–1027.

Stevens, R. and Cowey, A. (1972). Enhanced alternation learning in hippocampectomized rats by means of added light cues. *Brain Research*, **46**, 1–22.

Stevens, R. and Cowey, A. (1973). Effects of dorsal and ventral hipocampal lesions on spontaneous alternation, learned alternation and probability learning in rats. *Brain Research*, **52**, 203–224.

Stone, J. and Fukuda, Y. (1974). Properties of cat retinal ganglion cells; a comparison of W-cells and X- and Y-cells. *Journal of Neurophysiology*, **37**, 722–748.

Straschill, M. and Hoffman, K.-P. (1970). Activity of movement sensitive neurons of the cat's optic tectum during spontaneous eye movement. *Experimental Brain Research*, **11**, 318–326.

Straschill, M. and Rieger, P. (1973). Eye movements evoked by focal stimulation of the cat's superior colliculus. *Brain Research*, **59**, 211–227.

Stryker, M. P. and Schiller, P. H. (1975). Eye and head movements evoked by electrical stimulation of monkey superior colliculus. *Experimental Brain Research*, **23**, 103–112.

Sutherland, N. S. and Mackintosh, N. J. (1971). "Mechanisms of Animal Discrimination Learning". Academic Press, London and New York.

Szekely, G. (1973). anatomy and synaptology of the optic tectum. *In* "Handbook of Sensory Physiology" (Ed. Jung), vol. 7, part 3, pp. 1–26. Springer-Verlag, Berlin.

Thompson, R. (1969). Localization of the "visual memory system" in the white rat. *Journal of Comparative and Physiological Psychology*, **69**, 1–

Trevarthen, C. B. (1968). Two mechanisms of vision in primates. *Psychologische Forschung*, **31**, 299–337.

Updyke, B. V. (1974). Characteristics of unit responses in superior colliculus of the cebus monkey. *Journal of Neurophysiology*, **37**, 896–909.

Vetter, R. J. (1975). Visual localization and discrimination in squirrel monkeys with bilateral lesions of the superior colliculus. *International Journal of Neuroscience*, **6** 215–221.

Weinberg, D. and Stein, D. G. (1978). Impairment and recovery of visual functions after bilateral lesions of superior colliculus, *Physiology and Behaviour*, **21**, 323–329.

Weiskrantz, L., Warrington, E. K., Sanders, M. D. and Marshall, J. (1974). Visual capacity in the hemianopic field following a restricted occipital ablation. *Brain*, **97**, 709–728.

Weldon, D. A. and Smith, C. J. (1979). Superior colliculus lesions and environmental experience: nonvisual effects on problem solving and loco-motor activity. *Physiology and Behaviour*, **23**, 159–165.

Wilson, P. D. and Stone, J. (1975). Evidence of W-cell input to the cat's visual cortex via the C laminae of the lateral geniculate nucleus. *Brain Research*, **92**, 472–478.

Wilson, M. E. and Toyne, M. J. (1970). Retino-tectal and cortico-tectal projections in *macaca mulatta*. *Brain Research*, **24**, 395–406.

Winterkorn, J. M. (1975). Visual discrimination between spatially separated stimuli by cats with lesions of the superior colliculus—pretectum. *Brain Research*, **100**, 523–541.

Wood, B. S. (1975). Monocular relearning of a dark–light discrimination by cats after unilateral cortical and collicular lesions. *Brain Research*, **83**, 156–162.

Wurtz, R. H. and Goldberg, M. E. (1972a). Activity of superior colliculus in behaving monkey. III Cells discharging before eye movements. *Journal of Neurophysiology*, **35**, 575–586.

Wurtz, R. H. and Goldberg, M. E. (1972b). Activity of superior colliculus in behaving monkey. IV Effects of lesions on eye movements. *Journal of Neurophysiology*, **35**, 587–596.

Wurtz, R. H. and Mohler, C. W. (1976a). Organization of monkey superior colliculus: Enhanced visual response of superficial layer cells. *Journal of Neurophysiology*, **39**, 745–765.

Wurtz, R. H. and Mohler, C. W. (1976b). Enhancement of visual responses in monkey striate cortex and frontal eye fields. *Journal of Neurophysiology*, **39**, 766–772.

Yarbus, A. L. (1967). "Eye movements and Vision". Plenum Press, New York.

3 Representing Ourselves: Mental Schemata, Computational Metaphors, and the Nature of Consciousness[1]

K. OATLEY

*Department of Experimental Psychology,
University of Sussex*

> . . . . . . human kind
> Cannot bear very much reality.
> 'Burnt Norton'

1 Introduction

Consciousness is a peculiar issue when considered in a natural scientific context. Scientific methods work best in investigating certain phenomena "out there" in the external world, whereas consciousness, of all psychological issues, is not "out there". For the most part interest in consciousness is interest in one's own inner world and also in the subjective experience of others—together perhaps with an interest in increasing the extent of, or changing the state of, our conscious awareness.

In this Chapter I will consider the relationship of the world within (the constructions of our mental schemata) to the external world. I will examine how some matters become conscious while others are (in various senses of the term) unconscious. To conduct this enquiry I shall explore the uses of computer programs as metaphors for our own

[1]This chapter is written in a tradition of theoretical psychology deriving from the work of Max Clowes and Sylvia Weir. I am grateful to both of them for much discussion on subjects included here. I am also particularly grateful to Judith Katz for discussion on her insights into how mental schemata function in emotions and social interaction. Steven Draper and Heather Wood read a draft of the manuscript and made helpful suggestions. I thank them for those and for helpful discussion. I also thank Mary Walton for typing the manuscript. The poetry quotations in this chapter are from T.S. Eliot's "Four Quartets".

mental processes, arguing that they are the best vehicles we have currently available for formal understanding of the principles and properties of mental schemata.

I will refer to two new theories about the nature and function of consciousness: Jaynes's (1976) theory of the evolution of consciousness and Humphrey's (1977) theory of conscious introspection as a method of social knowledge. I will also draw on two rather old theories of different kinds of unconsciousness: Helmholtz's (1866) theory of unconscious inference, and Freud's (e.g. 1926) theory of unconscious defense mechanisms, as well as various programs from the literature of artificial intelligence.

2 Metaphors and theories

2.1 Schemata and consciousness

How is our inner world constructed? Much of what we know we have learned by doing. In Piaget's (e.g. 1974) analysis mental "schemes" arise as internal symbolizations of external actions. And Dewey (e.g. 1900) argues we learn best by self-motivated active experimentation with the world. So our schemata assimilate new data in our more successful attempts at action and accommodate in response to our mistakes.

Presumably, as well as action-based schemata there is a category of primary perceptual experience, e.g. the baby's pleasure when being cuddled, or when sucking at the breast.

So, it is as if there is a basic layer of representation, where actions are internalized as inferences, and where the structure of the world outside is internalized as what Craik (1943) has called an inner model, derived from perception. The symbolic manipulations and the internal model on which they take place are analogous to actions and objects in the outside world. As Clowes (personal communication) has put it in computational terms: we have actions and the structure of the outside world, and in a program these are represented by procedures and a data base on which they operate.

It is reasonable to suppose that it is to this basic layer of representation that we can attribute one aspect of consciousness, which I will call awareness. Thus we may act in deliberate awareness when actions are directed towards some goal. This sequence of actions is generated by a schema. And when perceiving we are consciously aware of that which our schemata can construct, and to which we pay attention.

A further aspect of consciousness is that as well as doing, we can think about what we are doing, and as well as perceiving we can reflect upon our experience. I will call this "reflective consciousness". In the building up of our schemata during childhood it seems that this second aspect of consciousness grows only slowly. We create extensive mental schemata without self-conscious direction of thought, and we assimilate perceptions without necessarily reflecting on them. This aspect of consciousness seems to require a second layer on top of the basic representational one. It involves what Bartlett (1932) called the ability to "turn round upon" our own schemata. In this phrase I take it Bartlett refers to our ability as adults to direct our awareness. Here is a domain that we more usually recognize as metaphor. We consciously (and often in externally or internally expressed language) bring to bear something old upon something new; some aspect of our understanding or experience which is already part of our mental schemata on something we know about in some way but which we do not yet properly perceive, or can't yet make such sense of.

Here from 'The Dry Salvages', is a metaphor of the future, to be made sense of in terms of the past.

> . . . .the future is a faded song, a Royal Rose or
> a lavender spray
> Of wistful regret for those who are not yet alive
> to regret,
> Pressed between the yellow leaves of a book that
> has never been opened.

Different aspects of our mental schemata are, as it were seen in terms of each other. As we go through life a large part of the enrichment of meanings comes from taking part in just such metaphorical relationships with the world.

One meaning of the unconscious, particularly as it is referred to in psychoanalysis is that as adults we are not always able to make sense reflectively of some things that we do or feel. Psychoanalytic theories assert that much adult experience is metaphorically based on rather early primary experiences such as sucking at the breast. This sense of the unconscious then is that some adult experience and behaviour is part of a metaphorical structure whose primary root was in early childhood, and which therefore, never was in reflective consciousness. So on this basis kissing may get at least some of its meanings of intimacy, security and excitement from our early experiences of simultaneously sucking and being held.

2.2 Metaphor in psychology

As psychologists we struggle to make sense of the unfamiliar, because though our own thoughts are familiar to us, how they come about is not. Though we are aware of the products of our mental operations, we are not aware of the processes by which these are achieved. We need therefore metaphors for mental processes to help us make sense of them.

Implicitly or explicitly psychological investigation has been structured around metaphors drawn from the furniture of our ordinary world. These metaphors tend either to be physical or social. Here is an example of the physical kind.

Regarded as an optical instrument the eye is a camera obscura. This apparatus is well known in the form used by photographers. A box constructed of two parts. . . .etc.   Helmholtz, 1868, "Popular Scientific Lectures". p. 97

This comes near the opening of a lecture in which Helmholtz goes on to talk about his theory of perception as a process of unconsciously drawing conclusions: conclusions of which we are consciously aware when we see.

Next is an example of a "social" metaphor—from Freud's "New Introductory Lectures" explaining his notion of thinking carried out by the ego.

Thinking is an experimental action carried out with small amounts of energy, in the same way as a general shifts small figures about on a map before setting his large bodies of troops in action.   Freud, 1933, p. 122

In these metaphors we are asked to imagine the eye as a camera, or thinking as like a general planning strategy before committing his troops in real battle. This metaphorical or analogical structure: seeing one thing as another becomes central to cognition. By means of it we understand something unfamiliar in terms of something more familiar, or more imagineable, or in terms for which we have more ready knowledge and intuitions.

Though analogies from physics seem adequate (in some ways) for the eye, there is a difficulty when approaching our own mental processes. What sufficiently creative, flexible processes which use knowledge are there in the physical world for us to liken our own mental operations to? How can we give the largely unconscious processes underlying thought, language, perception and our own motives, substance and structure? If we choose metaphors from the personal or social world (thinking is like the general planning his strategies) we are in danger of making infinite regresses; as we wonder what goes on in the mind of the little general inside our mind.

Clowes (e.g. 1971) has argued that artifical intelligence in its relation to psychology is the construction of programs to serve as computational analogies or metaphors of representation, meaning and inference, for our own mental processes. Events suitable as analogies do not (otherwise) occur in the physical world.

In academic psychology nowadays the choice for making familiar the workings of the mind seems to be the use either of metaphors from the ordinary world, or from the world of computation. So, memory (for example) can be seen as storage in boxes or filing cabinets, as decay like the fading embers of a fire, as interference like the footprints of people obscuring the footprints of gulls on an early morning beach, and so on. Alternatively it can be seen in terms of the more powerful computational metaphors of knowledge and inference which emerge from attempts to write programs to hold conversations in English (e.g. Winograd, 1971).

Though evocative because they draw on already elaborate schemata the metaphors from the more ordinary world do not go very far. They touch upon simple issues like storage, without really impinging upon much that is central to mental activity, e.g. its creativity or its use of knowledge and inference (cf. Clowes, 1973).

So computation in artificial intelligence can be seen as an activity in which we make familiar to ourselves (perhaps by the actions and experience of programming) some of those processes of inference etc. which might plausibily be fundamental to our own mental life— processes which are unfamiliar because unconscious, and unfamiliar also because they do not occur in the physical world.

Take the example of seeing. According to Helmholtz after a visual scene has been imaged in the camera obscura of the eye, the main task is one of interpretation of this image. This interpretative process is unconscious and is like thinking. So just as we might when travelling by train in a country where we could not speak the language consciously infer that a sign above the window is a warning against leaning out of the window, we unconsciously infer that the pattern of reflections and (apparently) moving images is a window.

According to this view, when we see something "We see it as we interpret it" (Wittgenstein, 1953). We attribute to it meaning in terms of a construction of our mental schemata. And this is true even of the most lowly perceptions. To use another of Helmholtz's examples: if you press gently on the right side of your closed eyelid with a finger while directly your eyes to the left, you will see the resulting phenomenon as light. It is a patch or ring of light seen in the direction that light would normally have to come from (i.e. from the far left) to affect the part of the retina which you are stimulating with your finger. This is the result not of direct perception in any sense, but of inference, in this case a mistaken one, that there is some light coming from the left.

The role of computation in understanding this process of unconscious inference is that by setting ourselves the task of creating an artificial perceiving process we can explore a whole variety of the inferences that have to be made in order to see. We can thus convince ourselves not simply that perception does involve inference (as with Helmholtz's demonstration) but inform ourselves as to the possible nature of unconscious thinking processes. (And just as seeing is interpretive, so understanding our own perception can be interpreted with the metaphor of the computer program. The program is external and explicit and so can become more comprehensible where our own unconscious processes are internal and implicit.)

2.3 A computational metaphor for perception

Consider, for instance, the program of Roberts (1965), one of the earliest but most psychologically important perceptual programs. In part of the program a search is made for cues in a picture, which at this stage of processing is a two-dimensional line drawing (see Fig. 1).

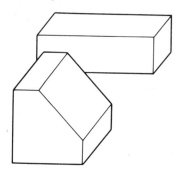

FIG. 1. Line diagram of a scene (after Roberts, 1965).

Cues are two-dimensional configurations which the program can process the picture to discover. Cues serve the function of identifying which prototypes (i.e. stored representations of three-dimensional objects) can be projected on to the picture. The purpose of this is to see that part of the picture "as" a two-dimensional projection of the selected three-dimensional prototype.

In order to see anything at all the program therefore needs to have in it various kinds of knowledge. It needs first a knowledge of cues (which in this case are arrangements of two-dimensional figures, triangles, quadrilaterals, hexagons) appropriate to the world the program operates in. Secondly, it has a set of prototypes, which are three-dimensional descriptions (in contrast to the cues which are descriptions not of objects but of possible parts of a 2-D picture). In this program the prototypes are a cube, a right-angled wedge, and a hexagonal prism. Thirdly the program has a theory of transformation which operates on the prototypes. The transformations (a) stretch and rotate the proto-types (e.g. to produce from the cube a cuboid in a particular orienta-tion) and (b) work out what the two-dimensional projection on to a screen of the three-dimensional prototype would be. It is the second and third kinds of knowledge (prototypes and the theory of transformation) that operating together correspond to what psychologists such as Bartlett (1932) and Neisser (1976) have called constructive mental schemata.

In the example of Fig. 1, then, at one point the program identifies a cue of two quadrilaterals sharing a common line: the two quadrilaterals nearest the top of the picture. This invokes the cube prototype and operates the rotating and stretching transforms, and the rotated stret-ched cube is then projected on to the appropriate part of the picture to see that area "as" a two-dimensional representation of a partly obscured cuboid, see Fig. 2.

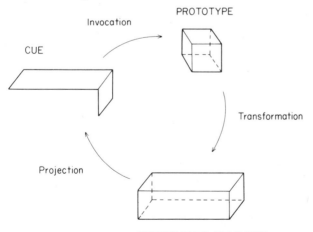

FIG. 2. In Roberts's program working on the picture of Fig. 1, a cue of two adjoining quadrilaterals invokes the 3-D cube prototype. The prototype is part of a constructive schema which applies rotation and stretching transforms to produce a 3-D schematic fragment. This is further transformed into a 2-D projection and tested against the picture data.

Without internal knowledge (of cues, prototypes and theories of transformations) a program might be able to process pictures (in some way) but in no sense could it see pictures as meaningful. To see something we must see it "as" something we know about, and to that "something" there are connected further inferences and potential actions. These are the meanings we supply from inside our heads; projecting them into the data of our retinal images to make sense of them. (For more extensive exposition of Robert's program in this vein see Oatley, 1977 or 1978).

2.4 Projection of implicit theories and modes of unconsciousness

This theory of unconscious inference in perception establishes a sense of what it means to be aware of something in one's perception. We are aware of the conclusions that our perceptual processes reach as we project our schematic knowledge on to the data of our retinal images.

What we are doing when we see, therefore, is to project aspects of an implicit theory (or schema) on to the world, and thereby to make sense of it within the terms of that theory. (Gregory, 1973, pursues the idea of seeing as being like the application to evidence of hypotheses in scientific theories.)

This projective process is, as Clowes (1971) has put it, a bit like hallucination. When looking at a two-dimensional picture such as Fig. 1:

> . . . it is as if we were able to hallucinate edges, surfaces, and corners on to the picture, *consistent with what would make three-dimensional sense* out of the picture. An important component of that sense is of course a knowledge of perspective . . . as well as expectations about the sorts of objects we may be dealing with (italics in original).

This theory also makes clear a number of senses of what it means to be unconscious of something, and the sense of what it might be to become conscious of that thing.

2.4.1 *The unconsciousness of unconscious inferences*

Just as the theory of Helmholtz makes clear that we become aware of the conclusions of inference processes, it makes clear that we are unaware of the processes by which we reached these conclusions, and this is the sense of "unconscious" in Helmholtz's use of the term. Not only are we unaware of them, Helmholtz argues, but we cannot by thinking about it consciously change an unconscious inference. We cannot for instance by taking thought alter the impression made of light to the left when we rub our eyelid on the right.

Though the metaphors of vision programs give us a structured sense of the nature of the relationship we have to our perceived world, they do not give us any introspective access to the workings of our perceptual processes, or the means directly to change our implicit theories.

2.4.2 *Unconsciousness as confusing inner and outer*

Hallucinations (and dreams) are no doubt produced by the same constructive schemata as operate in more usual daily perception, though working without the guiding function of cues. Feelings too sometimes can be projected, so that anger for instance which originates in our self, can be experienced as coming from someone else, as Freud (1911) proposes. For example I may be angry with him but it may be unnacceptable for me to allow that I am feeling destructive or cruel so instead I feel frightened and persecuted as I experience him as being angry with me. This structure of seeing "as" thus leaves room for misattributions of many kinds: seeing what is within as outside, or what is outside as within. And part of each person's reflective consciousness is concerned with the separation and interaction of inner and outer worlds. Some kinds of unconsciousness, then, will be the unawareness of misattributions.

2.4.3 *Unconsciousness as being without an appropriate schema*

Because of the constructive qualities of schemata, quite new things can be experienced in the outside world. For instance Roberts' program sees the object in the foreground of Fig. 1 by constructing it from two stretched cubes and a right-angled wedge. Evidently within this theory, although we see in terms of what we already know, there is a creative quality of being able to construct quite new combinations of what we know.

Even so, often we are not able to make sense of things with existing schemata, or at least not adequate sense for the purposes we have in mind. One is in a largely meaningless world when one first looks down a microscope, or when one begins to look for entopic phenomena (after images and the like) in studying perception. One is also in something of this position when beginning to explore inner worlds, of dreams for instance, or of certain kinds of emotional experience. Here we need to embark on a process of perceptual learning, aided if possible by the provision of pointers to the cognitive schemata that will make sense of the new experiences.

2.4.4 *Unconsciousness as being unaware of the origins of an interpretation*

As briefly mentioned in section 2.1 some of our actions or experience might seem strange because founded on schemata constructed in early childhood, when the ability to turn round reflectively on our schemata was not present.

We may see someone as "friendly", "sexy", "irritable" or whatever. Certain cues will have enabled us to project our implicit theory of not only what it is for someone to be, e.g. friendly, but also what to do about it. Our theory almost certainly will carry along a vast quantity of experience from previous interpersonal encounters, including probably our earliest relationships. Moreover it will identify primarily the data about the person which will confirm our theory, and make it useful for our current purposes. Other data will tend to be dismissed as irrelevant. Such implicit theories, that is to say, are not always tested very extensively. And yet some of our modes of relating (e.g. of dependency) might well be more appropriate to childhood than adulthood. Nor are we always aware of why we react to people as we do.

2.4.5 *Unconsciousness of other people's meanings*

The theory makes it clear that schemata, though they are symbolic abstracts of reality, can reflect it in very individual ways. Representations will be more or less effective for the purpose to which they are put. (This is perhaps one of the most fundamental lessons of artificial intelligence research.) So people who have different purposes will tend to develop different representations of the world, different implicit theories.

These differences of purpose and perception in the world of things can be quite harmless, despite the fact that the same thing can be seen quite differently by two different people. For instance, for the purpose of passing an exam in physics seeing the motions of a pendulum in terms of a second-order differential equation is appropriate. But for the purpose of capturing the attention of a kitten, seeing the pendulum as a plaything, is more to the point. But when similar differences of implicit theory are projected not on to things but people, difficulties can arise, and we can be completely unconscious of the reason.

Moreover, when it comes to interacting with another person, there comes the possibility of creating new interpersonal meanings, not possible with things. Someone might mean to say something and a second person might understand the meaning of what is being said. So a meaning is understood in a different sense than of understanding the properties of a pendulum, which had no intention of creating a meaning.

Moreover when interacting with another I might have a view (say of why I was late) and the other might have a different view. (Here we have a disagreement.) But as Laing *et al.* (1966) point out it will also be relevant what the other's view was, a view I may not be able to, or wish to grasp. Thus it also becomes relevant in our interaction just what is my understanding of the other's view of my being late. We have only each other's behaviour, words, and our implicit theories, on which to base our interpretations. There are very many opportunities not just for disagreements but for complete misunderstandings. We can be quite unconscious of what might go on between us, that is to say it can become hard to make sense of it. For though the possibilities of making mutual meanings is tremendously enriching, as these multiply so too do opportunities for projection, illusion, delusion, collusion. . . .

2.4.6 *Unconsciousness as being stuck inside some too rigid implicit theory*

Perhaps most characteristic of the relationship of our inner schemata to the outer world is the possibility of being stuck inside an implicit theory. Theories articulate some data, and reject others as noise. They make sense of the world. They seem resistant to change, perhaps because disconfirmations of theories are painful, or perhaps because in society some changes of theory are punished, or perhaps because the consequences of change are too costly; most likely for all three reasons. Here is an illustration of entertaining a particular implicit theory.

Imagine two people: Alfie and Betty, who are married. Betty, after some careful (and agonizing) thought gives Alfie a set of records for his birthday. She doesn't much like giving birthday presents, and doesn't think herself very good at choosing them appropriately, either for persons or occasions. She has at times wondered whether this is because she is really too self-absorbed to have much of a sense of what the other person would really like, and has thought that if she cared more selflessly for the other she would not find it so difficult to find the right present. She gives the records to Alfie, who thanks her for them in a rather perfunctory way, assures her that he likes the present very much and puts one record on. Just to show. Betty notices that he doesn't play the second side, and was in any case distinctly ungracious in his receiving of the present.

Betty has her theory of her own ineptitude at buying presents confirmed, simultaneously is a bit depressed and self-blaming about the episode. She resolves to do better next time and wonders how she might more effectively show her love for Alfie; how she might reach him, as it were.

If there were a third person, say Betty's sister Gaby, at the scene,

Gaby might also be struck by the churlishness with which Alfie received the present, wonder why he was reluctant to accept a symbol of affection from Betty, and speculate on whether he no longer loves Betty (and thus feels guilty about accepting a present from her). Maybe, even (she wonders) he is having an affair. Of course, as in many social interactions neither Betty nor Gaby is likely, for various reasons, to know "the truth" of the matter. For we can't see truths directly only make interpretations. But one thing is clear. Whereas Gaby (who doesn't really like Alfie all that much anyway, and is a bit envious of her sister's married status) could see Alfie's ungraciousness as indicating that he found it difficult to receive a present because he did not love Betty, there is nothing in Betty's scheme of things (schema) that would allow her to see his act in those terms. Her life is built round the "fact" that they both love each other and always will. Only later, if he were to leave her for a new lover, might she start to be conscious of the meanings of various things in their life together in a different way.

In this scene Betty can only be conscious of what the implicit theories of her life can conceive. If a discordant note is struck, then it tends to be seen not as a counter-instance requiring some alteration of her theory, but as an implication of her own already existing theories. So Betty (and all the rest of us) in a certain sense are conscious in our perceptions typically of what there is both some external evidence for and accords with the purposes and attitudes built into our mental schemata.

It is well known that in many circumstances we are reluctant to seek for disconfirmations of our hypotheses (see Jenkins and Ward, 1965; Wason, 1968). The theory of perception embodies in Roberts' program provides one reason why. We can't easily see disconfirmations as disconfirmations. If something can't be seen in terms of current mental schemata, it can't be seen at all.

Not only that but an attitude of seeking deliberately for disconfirmations of one's most deeply held implicit theories, though no doubt admirable by the canons of Popper's (1963) scientific procedures, would be odd in one's personal relationships. Though Betty might have been too deeply embedded in one particular implicit theory to be sensitive to tell-tale cues that might signal other interpretations, adopting a continually sceptical view of all that passed in a relationship would quite rightly be regarded as paranoid and crazy. It is the implicit theories (metaphors) that give our lives meaning.

If we take the metaphor of perception provided by Roberts' program seriously, we may also perceive that it's not necessarily much good simply exhorting ourselves to look for disconfirmations (by means of some superordinate theory of how to be sceptical in the world). More plausibly if we knew more about the content of what we were projecting on to the data of the world, we would be more reflectively conscious of the sorts of conjunctions we habitually placed on events. When we are more conscious of the content of our implicit theories (our inner world), we give ourselves the possibility of becoming conscious of more things in the outside world. (Perhaps this is done by courting a wide variety of experiences and hence acquiring a wider variety of schemata to project. This matter will be discussed further later in the context of Humphrey's theory.)

Certainly we can imagine that if Betty had been more conscious that the combined projection on to events of her emotional dependence on Alfie, and a self-deprecating attitude towards herself would more or less force her to see anything that seemed discordant in her relationship as "her fault", then she might have been able to wonder what was going on in Alfie to make him so ungracious in the receiving of the birthday present (particularly when one of the things that he really liked most in the world was records). But we can observe here (a theme that will be taken up in the next section) that it would be painful to Betty in the extreme to think the thoughts that Gaby had thought. As Freud pointed out, unconsciousness has its uses.

2.4.7 *Summary of "projection of implicit theories"*

I have outlined above six modes in which one might speak of being unconscious of something. All arise from the fundamental nature of our relationship to the world, as mediated by mental schemata, the implicit theories which we project on to evidence in the world to make sense of it. We can be aware of the conclusions our implicit theories draw. We are unconscious in various ways of what they can not encompass.

The computational metaphor illuminates these matters principally by making explicit the structure of the relationship between the cues in the data and the schemata they invoke. So Roberts' program is not exactly a theory of how people see, but a metaphor for schema-based seeing. By considering it we can consider what are the cues that evoke our mental schemata, what are the schemata that we project, and what are the consequences of this relationship between inner and outer worlds.

All these modes of unconsciousness can be thought of basically as "unawareness", using the terminology that the constructions of the perceptual schema are what we are aware of. But we can reflect upon them too, that is to say turn round upon the relevant schemata. And in all these modes except the first it seems that this kind of self-conscious reflection upon experience, or the thinking about what we are doing, bringing one aspect of our experience metaphorically to bear on another might be important in enlarging our consciousness.

In the next section I will consider a different kind of unconsciousness, caused not so much by a failure of schemata to apprehend data that are fragmentary and inconsistent, but by the actively energetic attempts we make to mould our conceptions of the world in ways that have more to do with what is comfortable than with what is true.

3 Feelings

3.1 Feelings as matches and mismatches of data with schemata

Perception is a process whereby we make sense of the world outside in terms of the meanings of a world within. Weir (1975) has suggested that the experience of feelings or emotions is due to the world outside either matching the world within (giving rise to feelings of contentment, of satisfaction, etc.) or not matching it (giving rise to feelings of anger, disappointment and so on).

Weir has made this suggestion on the basis of her perceptual program which derives cues from sequences of frames in a simulated display of Michotte's (1963) causality experiments. In Michotte's displays a dot moving towards another one is seen phenomenally to knock the other out of the way (like a billiard ball), trigger or launch the other, creep over the other etc., according to various conditions of the observer and display. In turn these different conditions cue the selection of different schemata, which are associated with different meanings, and which then match or fail to match subsequent frames of the display.

For inanimate objects, like billiard balls, a failure of expectations, e.g. if a cue-ball on a billiard table instead of knocking a red ball out of the way bounced back off it while the red one remained still, would cause some feeling of surprise, and curiosity. This failure of expectations, as the implicit projected theory fails, might well be taken as a signal either to change the theory (e.g. to wonder whether the cue-ball wasn't a billiard ball but a ping-pong ball) or to investigate the situation more closely or both. In the more important matters of our aspirations or relationships the feelings involved are not necessarily just surprise or curiosity, nor is the revision of the implicit theory so straightforward. In the case of Betty for instance any such gross mismatch (disconfirmation) of her theory that she and Alfie would always love each other exclusively, with evidence from the outer world would not lead only to surprise. If she discovered a letter from Alfie's lover, read it, and found it to contain unmistakable indications of sexual involvement she would experience quite other feelings as well. Typically, as Katz (1978) has pointed out in an excellent paper on the relation of mental schemata to a typology of the emotions, a variety of emotions might occur, depending upon which aspects of the situation she focused on, and what implications for her life might be involved. If she focused on her own loss, she would feel grief; if on her own "failure" then despair; if on wanting Alfie back, then longing; if on her husband's perfidy then anger; if on the other woman then jealousy; if on what the neighbours might think then embarrassment; if in moral terms (i.e. a mismatch with what Katz calls schemata of the ideal self) then perhaps she would feel guilt or shame, and so on.

If Alfie were to leave her for someone else, i.e. where as Katz points out a central aspect of a person's life (and mental schemata) is overturned, exploration of a whole set of implications and the creation of some new implicit theory of herself in the world would be likely to take months or years. This is often nowadays referred to as the reaction of grief, or mourning, even when the event that precipitates it is not death.

Katz makes it clear that what tends to occur is not just that different people might feel different things. The same person, e.g. Betty, will be conscious of a sequence of feelings as she tries out various explanations, or calls in new pieces of mental schema to explain to herself what has happened, or what she will do. So she will be conscious in turn of resentment as she blames him, depression when she blames herself, despair when she thinks of the future. And these feelings will reverberate in a wavelike fashion throughout her life when in trying to make sense of the crisis new aspects of the event become clearer, and new meanings enable her to make new connections between events.

How does the theory of mental schemata, as expressed in programs such as that of Roberts and Weir inform these matters? The programs give a firm and formal grounding to the theory of mental schemata. And it is to this kind of theory that the phenomologically directed arguments expressed in the tale of Alfie and Betty can be connected. There is in other words a domain of *meaning* at which both the computational metaphors of mind and the critiques of experience can meet. And in meeting they disperse at least some of the arguments about the incompatibility of mechanism and humanism.

3.2 Mismatches of schemata and the psychoanalytic theory of object relations

This cognitive theory also makes some important connections with psychoanalytic theory. Winnicott (1965) for instance has argued that at the core of emotional development is the idea (or in the terms of the current argument the schema) that a very young baby has of his or her mother, or perhaps of the mother's breast. Satisfaction and affirmation arise when the mother creates in the actual, outside world, just that event which the baby's schema had conceived. For instance the breast actually arrives in the mouth, and the mother's arms actually are safe and supporting. But sometimes reality does not match the internal idea. Then quite different things happen. The mismatch, according to Winnicott gives rise to hatred (that feeling which tends to occur whenever the outside world does not do just what we want). The virtues of that painful state are that the child can thereby come to distinguish self and fantasy, from non-self and outside reality. Failures of schema and actuality to match "have value in so far as the infant can hate the object, that is to say retain the idea of the object as potentially satisfying while recognizing its failure to behave satisfactorily" (Winnicott, 1965, p. 181). "Object" in this passage is a psychoanalytic term, meaning the recipient of one's emotional attachment, as in the phrase "the object of my affections". Winnicott here means by it specifically the baby's mother or mother surrogate.

If the mother were absent for a period that was too long for the baby to tolerate, a harmful discontinuity in experience, and thence psychopathology, could occur, as the painful feelings which perhaps in a baby amount to feelings of annihilation, are disowned or projected in self-protective distrustfulness.

It seems important to note that though the terminology is different, psychoanalytic and cognitive theory come quite close enough together for communication in this kind of formulation.

In psychoanalytic theory, then, the main cause of unconsciousness is not so much a failure of schemata to apprehend reality, but a flight from the pain of some fundamental mismatch, or from the conflict that the mismatch signifies. One might expect that if mental schemata were somehow dispassionate, a mismatch would lead simply to a revision of the implicit theory. And the revised theory would be an improvement capable of encompassing a broader range of events. As it is, some mismatches give rise to strong feelings which are intolerable so that the feelings themselves are disowned. And rather than a schema changing it thereby becomes frozen, and events are denied or distorted.

Freud called these processes defence mechanisms. They arise from intolerable anxiety (which is perhaps the fear of further mismatches). Most fundamentally these defences involve distortions of one kind or another. We might for instance repress the fact that we hate someone whom we love but by whom we feel catastrophically let down. This is the kind of reality that human kind cannot bear very much of.

3.3 Containment metaphors for feelings and the strategy of pretence

There is a good deal of theorizing both formal and informal which takes feelings, particularly anger, as capable of being stored, bottled up, held down. No doubt this is at least partly due to some of the Freudian metaphors of repression, of libido being contained "in" the unconscious. As a result it has indeed become part of common talk to refer to feelings being bottled up. Presumably it is an aspect of common consciousness to experience them as being so. But though the time interval between an event (e.g. Betty's reading the significant letter) and an upsurge of anger (perhaps months later) might plausibly be thought of in terms of some sort of storage, or bottling up of the anger, that metaphor seems unhelpful and unilluminating. Katz (1978) points out that it is much more apposite to suppose that though a significant event might occur at some particular time, the initial feeling might be only of numbness and unbelief. This is not because of storage of other feelings, but because the easily available mental schemata fail to construe the event. Only later as different aspects of the significance of the event are reviewed (as Betty mulls obsessively over the implications) then grief, anger, etc. are felt at the time when those particular attributions (of personal loss, or blame of Alfie) are made. Certainly having feelings occurring too long after the event to be appropriate is a common experience. But not because these feelings were there, but were stored (or bottled up by repression), not expressed at the time and so burst out later. Repression as a process of defence may well occur—but it seems better described as a selection of meanings (and thus of feelings) by focusing on one rather than another aspect of events. It could be due to a distortion of mental schemata that represent reality, or an implicit theory that is in some respects inadequate or undeveloped, rather than by storage.

The notion of expressing ones feelings also seems to arise from the idea of feelings as some kind of liquid substance (maybe boiling water) to be stored, contained or released. If we feel pleased to see someone, or angry with them we communicate our pleasure (the match of a mental schema with happy associations to an outer reality of the person's presence) or our displeasure (a mismatch of mental schema with what is wanted) through our behaviour of gestures and words. There is some sense of making explicit and external that which was within (e.g. pleasure or displeasure). But is that not more probably due to a feature of consciousness that allows one (to some extent) to choose how to behave, or what to say and what not to say, rather than more simply acting in some automatic way?

The point has been made by a number of writers, e.g. Snell (1953) as well as Jaynes (1976) whose work will be discussed in a later section, that one of the changes in consciousness recorded in Homer's "Odyssey" was that Odysseus was seen and admired for his craftiness, his guile and ability to deceive. By contrast Achilles in the earlier poem "The Iliad" just acted; doing the bidding either of his warrior instincts or the gods. And Jaynes argues that in "The Odyssey" we have a portrait of a new kind of consciousness of which this craftiness is a feature. (Jaynes argues that it is the dawning of the first real consciousness in the modern sense of being self-conscious, capable of reflecting on ones actions and choosing.)

Consciousness, then implies some notion of autonomy (as opposed simply to acting automatically, unreflectively). It carries with it some ability to choose whether to behave or speak in this way or that and thus also the ability to pretend. So that rather than saying within the storage metaphor of feelings that this feeling or that is let out or kept in, one might enquire how far some particular person was deciding to behave in the way of implying these meanings or those and in more extreme forms even of whether he or she is pretending in his or her words or actions, or being in bad faith (Sartre, 1958), and whether the pretence was known to the actor or not.

The notion of the unconscious in the psychoanalytic sense is closely bound up with this issue of pretence—not so much in the conscious present of the adult but in the more distant foundations of interpersonal strategy of the child on which subsequent schemata of how to relate to others are presumably built. In childhood as part of socialization it is (for some people) often necessary to pretend that one is not angry. Otherwise one will be punished or rejected by a parent on whose love we are emotionally all too dependent. And such pretences (management as it were of the consequences of mismatches in our schemata) about either wishes or actualities become part of a habitual and even compulsive way of seeing the world and being in it. The formation of these strategies with long-lasting consequences is described by Horney (1942). So Betty, for instance, might have found it easier to live when a child by distorting both her own feelings and her view of reality. She might have pretended that when her wishes and her mother's did not coincide that she was not angry or frustrated. Instead she might have cultivated in these circumstances an attitude of apologetic compliance — to which her mother would respond more acceptingly where she did not respond to angry tantrums. The child's experiments in her original management of difficult feelings, and the ways in which these decisions to deceive herself and others by tailoring somewhat her own sense of reality is not necessarily conscious. Thus when a disagreement occurs Betty feels invariably in the wrong and must do whatever she can to heal the rift. But they sprang in the first place from some ability of choice which is itself the seed of consciousness. For, as Freud was arguing in his analogy of the general shifting his troops about as toy figures on a map, to be able to think is to be able to think of the possibilities of different actions, different strategies. To be unaware is to be driven automatically by a necessity of some kind, whether instinctual or otherwise.

3.4 Information, energy and Colby's simulation of Freudian defence mechanisms

The issue of whether we see feelings as some kind of fluid to be bottled up or released is part of a larger issue of the appropriateness more generally of metaphors in the mental world drawn from machines which deal primarily with energy. The steam engines of the nineteenth century no doubt transformed for the Victorians their consciousness of their relation to the world, and it was into this world that Freud came. His theory of libido, that which gives energy to action, has noticeable similarities to the head of steam in the steam engine's boiler, with its capacity either to move the engine purposefully, to leak out here or there through tell-tale imperfections in the pipes, or occasionally to cause explosions with devastating results.

One theorist commited to replacing the original energy models of Freud is K.M. Colby. For many years a practising psychoanalyst Colby has since the early sixties been developing computational models of just those Freudian defence mechanisms which were described in terms of libido, cathexis and so on.

In his earlier simulations (e.g. Colby, 1963, 1965) he explored ways in which the conflictual beliefs of a woman undergoing psychoanalysis might be represented computationally. This woman believed that her father abandoned her when she was small, but because of conflicting requirements e.g. of "oughts" and "musts" (strong super-ego beliefs) such as "I must love my parents" she was unable consciously to accept that she hated him for this.

Colby's early programs are in many ways unsophisticated by the standards of much research in artificial intelligence. The decisions taken by the program are on the basis of numerical values of parameters representing "emotional charge", "credibility", "imperative level" (which is highest for "musts", next highest for "oughts" and so on) attached to various parts of statements which are printed out by the program. The unsatisfactory nature of this scheme is that there is no sense in which the program actually understands what its beliefs are, or what it prints out. Instead tables (matrices) containing numbers corresponding to features of statements of beliefs are addressed, and decisions about what words to print out are taken on grounds of arithmetic.

Nonetheless, a careful working through Colby's program gives a sense (quite different from that of the steam engine) of how substitutions in a symbolic structure might take place: how "I hate father", because it is unacceptable, may be substituted by deflection into hating someone else, or by substitution of weaker synonyms of hate (e.g. "I see faults in father"), or by projection as in "father hates me" etc. That is to say the program is a statement of how representations of the world may be modified to fit very strongly held implicit theories such as "I must love my parents".

According to Freud humans must struggle for consciousness on two fronts. Not only does consciousness grow out of an originally unconscious state (of instinctual motives) but at the same time that we become aware of these motives and feelings many of them are prohibited by parents (or other members of society) and are then distorted. So the Freudian unconscious is a kind of secondary unconsciousness—of mental contents that might be conscious, but do not easily fit in to the way in which for various reasons we prefer to describe ourselves to ourselves. Hence some mental contents are denied in various ways.

In section 2.4 on the projection of implicit theories, I indicated six types of unconsciousness which arise as a result of schematic perception of the world. The Freudian defensive unconscious does not so much arise as a property of schemata as from the nature of human interactions, particularly in the family.

On this account the reason why some aspects of mental life remain unconscious is that there are advantages to being able to deceive others (as did Homer's Odysseus or Betty with her mother). And Johnson-Laird (1979) has argued that to deceive well it is best to deceive oneself at the same time lest tell-tale signs emerge. This implies therefore that some parts of our mental world are going to become inaccessible to other parts. It would also give a reason why there may be advantage (in evolutionary and/or cultural terms) in some of our motives becoming or remaining unconscious, i.e. unknown to ourselves.

What does become conscious though is a set of conclusions, or percepts, some of them tailored to fit more comfortable versions of reality. It is a set of stories (and images) that we can tell ourself and others about ourself and others. How did this arise, and why?

4 The evolution and function of consciousness

4.1 Jaynes's theory of the bicameral mind

Some of the most interesting new ideas on the issue of how consciousness arose are to be found in Julian Jaynes's book "The Origin of Consciousness in the Breakdown of the Bicameral Mind". Although Jaynes is somewhat cavalier with some of the evidence (particularly anthropological), here is an interesting idea: that consciousness as we know it came into being around 3000 years ago.

Before that time, Jaynes argues, peoples' lives were directed by two kinds of process: first a roughly speaking motivational one, so that people might look after themselves, eat, flee from danger, interact socially and so on, much as might more sophisticated and verbal chimpanzees. Secondly, in the course of evolution of groups larger than those in which members could be socially controlled by immediate face to face contact (e.g. as villages or other settlements arose) a mechanism emerged whereby one person could control the rest of the tribe (or group) while out of view or earshot. This mechanism took the form of verbal pronouncements, admonitions, injunctions, and the like, uttered by the chief, and internalized by the population. These commands would come to mind particularly in situations of stress or where some task of importance to the group was to be performed. And they would be heard, Jaynes argues, as voices, as auditory hallucinations perhaps not unlike the hallucinations of schizophrenics in our own age. (Indeed Jaynes argues that this aspect of schizophrenia involves a throw-back to this earlier state of evolutionary development.)

It is this state of having two chambers of personal govenrment (like two chambers of parliament), the individual instinctual one and the autocratic one heard as voices of authority telling one what to do that Jaynes calls the bicameral mind. It is the breakdown of this relatively simple method of group social control by means of the voices, when social conditions became more complicated, which led to consciousness. Consciousness is a more complex development in which people describe to themselves the reasons for what they are doing. In conscious thinking people work out what a best plan of action is by the kind of inner experimentation hinted at by Freud's metaphor of the general and his maps.

In the bicameral period, Jaynes argues, people heard the voices particularly in times of stress. As kings died, and their voices continued to be heard, the kings became the gods, i.e. people whose voices could still be heard though they were dead. In the evening of the bicameral age as the voices of gods faded a new caste of people, priests and oracles who supposedly were still in touch with these voices was needed to act as intermediaries as people struggled to make their own conscious decisions.

In some of the world's earliest writings, e.g. "The Iliad", there are many passages in which the original relationship with the voices is portrayed. So Achilles and other heroes hear the voices of gods telling them what to do. What Jaynes argues is that the idea of people being commanded by the hallucinated voices of gods should be taken literally.

Nowadays, of course, we hear these same voices saying we ought to do this, or we must not do that, but we hear them inside our heads. Psychoanalytically inclined people term them the superego. They are accompanied by perhaps another voice reasoning, thinking things out, by images, by our reflections and re-orderings of experience. What Jaynes is arguing is that there was a stage in which this second voice of our ego, of self-reflective consciousness, was not present. The only voice represented the admonitory wisdom of the tribe, and that was heard not within, but from outside, like the voice of a god.

Within the projective theory of perception described here one is not especially surprised that there should be hallucinations. In any percept of a social event there is always for us humans the issue of how much should be attributed to the actors being observed and how much to our own projections. Thus it seems not inherently implausible that a set of particularly important memories of authoritative injunctions, presumably carrying with them some enforceable sanctions, are heard as outside rather than inside. We nowadays make a sharp distinction between experiencing percepts outside and our imagery and memories within. But there are obviously other ways of dividing up experience.

The properties of consciousness, then, as described by Jaynes, are that a new and sophisticated kind of internal language and imagery grew up. So we have internal models or representations of the outside world (as postulated in Craik's 1943 theory of thinking and as described in some form in all theories of mental schemata (including the brief account given in section 2.3 of the inferential processes of Roberts' program). But in addition to this representational ability which must be shared by many animals, there is the representation of internal visualizable mental images and verbal discussions. This is the reflective consciousness, referred to in section 2.1 on "Schemata and Consciousness". The metaphorical structure in which we see the events in the outside world as meaningful, in terms of our own meanings, is depicted to ourselves in what Jaynes calls "mind space", a metaphorical area in which we can create inner scenes, talk to ourselves about them, and imagine what if we were to do this or that.

Some basic features of consciousness, according to Jaynes are as follows:

1. Spatialization: this is thinking in terms of spatial images and spatially separated events. Even time is conceptualized as laid out in space, including pictures and diagrams. Images provide an important mode of our inner thought.

2. Exerption: we abstract, or make exerpts of the particular matters when following a train of thought or a stream of consciousness. (In "stream of consciousness" the stream is an example of a metaphor of spatialization.)

3. An image of the self is represented in this internal world: this imagined self can move about, try things out in this vicarious space, Jaynes also makes a distinction between this image of the self and the other image of the self in which we not only imagine how we might do something but imagine a view of ourselves doing it from the position of another observer.

4. Narratization: this is the telling ourselves stories about what we are doing, or have done, giving reasons for our actions and so on. An inference from Jaynes' idea would be that the creating of and responding to novels, stories, films, plays is enabled by this internal storytelling ability. They are externalized varieties of what we typically create individually in our minds. Jaynes argues that poetry on the other hand with its metre, and its somewhat hypnotic quality is the descendent of the gods' voices.

5. We typically seek to make compatible the events in our imaginal mind space. As part of our making sense of our lives we have to fit things together—possibly tailor this notion to that requirement as discussed to some extent in the previous sections. Here is the resolving of cognitive dissonances (Festinger, 1957), the operation of defences (Freud, 1926), or even the rewriting of history (Orwell, 1949). But this possibility presumably holds within it also that most important capacity, namely the prerequisites for psychological change as when Betty was able to re-interpret Alfie's gracelessness, or when in response to mismatches of the inner and outer, or other kinds of contradiction of our implicit theories, growth and change of mental schemata occur.

Jaynes hereby gives some useful definitions of some of the characteristic features of modern consciousness, as well as a somewhat speculative account of its coming into being. But what of its function? From Jaynes' point of view it is mainly a more sophisticated strategy for making decisions in the world. It is the evolution of a new form of personal government to replace the bicameral system, or the invention of the map in Freud's metaphor of the general and his plans of attack.

The idea of mental models within which we can try out "what if" has been with us for some time, e.g. in Freud's metaphor of the general. Let us say this: schematic representation gives to perception the possibility of reflection (as argued earlier in this chapter), and this allows the possibility of making a range of different interpretations, and of creatively making sense of things. In a similar way mental schemata confer equivalent advantages to action, in the planning of actions, and the fitting of plans to our purposes.

In the domain of actions, the schema allows reflective vicarious planning within the internal model before committing oneself to actions which could be costly or dangerous. In computational terms Draper (personal communication) has pointed out to me that this idea is well represented by Sussman's (1975) program HACKER. This is a program which itself writes programs and acquires skill in doing so. HACKER runs any new code it writes in CAREFUL (i.e. virtual) mode, checking carefully for errors (bugs) before running the new code for real. Of course when a mistake does occur for real this is an invitation for the program to classify the bug for future reference and repair itself by writing some new code. Just as when we make a mistake in action we might take it as evidence of something that we were not simulating mentally very completely, i.e. we were not conscious of all the relevant considerations while running the problem in virtual mode. So we learn from the mistake, and try a modified plan.

Though this gives an important rationale for reflective consciousness both in perception and action, one matter still is left out. Why are some aspects of this representational activity conscious and open to introspection?

It is to this issue that I now turn.

4.2 The function of introspective consciousness

What we are aware of are percepts of the outside world and ourselves acting in it. At the second level of inner reflective consciousness are the meanings expressed in language, the conclusions of reflective thought, the conjectures, narratizations and images of mind space, and to some extent theories of our own motivations and feelings. What, then is the reason why this particular set of features is or can be conscious, and comprises our experience?

There are explanations of reflective consciousness drawn from the world of computation, e.g. Minsky's (1968) idea that in a complex computational system there needs to be a representation of the representational processes, or Johnson-Laird's (1979) suggestion that where there are a number of parallel processes going on in patterns of inference, a higher level of monitoring and arbitration is needed. With parallel processing two procedures might both be waiting for the result of the other. These ideas are about process, however, and it is still not clear why such higher level models or monitors should be conscious as such.

More appealing here is an idea of Humphrey (1977). Humphrey also starts with the assumption that to cope effectively with the world people need a model of external reality within which to experiment, plan, and make meanings. Like Jaynes he argues for the evolutionary importance of this representational ability. But unlike Jaynes, he places the emergence of consciousness far back in our animal past.

Introspective consciousness, in Humphrey's hypothesis, is the means by which social animals infer what other animals are up to, what others might be seeing, feeling or intending. To be conscious is to be able to introspect our own feelings etc., and to be able to introspect them as if we were in various situations that we are not in. Thereby we can infer by analogy what other members of our own species might be feeling and intending in the positions that they are in.

Using methods of natural science people have constructed enough of a theory of physics and its practical applications to land rockets on the moon, make television cameras, and contraceptive pills. The social world however remains more resistant to natural scientific investigation. Following a hundred years of natural scientific psychology, for instance, a behaviourally derived analysis remains inadequate. Humphrey suggests that

... if a rat's knowledge of the behaviour of other rats were limited to everything that behaviourists have discovered about rats to date, the rat would show so little understanding of its fellows that it would bungle disastrously every social interaction it engaged in; the prospects for man similarly constrained would be still more dismal.

What this suggestion may amount to is the idea that in the physical world perception and action require an internal theory of physics, built up partly by evolution on the basis of many experiments, and recapitulated in personal development by a growing effectiveness of description as described by Piaget and his followers (e.g. Flavell, 1977) and put within the structure of computational theory by Minsky and Papert (1972). So, for visual programs like that of Roberts and his successors (e.g. Guzman, 1969; Clowes, 1971b; Falk, 1972; Waltz, 1975; Marr, 1975; Mackworth, 1976) what is at issue is interpretation of pictures by means of an internal theory of the properties, 3-D geometry, reflective qualities etc. of solid objects. Thus as described earlier a cue can evoke some particular piece of this internalized theory of physics in order to see a picture or retinal image as depicting a 3-D object of a particular shape and size.

In the interpersonal world, on the other hand, Humphrey is arguing, there is no such analysis. We don't so much work by means of some general internalized theory of social interactions, inferring that if a person makes this or that particular gesture he or she intends to do such and such. Rather if the matter is one of interest to us we infer by analogy from what we introspectively imagine we might think, feel or do in that position. It seems likely that we also use the cues of gestures and intonations and suchlike to address our interpersonal theories. But the nice idea of Humphrey is that the interpersonal model or schema is actually our own self, our own feelings and our own range of experience which we can interrogate by introspection. (This is in distinction to having a schematic model as a separate mechanism within our head, which is the case for representations of things physical.) The metaphorical or analogical relationship to the outside world is the same, and the idea of cues to address the appropriate feelings and ideas would also be similar. This, perhaps is the basis for plays, novels and films being able to evoke feelings, although the situation is purely analogical.

Several interesting issues arise here: one of these again being the issue of inside and outside. We infer what another person might be feeling by identification, which is a form of projection. We might be sceptical about Jaynes' idea that voices of authority were heard as hallucinations in ancient times. But if Humphrey's idea is correct, and there seems a deal of inherent plausibility to it, we find it in modern times not so odd that aspects of our own feelings should be attributed to others as part of our perception of them.

If this act of empathetic perception is indeed part of our dealings with others this gives ample reason why certain kinds of social interaction might become difficult. People with too many preoccupations or emotional needs of their own for instance might not always have the flexibility of empathetic representation sufficient to allow their feelings to respond to the other person's situation as such, and their perception of the other might therefore be very much mistaken.

There is also a question of how adequate this empathetic identification process is. There is no shortage of examples in everyone's experience of how fallacious the assumption is that other people necessarily think and feel as we do. It seems clear then that in order to have a real relationship with another person, as well as this empathetic capacity, we need the means for constructing an inner model or representation of that specific person, as we get to know him or her. Again, there is a possibility of confusion of inner and outer as our emotional needs and that person's own characteristics and best interests may, because of the obscurities of our consciousness, become entangled.

5 The effectiveness of the computational metaphor

How far then do computational metaphors illuminate the issues discussed in this chapter? They do in so far as it has only been with the help of computation that we have begun systematically to investigate and experiment with representations of knowledge. No artificial intelligence programs have been written without some basic grappling with the problems of how the task domain is to be exerpted, and represented in such a way as to make the inference necessary to the task. So in that sense the whole of artificial intelligence is an exploration of just those representational processes of which human consciousness (in Jaynes' sense) is an example. And by grappling with new ways of representing the world we will necessarily expand our own consciousness.

Part of the problem though is that it is best to write programs oneself for the newer insights to be transferred into one's own mind. Spatializations, as Jaynes says, are favourite vehicles for many of our mental metaphors. Presumably this is because moving, and seeing in space, manipulating a world that responds (in part) mechanically gives us a set of intuitions and understandings about spatial relationships, and a facility of spatial inference, that makes it worthwhile to see other (less familiar) things in terms of the spatial metaphor. For computational metaphors really to work, just as we have already a familiarity with spatial relationship so we must acquire some personal experience of computation. There is no very satisfactory way round this. So when I say that programming in artificial intelligence provides metaphors of representation, this will only really be true for people who have actually written programs. This is artifical intelligence's most disabling weakness at present, because very few of us have written computer programs, and even fewer have written programs to do much more than carry out calculations. To explain a computational metaphor, except by providing the experience of programming, is a bit like trying to explain the theory of harmony to someone who has never played a musical instrument. One can by following a published account of a program carefully acquire a sense of how knowledge is represented and used to accomplish some end. But this is much easier for the person who has programmed than for the one who has not.

This situation will change gradually, as more and more people have experience with programming. It is clear too that the LOGO project initiated by Papert (e.g. 1973) in which children write programs to draw a picture, drive toy vehicles about, make animated cartoons, compose music or poems and so on, provides ideal experience. Here children can productively deploy the computational metaphor not just in the domains in which they write programs but perhaps, as Papert argues, in other aspects of their thinking too. This might be a new departure of human consciousness, perhaps beyond that of the spatialized metaphors such as those that stalk through this sentence.

There are several ways in which questions of whether the advent of computational metaphors illuminate the representational issues raised in this paper can be answered.

5.1 Languages of representation

First, with the development of programming languages which deal directly with representation, computational ideas and experience can enrich our understanding of our own mental processes. In ordinary language spatialization is the common mode of most consciousness up to the end of the twentieth century. It may be that other metaphors derived not so much from talking and moving about in physical space, but from the use of knowledge and the making of inferences in programs will be able to deal more penetratingly with some of our mental experience which is at present obscure. Though this is a somewhat science fiction idea, people's conscious experience of themselves in their world has changed quite substantially during the course of history. One way of seeing this is in the history of representational art. Thus Snell (1953) and Auerbach (1953) have shown in literary representation and Gombrich (1960) in the history of painting how people have changed their representation of reality. People have seen their world and consequently their idea of themselves in the world in different ways. They have had different theories about themselves in the world, different consciousness.

5.2 The technological fix?

Experience with computation may provide us with an extended repertoire of metaphors and hence the possibilities of a potentially richer and more incisive consciousness. But it is also possible that the experience of this particular piece of technology may change our consciousness in specifically harmful ways. As Weizenhaum (1976) points out "When [in prehistoric time] hunters acquired spears, for example, they must have seen themselves in an entirely new relationship with their world".

Weizenbaum goes on to argue that the invention of the clock, as an automatic device, marked a new departure in man's alienation from nature. Rather than relying on nature as in the coming of dusk or the feeling of hunger as indications to head homewards, or to eat, now we see time as precisely ordered and divided into minutes and hours. "The rejection of direct experience" continues Weizenbaum "was to become one of the principal characteristics of modern science". For Weizenbaum the computer is simply one of the more recent technological innovations which transforms our sense of ourselves in relation to nature and our fellows. The possibility is that we continue to cultivate a consciousness of other people as things to be operated upon in some way. Life is seen as presenting "problems"—and problems need to be solved. The view arises of the technological fix, perhaps in the inner world as well as the outer.

Going along with this view is a sense of omnipotence. The world of the computer program is the world that can be completely created and controlled, and Weizenbaum offers us a portrait of the compulsive programmer, apparently symbiotically attached to the machine, working at all hours on writing more bits of an ever growing program to create and control yet more and more of the computational universe. The omnipotence has an addictive quality. If, moreover, we see this as a microcosm of either the physical world, the world of other people, or the world within, we would be involved in serious delusions.

If this criticism is taken seriously (as it must be) then the metaphors drawn from computation though perhaps more expressive, more articulate, and more extensive, than those drawn from others aspects of technology (e.g. where memory is likened to filing cabinets, tape recorders and so on), are none the less being drawn from technology and thence a particular relationship with the world. Thus we run a danger of acquiring a consciousness of ourselves as some "thing" to operate on, to reprogram, to change. And the wisdom of this can be seriously doubted.

But although Weizenbaum is correct in saying that we live in a time and in a culture where manipulation of the outer world is a preoccupation; and although he is correct too about the dangers that programming exposes for omnipotent control over a computational world the important function of computation as a metaphor for mental processes rests on other foundations. One foundation is that it is our *own* understandings about representations, inferences and the like with which we experiment in the context of an exacting discipline of logical entailment. We do this to make the organization of knowledge in representation and inference more familiar, more comprehensible to us as human beings. Large programs that carry out complicated functions easily become incomprehensible, and are for psychological purposes useless. A second foundation is that as with anthropology, where the meeting with a different culture confronts us with our own, so the creation of artificial intelligence confronts us with our own natural intelligence. In the comparison we can find out more about what it is to be human.

Computers are indeed used at present in our bids to control and manipulate the outer world. But that function is not intrinsic to computation. When writing was first invented, all it was used for was to make lists and inventories, as a sort of aide memoir. And though this memory function of writing is still important, its uses have multiplied, and now embrace novels, letters, the composition of music and so on. Likewise the computer as the controller of data or machinery, is simply the computer in its early infancy. For psychology it needs to be seen as a creative medium which unlike other media is capable of executing the patterns of inference which are its programs.

5.3 Process and content

Computational metaphors (or cognitive psychology more generally) though possibly being helpful about the processes of mental life, are not necessarily helpful about praxis, nor about the content of our inner world.

A theory of perception, such as that of Helmholtz, or Bartlett or Roberts which rests on the idea of projection of constructive schemata, in an effort towards meaning and interpretation, is a step in an insight about our relation to the outer world. But it is only a first step, and quite a small one at that. Simply being conscious that perception has a projective quality helps little unless we know what is being projected. The knowing of projective processes need not itself change our consciousness or make us more perceptive.

This cognitive view of perception does however point from the position of more formal branches of academic psychology towards a next step in approaching the issue of consciousness. For Betty the move in the direction of being more conscious of what goes on in the outside world involves being more conscious not so much of the mechanisms of her inner world, but the content: the particular conclusions her implicit theories necessarily lead her towards regardless of evidence.

This means departing now from the (scientific) generalities of the principles of perceptual processes (such as might be illuminated by Roberts's, 1965, or other programs) to the more particular and personal meanings of an individual's own mental schemata; our own implicit theories and inner meanings. Thus it is not just the hypothesis that there are mental schemata which is at issue but the particular personal content of what is projected. It is the knowledge of this which would really change our consciousness, and this knowledge is not typically gained by the methods of natural scientific enquiry by which we investigate what is out there. Rather, for these theories or computational metaphors to have not just explanatory significance but some possibility of insight which will transform our implicit theories and increase our consciousness two further steps must be taken.

One step suggested by the general theory of mental representations is that what is needed to change theories are mismatches, experienced quite often as mistakes. Seldom of course do we court mistakes, though there are forms of activity that have that quality. One view of psycho-analysis for instance is that in transference we project our theories about how to relate on to the therapist, who acts and gives interpretations in such a way as to allow the client to experience these projections as mistaken. The relationship with the therapist can then be experienced as more benign than some earlier ones on which so much later experience including the current transference projections were founded. Psychotherapy however is not to everyone's taste, and life has a way of confronting us one way or another with our own mistakes, the internal contradictions in our implicit theories.

A second step which is closely related to the first is that in order to extend our consciousness we must have new experiences. This includes according to Humphrey's theory the idea that to be aware of what another person might be feeling we need first to have experienced that particular feeling ourselves.

It is scarcely very new to argue that self-knowledge and the broadening of our experience are seeds of changes in consciousness. But the conclusion is no worse when approached via a consideration of the properties of mental schemata than from some other direction.

> . . . . the end of all our exploring
> Will be to arrive where we started
> And know the place for the first time.
> 'Little Gidding'

References

Auerbach, E. (1953). "Mimesis". Princeton University Press, Princeton.

Bartlett, F. C. (1932). "Remembering". Cambridge University Press, Cambridge.

Clowes, M.B. (1971). Artificial intelligence as psychology. A.I.S.B. Bulletin No. 1.

Clowes, M.B. (1971). On seeing things. *Artificial Intelligence*, **2**, 79–116.

Clowes, M.B. (1973). Man the creative machine: a perspective from artificial intelligence research. *In* "The Limits of Human Nature" (Ed. E.J. Benthall), pp. 192–207. Allen Lane Press, London.

Colby, K.M. (1963). Computer simulation of a neurotic process. *In* "Computer Simulation of Personality" (Eds S.S. Tomkins and S. Messich), pp. 165–180. Wiley, New York.

Colby, K.M. (1965). Computer simulation of neurotic processes. *In* "Computers in Biomedical Research" (Eds R.W. Stacy and B.D. Waxman), vol. 1, pp. 491–503. Academic Press, New York.

Craik, K. (1943). "The Nature of Explanation". Cambridge University Press, Cambridge.

Dewey, J. (1900). "The School and Society". Reprinted as a combined volume "The Child and the Curriculum" and "The School and Society". University of Chicago, Chicago (1956).

Eliot, T.S. (1944). "Four Quartets". Faber and Faber, London.

Falk, G. (1972). Interpretation of imperfect line data as a 3-dimensional scene. *Artificial Intelligence*, **3**, 101–144.

Festinger, L. (1957). "A Theory of Cognitive Dissonance". Stanford University Press, Stanford.

Flavell, J.H. (1977). "Cognitive Development". Prentice Hall, Englewood Cliffs, New Jersey.

Freud, S. (1911). Psychoanalytic notes on an autobiographical account of a case of paranoia (Dementia Paranoides). "Standard Edition of the Complete Works of Sigmund Freud", vol. 12 (1955). Hogarth Press, London.

Freud, S. (1926). Inhibitions, symptoms and anxiety. "Standard Edition of the Complete Works of Sigmund Freud", vol. 20 (1960). Hogarth Press, London.

Freud, S. (1933). "New Introductory Lectures on Psychoanalysis". Pelican Books, Harmondsworth, Middlesex. (1973).

Gombrich, E.H. (1960). "Art and Illusion". Phaidon, London.

Gregory, R.L. (1973). The confounded eye. *In* "Illusion in Nature and Art" (Eds R.L. Gregory and E.H. Gombrich), pp. 48–95. Duckworth, London.

Guzman, A. (1969). Decomposition of a visual scene into three-dimensional bodies. *In* "Automatic Interpretation and Classification of Images" (Ed. A. Grasselli), p. 243–276. Academic Press, London and New York.

Helmholtz, H. von (1866). "Treatise on Physiological Optics" (Ed. J.P.C. Southall), vol. III. (1962). Dover, New York.

Helmholtz, H. von (1868). The theory of vision. *In* "Popular Scientific Lectures" (1962). Dover, New York.

Homer, "The Iliad", Penguin, Harmondsworth, Middlesex. (1950).

Homer, "The Odyssey", Penguin, Harmondsworth, Middlesex. (1946).

Horney, K. (1942). "Self-analysis". Routledge and Kegan Paul, London.

Humphrey, N.K. (1977). Nature's psychologists. Paper based on the Lister Lecture delivered to the British Association for the Advancement of Science, September 1977. *In* "Consciousness and the Physical World" (Eds B. Josephson and V.S. Ramachandran). Pergamon Press, Oxford.

Jaynes, J. (1976). "The Origin of Consciousness in the Breakdown of the Bicameral Mind". Houghton Mifflin, Boston.

Jenkins, H. and Ward, W. (1965). Judgements of contingency between responses and outcomes. *Psychological Monographs*, 79, whole no. 594.

Johnson-Laird, P.N. (1979). Language and human mentality. *In* "Psychology Survey 2" (Ed. K. Connolly). Allen and Unwin, London.

Katz, J.M. (1978). Discrepancy, arousal and labelling: towards a psychosocial theory of emotion. Paper presented to the World Congress of Sociology, Upsalla, Sweden, August, 1978.

Laing, R.D., Phillipson, H. and Lee, A.R. (1966). "Interpersonal Perception". Tavistock Publication, London.

Mackworth, A.K. (1976). Model driven interpretation in intelligent vision systems. *Perception*, **5**, 349–370.

Marr, D. (1975). Analysing natural images: a computational theory of texture vision. MIT Artificial Intelligence Laboratory Memo No. 334.

Michotte, A. (1963). "The Perception of Causality". Methuen, London.

Minsky, M. (1968). Matter, mind and models. *In* "Semantic Information Processing" (Ed. M. Minsky), pp. 425–432. MIT Press, Cambridge, Massachusetts.

Minsky, M. and Papert, S. (1972). Artificial intelligence progress report. MIT Artifical Intelligence Laboratory Memo No. 252.

Neisser, U. (1976). "Cognition and Reality". W.H. Freeman, San Francisco.

Oatley, K. (1977). Computational metaphors for perception. Open University Cognitive Psychology Course D303, Block 2, Unit 8. Open University Press, Milton Keynes.

Oatley, K. (1978). "Perceptions and Representations". Methuen, London.

Orwell, G. (1949). "Nineteen Eighty Four". Secker and Warburg, London.

Papert, S. (1973). Uses of technology to enhance education. MIT Artificial Intelligence Laboratory Memo No. 298.

Piaget, J. (1974). "The Child and Reality". Frederick Muller, London.

Popper, K.R. (1963). "Conjectures and Refutations". Routledge and Kegan Paul, London.

Roberts, L.G. (1965). Machine perception and three-dimensional solids. *In* "Optical and Electro-optical Information Processing" (Eds J.T. Tippett *et al.*), pp. 159–197. MIT Press, Cambridge, Massachusetts.

Sartre, J. P. (1958). "Being and Nothingness". Methuen, London.

Snell, B. (1953). "The Discovery of the Mind". Harper and Row, New York.

Sussman, G.J. (1975). "A Computer Model of Skill Acquisition". American Elsevier Publishing Co., New York.

Waltz, D. (1975). Understanding line drawings of scenes with shadows. *In* "The Psychology of Computer Vision" (Ed. P. Winston), pp. 19–91. McGraw-Hill, New York.

Wason, P.C. (1968). "On the failure to eliminate hypotheses. . ." a second look. *In* "Thinking and Reasoning" (Ed. P.C. Wason and P.N. Johnson-Laird). Penguin, Harmondsworth, Middlesex.

Weir, S. (1975). The perception of motion: actions, motives and feelings. *In* "Progress in Perception". Unversity of Edinburgh Department of Artificial Intelligence Report No. 13, 6–38.

Weisenbaum, J. (1976). "Computer Power and Human Reason". W.H. Freeman, San Francisco.

Winograd, T. (1971). Procedures as a representation for data in a computer program for understanding natural language. MIT Artificial Intelligence Laboratory Memo TR17.

Winnicott, D.W. (1965). "The Maturational Processes and the Facilitating Environment". The Hogarth Press, London.

Wittgenstein, L. (1953). "Philosophical Investigations". Translated by G.E.M. Anscombe (1968). Blackwell, Oxford.

4 Arousal

G. CLARIDGE

Department of Experimental Psychology,
Magdalen College, Oxford

Like many concepts in psychology, that of "arousal" has had a chequered history, opinion about its usefulness often being sharply divided. Some have regarded it as vague, describing a great deal but explaining nothing about consciousness. For others it has been the mainstay of their theories about behaviour and about individual differences in behaviour. In its crudest form arousal, or activation as it has alternatively been called (though a distinction, to be discussed later, between these two terms has sometimes been made), denotes an inferred state of central nervous excitability which, it is hypothesized, parallels observed behavioural variations along a continuum running from sleep, at one end, through drowsiness and normal wakefulness to extreme emotional excitement, at the other. In the recent history of psychology the idea can be traced to the writings of Elizabeth Duffy (1934). Attempting to integrate the concepts of emotion and motivation, she suggested that the distinction between them was largely superfluous and that emotion and the intensity, if not the directional, aspects of drive, could be subsumed under a common heading—that of activation or arousal. Duffy, who later (1962) reviewed the empirical evidence for her hypothesis, considered that shifts along the arousal continuum were reflected in changes in the physiological state of the organism, many of the changes being consonant with those originally described by Cannon (1929) as characterizing the strong emotions. These included the familiar alterations in somatic and autonomic functions such as muscle tension, heart rate, skin resistance, respiration, and blood pressure, to which Duffy added changes in the EEG and biochemistry of the individual.

Subsequent to Duffy's original formulation various other workers, notably Lindsley (1951), Hebb (1955) and Malmo (1959), adopted a similar theoretical position and the term "arousal" quickly became embedded in the everyday language of academic psychology. There are probably two, related, reasons for this ready acceptance of the concept. One has to do with trends in research on the neurophysiology of consciousness which were emerging at that time, the significant land-mark for psychology being the classic paper by Moruzzi and Magoun (1949) outlining the functions of the ascending reticular formation. Although Duffy's own earliest writings antedated that work, the demonstration of a possible neural basis for the psychological construct of arousal gave considerable impetus to the idea. Representative of this interest was a paper of great theoretical importance at the time, by Samuel (1959) who, on the basis of currently available findings, discus-sed in detail how reticular mechanisms may be implicated in beha-viour. In that review Samuel drew attention to two features of the neurophysiological evidence which were considered of particular signi-ficance for psychology. One was the existence of physiologically dis-tinguishable brain stem and thalamic reticular systems which appeared to be responsible for, respectively, tonic, or long-lasting and phasic, or short-duration, arousal responses. The other was the demonstration of ascending and descending, both excitatory and inhibitory, connections between the cortex and the reticular system, a feedback arrangement which had the right kind of flexibility to account for the subtle varia-tions and shifts in attention and arousal which psychology felt it needed to explain. These two points of emphasis have remained important in arousal theory, even though the neurophysiological data have since gone beyond those reviewed by Samuel and focus has shifted to include other brain areas, such as the limbic system, which appear to be implicated.

The second reason for the popularity of the concept of arousal concerns the rise of psychophysiology as a discipline within psychology. For more than a hundred years, but in this century ever since the pioneering work of Darrow (Gullickson, 1973), researchers have been trying to make sense of recordings taken from the surface of the body, initially of the autonomic and somatic nervous systems and then later of the EEG. These measurements have always been assumed to form a dual interface between body and brain and between brain and mind. It is not surprising, therefore, that "arousal" was seized upon as a useful explanatory construct, as an easily manageable way of interpreting physiological changes observed peripherally during different states of emotion and consciousness, while also forming a conceptual bridge with the direct study of the brain possible in neurophysiology. It would be beyond the scope and purpose of this chapter to give a detailed descrip-tion of the different measures used by psychophysiologists as putative indices of arousal; in any case comprehensive accounts are available elsewhere (Greenfield and Sternbach, 1972; Hassett, 1978). However, a brief summary is appropriate.

Because of its obvious role in emotion some aspect of the activity of the autonomic nervous system has been the most common source of measurement for psychophysiologists. And there some feature of electrodermal activity has probably been the most popular index, partly because of relative ease of measurement and partly because it has proved extremely sensitive to subtle variations in attention and awareness. Another advantage is that it is possible to recognize several measurably distinct features of electrodermal activity. Thus, the individual's "tonic arousal" may be said to be represented in the slowly drifting baseline observed in recordings of electrodermal activity. Frequently superimposed on this baseline are rapidly fluctuating changes in level of short duration, so-called spontaneous electrodermal responses which have also been considered an index of arousal. The electrodermal response proper, that is the reaction to a known stimulus, has a number of definable features—latency, amplitude, recovery rate—all of which have been studied in their own right as indices of some aspect of arousal.

Another class of autonomic responses commonly studied have been those derived from the cardiovascular system, most usually heart rate, but also blood pressure, skin temperature, and blood flow, either in a digit or a limb or as penile plethysmography in the study of sexual arousal. Changes in arousal are also monitored sometimes through alterations in respiration, in the digestive system, or pupil of the eye. Finally, although not autonomic in origin, electromyographic recording from the voluntary musculature—in a limb or the face—has been used by some as a favourite technique for detecting alterations in arousal.

All of the above procedures assume that the responses observed reflect psychologically significant changes in central nervous state. But of course the physiological systems in question also subserve purely bodily functions, helping to maintain the physical integrity of the organism and being subject to influences that have nothing to do with psychological variables. The cardiovascular system provides a good example. Its various components—represented in heart rate, blood pressure, and peripheral resistance—show a complex pattern of adjustment due to factors such as posture and external temperature. This will especially complicate the interpretation of cardiovascular indices when, as is sometimes the case, they are used to try and monitor phychologically mediated reactions in the freely moving individual, by means of remote recording methods, such as telemetry. Another aspect of this dual function of the peripheral nervous system concerns individual differences. The effects of age, disease, and other idiosyncrasies will attenuate or distort correlations that the psychophysiologist may seek with factors like personality. Some caution is therefore necessary when interpreting peripheral psychophysiological measures, though it is also worth mentioning that the more commonly used indices, like eletrodermal activity, are actually quite robust in this respect.

Although not entirely free from some of the difficulties mentioned, the EEG is assumed to reflect solely changes in the organ in which fluctuation in arousal are presumably occurring. Two features of the EEG have been of interest. One is the background EEG, particularly the shifts in frequency and/or amplitude that occur in altered states of consciousness: towards synchronized alpha rhythm and slower waveform during relaxation and towards low voltage fast activity during mental activity. The other, usually dependent for its detection on the use of electronic averaging techniques, is the response of the brain to discrete stimuli or sets of stimuli. Several parameters can be studied; the latency, amplitude, and wave-shape of the averaged evoked response itself as well as the characteristics of the so-called CNV (contingent negative variation) or expectancy wave, a late slow (d.c.) negative component which builds up in experimental situations where a warning signal alerts the subject to anticipate a second stimulus. All of these features have generated considerable research by psychophysiologist, looking for precise measures of cortical activity during arousal and attention (Regan, 1972).

Although many psychophysiologists would confine the definition of their measurement techniques to those involving direct recording from the surface of the body, there are a number of other procedures which have sometimes been used in the context of arousal theory and which should be mentioned briefly (a more detailed account has been given elsewhere: Claridge, 1970). They include, on the one hand, various sensory and perceptual measures such as critical flicker fusion and two-flash threshold and, on the other, several drug techniques, notably the sedation threshold, that is the amount of injected barbiturate required by the individual to reach a behaviourally or physiologically defined change in consciousness (Shagass, 1954; Claridge and Herrington, 1960). The former especially might be more strictly described by some as measures of "performace"; nevertheless they have often been interpreted as direct indices of some aspect of the individual's state of arousal.

Another set of measures which Duffy certainly included as indices of arousal involves assaying the level of various hormones, usually in blood or urine (Lader, 1975). Most common has been the estimation of the output of the catecholamines (adrenaline and noradrenaline) from the adrenal medulla or of the steroids from the adrenal cortex. Also studied has been the secretion of adrenocorticotrophic hormone (ACTH) as a measure of the activity of the pituitary–adrenocortical axis and of protein-bound iodine as a measure of thyroid function. Although developed and investigated more within "stress research" than in the context of psychological arousal theory, these measures have obvious relevance to the latter as peripheral, biochemical indicators of the central nervous state of activation.

Returning to arousal theory itself, the latter has found a number of applications in psychology, arousal often being conceived in its original form—as a single, global process underlying a broad continuum of wakefulness. One such application has been to the explanation of performance variations on tasks where fluctuations in conscious aware-ness seem to be particularly involved. Typical are vigilance tasks where sustained attention is required over a long period of time in order to detect infrequently occurring "signals" occurring against a monotonous or stimulus-free background (Mackworth, 1950). Performance on such tasks was an obvious candidate for explanation within arousal theory and J. F. Mackworth (1969) has reviewed the evidence for vigilance decrement as a physiological habituation phenomenon. One way of testing this hypothesis is to record psychophysiological indices of arousal simultaneously with the performance of vigilance tasks. Many workers have done so, measuring skin conductance (Surwillo and Quilter, 1965; Dardano, 1962; Andreassi, 1966), several autonomic variables such as heart rate and electrodermal activity (Stern, 1966; Claridge, 1967), and level of catecholamine secretion (O'Hanlon, 1965). As one might expect, given the environmental setting of such tasks, physiological arousal does decline during the period of the test. However, in general the correlations between such decline and decre-ment in vigilance performance have been disappointingly low or non-existent. Rather more promising have been studies of the EEG-evoked potential. These have allowed a more "fine-grain" analysis of the cerebral events occurring around the time of signals that are detected or missed during vigilance tasks. Thus, Haider *et al.* (1964) and later Haider (1967) showed that evoked potentials were absent or reduced in amplitude when vigilance signals were missed, a result which can be linked to the finding that evoked response amplitudes are greater during directed attention (Haider, 1967; Cigánek, 1967). An impor-tant conclusion to be drawn from work in this area and to be borne in mind for later discussion is the distinction, already mentioned, that has to be made between tonic and phasic aspects of arousal or, put another way, between those features which have to do with the organism's overall state of wakefulness and those concerned with discrete attentiveness.

Although arousal theory has particular relevance to vigilance, a wide range of other types of performance has been considered from a similar point of view. Out of that work two principles that have been considered significant appear to have emerged. One is the so-called inverted-U

principle emphasized, among others, by Hebb (1955). This principle
states that there is a curvilinear relationship between performance and
arousal, efficiency improving monotonically up to some optimum and
then declining thereafter. The hypothesis is actually a restatement of
the earlier formulated Yerkes–Dodson law relating drive to performance (Yerkes–Dodson, 1908), though the latter contained a corollary,
not always made explicit by arousal theorists, namely that the optimum
state of drive at which performance begins to decline rather than
continues to improve is an inverse function of the complexity of the task.
Psychologists working within an arousal framework have made considerable use of the inverted-U principle to explain their results. This
despite the fact that it is extremely difficult to demonstrate its operation
in any given individual, that is by relating his performance on some task
over a wide range of concomitantly recorded physiological arousal.
Mostly arousal theorists have used the principle to explain differences
between groups of subjects considered to differ in arousal, a point I will
take up again when discussing individual differences. For the moment
suffice it to say that the inverted-U hypothesis is almost too open-ended
in its explanatory power, allowing the experimenter to explain away
almost any combination of results!

The second, rather less quoted, principle incorporating arousal as a
mediating variable in performance is the "narrowed attention hypothesis" (Callaway and Dembo, 1958), alternatively named the "cue
utilization hypothesis" by Easterbrook (1959). This states that as
arousal increases the range of cues attended to in performance decreases, resulting in a focusing or narrowing of attention. In practice
the principle has proved difficult to handle, partly because tasks differ
in the extent to which narrowing or broadening of attention is advan-
tageous or disadvantageous for effective performance and partly
because it undoubtedly interacts with the inverted-U influence of
arousal on efficiency. Nevertheless, the notion that performance, in its
sensory input aspects, is under the modulating influence of some
process regulating attention is an important one which it has been
necessary to incorporate into more recent revisions of arousal theory.

A significant feature of attempts to relate arousal to psychological
performance, and indeed of the interpretation of the concept in general,
is the tendency to identify arousal almost exclusively with anxiety.
Experimenters trying to manipulate arousal in their subjects have
usually done so by inducing anxiety, with, for example, threat of
electric shock. Similarly, investigations of the physiological correlates of arousal have usually been carried out within the context of
the study of anxiety. With a few exceptions (e.g. Ax, 1953) anger has
rarely been studied from a similar point of view, while the physiology

of sexual arousal has been investigated extensively (Zuckerman, 1971), but the findings have tended not to be discussed within the framework of conventional arousal theory. Lader (1975), in discussing this question, considers several reasons for the almost exclusive concern of arousal theorists with anxiety. The latter is, he suggests, a frequently experienced emotion and, furthermore, is easily induced in the laboratory. It has also been commonly viewed as an overaroused state and therefore one which can be related to an existing theoretical framework within which to interpret experimental data, for example via the inverted-U hypothesis. Finally, he argues, many theorists of personality give great prominence to the individual variations that can be observed in anxiety-proneness and which are construed by such theories as trait anxiety.

Indeed, it is theories of individual variation in psychology that have made particular use of the arousal concept, as well as forming the springboard from which several revisions to arousal theory itself have been made. Before discussing that particular application of arousal theory it is worth pausing briefly to consider why the latter should be so. There are probably two reasons. One is that individual variations in personality present to the psychologist natural experiments which allow him to study the full range of some process, in this case arousal, which is otherwise only observed operating at some average level. Used in conjunction with some experimental manipulation, like drugs, it then becomes easier to dissect out different aspects of the underlying mechanisms. A second reason is that most personality theories utilizing the arousal concept have addressed themselves to abnormality as well as normality. This makes it possible to study the biological mechanisms of behaviour in an exaggerated and hence more clearly defined form. In some instances, as we shall see later, because of the particular way arousal mechanisms break down, it may be possible to discover characteristics of them which would not otherwise be observable.

As Lader points out, studies of individual variation have been based on an assumed identity between anxiety and arousal and his own work in the area attests to the usefulness of that interpretation. Thus, in a series of studies brought together in monograph form (Lader and Wing, 1966) it was demonstrated that neurotic patients high in anxiety showed significantly retarded habituation of the orienting response as well as generally heightened activity on a number of psychophysiological measures of arousal. Also found was a theoretically predictable reduction in physiological arousal, including habituation, in patients on sedative drugs. Attempts to construe anxiety as heightened arousal in normal samples, for example through correlations with self-report inventories, have on the whole been less satisfactory (Mangan, in press). This may partly arise from a distinction which I feel needs to be made between "arousal" and "arousability", paralleled in the distinction, in the descriptive personality sphere, between state and trait anxiety. Strictly speaking, arousability refers to the maximum degree of activation of which the individual is capable. Arousal as such describes the prevailing state of the individual at any given point in time. It seems probable that in patient samples, compared with normals, the two are more likely to coincide, given that the individuals concerned have succumbed, as a result of increased anxiety, to neurotic breakdown. Added to this, patient samples will cover a wider range of potential arousability; also many stressors used in the laboratory have little psychological significance, especially for normal subjects.

The distinction between arousal and arousability is also important because of its implication for the kind of measures chosen for study. Thus, many measures, particularly of autonomic function, are of such transient quality that it may require special conditions of extreme stress to bring out differences in arousability, as distinct from arousal. Other kinds of measure—and we have argued elsewhere (Claridge, 1967) that the sedation threshold is one such measure—may be more suitable for investigating the enduring differences in arousability which presumably underly trait anxiety. One method by which the suitability of such measures might be judged is the extent to which determination of them is seen to be significantly dependent on genetic factors, a criterion which the sedation threshold does indeed meet (Claridge and Ross, 1973).

Although arousal theory, including its application to personality, has given greatest prominence to the equation of over-arousal with anxiety, states of chronic under-arousal have also been seen as being important biological determinants of behaviour, including individual differences. Thus, Berlyne (1960), basing his views on a consideration of the hypothetical inverted-U function relating activation to behavioural efficiency, argued that deviations from the optimal arousal level in a downward direction are drive inducing, impelling the organism to seek out stimulation which will re-establish a comfortable state. The condition of under-arousal has been variously described as "stimulus hunger", the need for "arousal jag" and the "sensation seeking" motive. The last term was coined by Zuckerman (1974) who reviews the considerable work that has been done on sensation seeking from an individual differences point of view. The personality and behavioural styles considered by Zuckerman to characterize the sensation seeker do not concern us in detail here; suffice to say they are seen as individuals who prefer varied sexual, drug, and other experiences, to indulge in risky activities, like gambling, and to be represented in the abnormal field as primary psychopaths. Zuckerman argues that his biological investigations have been consistent with an interpretation of sensation seeking within an arousal framework and, incidentally, with some of the work on the psychophysiology of the psychopath (Hare, 1970). Two of his findings are worth quoting here because they illustrate particularly well some earlier comments about interpretation of the arousal concept. One is the demonstration (Zuckerman, 1972; Neary and Zuckerman, 1973) that high sensation seekers showed a predictably rapid habituation of the orienting response to a novel tone. Interestingly, however, the size of the initial orienting response itself was larger than in low sensation seekers. In other words, they appeared to be more *arousable* in the first instance but to sustain their arousal for a relatively short time. The result thus confirms the distinction made earlier between arousability and arousal. The second experiment of interest (Zuckerman *et al.*, 1974) investigated the "augmenting–reducing" response, that is the relative tendency for individuals either to amplify or diminish the magnitude of their response as stimulus intensity increases. The technique used was that developed and studied extensively by Buchsbaum using the amplitude of the averaged evoked potential as the response measure (Buchsbaum and Silverman, 1968; Buchsbaum and Pfefferbaum, 1971). Zuckerman and his colleagues found that high sensation seekers were characteristically augmenters compared with a relative tendency towards reducing in low sensation seekers. Augmenting–reducing has been regarded as reflecting the operation of a stimulus modulation mechanism regulating sensory input (Zuckerman, 1974) and therefore presumably more concerned with phasic than tonic aspects of arousal—a distinction drawn several times before in this chapter.

Accounts of the psychophysiology of trait anxiety and its opposite, sensation seeking, have represented largely *ad hoc* attempts to apply to personality perceived individual differences in arousal or arousability. Another offshoot of differential psychology which has had a major influence on arousal theory started from another direction. It arose out of an attempt to explain the biological basis of statistical dimensions arrived at through factor analysis of personality. Although others have made contributions (e.g. Cattell, 1972) the major influence here has undoubtedly been Eysenck (1957, 1960). The contribution of the Eysenck school—in its broadest sense—cannot be discussed in isolation from another important influence on arousal theory, one again having a different root in individual difference research but now inextricably linked to it both conceptually and empirically. I am referring to the work of Russian psychologists, originating in Pavlov's laboratory on "types of nervous system" (Pavlov, 1935). That work, which has recently been comprehensively reviewed by Mangan (in press), has attempted to discover the basic properties of the nervous system with regard to excitatory and inhibitory processes which might describe differences in temperament. Although couched in different language from that of Western psychology some of it overlaps conceptually with the latter and, indeed, Eysenck's first account of the biological basis of personality took over what most would now regard as an oversimplified interpretation of Pavlovian theory (Eysenck, 1955). Thus, Eysenck's early theorizing and experimental work focused on the personality dimension of introversion–extraversion which was visualized as being determined at the biological level by differences in the balance between excitatory and inhibitory cortical processes. An apparent similarity between the Russian notion of "excitation" and the Western concept of "arousal" eventually led Eysenck (1967) to revamp his theory of introversion–extraversion, his suggestion being that the introvert is more arousable, due specifically to greater responsivity of the ascending reticular formation. This revision coincided with a similar alignment of "excitation" and "arousal" by Claridge (1960) and a detailed rein-terpretation of Russian theory by Gray (1964, 1967), who translated the Pavlovian notion of "strength of nervous system" into a formulation which perceived the introvert as being more arousable and therefore having a "weaker" nervous system; that is, more susceptible to trans-marginal inhibition or diminution of response amplitude at weaker levels of stimulation than the extravert. Gray's interpretation therefore combined certain features of the inverted-U principle traditional in Western theory with the notion of an inhibitory regulating process intimately concerned in the control of arousal.

A second feature of Eysenck's revision to his own theory, and relevant in the present context, is his explanation of the biological basis of the second major personality dimension with which he has been concerned, namely neuroticism. The latter had previously (Eysenck, 1955) been regarded as a factor of emotional drive associated with the activity of the autonomic nervous system. As such it was seen as functionally in-dependent of the cortical excitatory process underlying introversion–extraversion. However, it was something of an embarrassment to the theory that neuroticism could, equally well with extraversion, be re-garded as a candidate for explanation in terms of arousal, for several reasons. Apart from its putative measurement with traditional auto-nomic indices of arousal, it relates to performance in a similar way (Claridge, 1960), as well as correlating with anxiety (Eysenck, 1959). In his revised theory Eysenck solved this dilemma by proposing a second "arousal" process responsible for variations in neuroticism. This he named "activation", which he identified physiologically with the activity of the visceral brain or limbic system. Two sources of cortical excitation were therefore recognized, one concerned with sensory arousal—mediated via the ascending reticular formation—and the other, of limbic origin, responsible for emotional arousal.

There is one other influence on arousal theory from the individual differences field which should be mentioned here, namely the explanation of psychotic states as disturbances in physiological arousal. As Lapidus and Schmolling (1975) point out in a recent review of the topic, there have been many varied attempts to interpret schizophrenia in this way. Some have been of interest, though of rather narrow thrust. Where successful they have usually taken the form of *post hoc* explanations of clinical or experimental observations in terms of principles lifted from arousal theory, such as the narrowed attention or inverted-U hypothesis (Venables, 1964). An example of the latter was an early attempt to explain the finding of extremely high physiological arousal in withdrawn retarded catatonic patients and their paradoxical increase in behavioural activity in response to barbiturates (Stevens and Derbyshire, 1958). On the whole, however, the psychoses have not yielded easily to an explanation as a single upward or downward shift in arousal and it is only in recent years that what has been a very chaotic field of enquiry has begun to take on some coherence. Because the results now emerging are so complex, and also because they have important general implications for arousal theory, an account of them will be deferred until later in the chapter.

The discussion so far has served as a background against which to judge the viability of the notion of arousal and as an account of some of the influences on its historical development. At several points ambiguities in and difficulties with the concept have been implied or stated explicitly and I would now like to look at these in more detail.

One difficulty concerns the measurement of arousal. Although it is true that shifts in the level of consciousness are accompanied by recognizable physiological change, individual indices of arousal are by no means interchangeable and hence correlations between different measures correspondingly low. Lader (1975), discussing autonomic measures, suggests that this is partly because the various possible indices are differentially sensitive over different ranges of arousal; for example, heart rate is more sensitive over the high and spontaneous GSR fluctuations more sensitive over the low range. Even confining oneself to a single autonomic system, such as electrodermal activity, the different measures available, such as skin conductance level and response amplitude, may or may not be correlated. A complicating factor here is the so-called "law of initial values" (Wilder, 1957), that is the tendency for level and response to be negatively correlated. Thus, responses occurring near the ceiling of the physiological system in question—and hence presumably at high "arousal"—may be smaller than those observed against a low level of background activity. This often forces psychophysiologists to resort to statistical corrections of their data, none of which is entirely satisfactory (Lacey, 1956; Benjamin, 1963; Heath and Oken, 1962). Another statistical manipulation which is sometimes necessary is that of "range correction" (Lykken, 1975). This is a method of allowing for the fact that individuals differ in the range of physiological activity over which they are capable of operating; hence responses of the same amplitude may have different significance looked at from the point of view of what they say about the psychological state of different individuals. Related to this problem is the fact that the autonomic system of course subserves peripheral bodily functions which have little or nothing to do with the central processes in which psychologists are interested—yet such factors will contribute to and be difficult to disentangle from the variance of measures used as indices of 'arousal'.

Even if these technical difficulties of measurement are overcome there remains the problem of patterning of autonomic response, throwing doubt on the notion of arousal as a change in physiological activity which is uniform across all individuals and all conditions. Apart from that associated with different emotional states and already referred to (e.g. Ax, 1953), two kinds of patterning can be recognized, one situational and the other individual in origin. The latter, "response specificity", refers to the tendency for some—though to complicate matters not all—individuals to show reliably characteristic profiles of autonomic response under arousal, some, for example, reacting maximally with increased electrodermal activity, others more typically through the cardiovascular system (Lacey *et al.*, 1953; Lacey and Lacey, 1958), Stereotypy of response due to the nature of the stimulus, or "stimulus specificity" has also been demonstrated (Davis *et al.*, 1955). The autonomic responses accompanying a change in arousal in a given individual at a particular time is therefore likely to represent the interaction between both of these factors (Engel, 1960). While these, not unexpected, complexities of measurement do not, in themselves, argue against the value of arousal as an explanatory concept, they do illustrate the dangers of oversimplistic interpretations of psychophysiological data.

A slightly different problem arises when one moves away from the measurement of arousal through autonomic indices to its measurement by means of the EEG. And here I am not referring to the two most obvious and often quoted difficulties with the EEG; first, that it is a relatively crude indicator of brain activity recorded from the outside of the skull and representing the composite electrical energy generated by large masses of cerebral tissue, and, secondly, that the waveforms observed are complex and not always easy to interpret in a psychologically meaningful way. Regarding the first difficulty, the human EEG is certainly crude but it is all the psychophysiologist has. At least it is a measure which should, in principle, bring him as close as possible to the "seat of consciousness". Looked at in this way its status is no worse, probably slightly better, than that of autonomic indices. The complexity of the EEG waveforms is certainly a problem and has preoccupied behavioural scientists ever since Berger first recorded voltage fluctuations from the human scalp. Reduction of this electric activity into a manageable form ranges from simple counts of the abundance, amplitude, or frequency of the alpha rhythm to more elaborate computer analyses of the whole frequency spectrum represented in the EEG. Although matching these physiological data to the more subtle aspects of mentation still proves elusive, grosser changes in "arousal" are fairly easily recognizable in the EEG.

EEG indices of arousal do not, however, relate in the manner one might naively expect to other types of measure, such as those of autonomic activity. Sternbach (1960) found no correlation between alpha index and a composite measure of autonomic response and considered that the two were independent of each other. Stennett (1957), on the other hand, did demonstrate a relationship—between skin conductance and alpha amplitude—though a curvilinear one; when looked at from the point of view of "arousal" the two types of measure covaried positively over the upper range, but in opposite directions over the lower ranges of electrodermal activity. Antedating both of these studies Darrow *et al.* (1946) also suggested that the correlation between EEG and autonomic measures was opposite in direction depending on whether the individual was in a resting or highly aroused state. They considered that this phenomenon provided evidence of opposing cortical and subcortical influences on cerebral function and offered a way of studying mutual cortical–subcortical regulating influences on arousal. Darrow's conclusions are of interest in that they anticipated one of a number of attempts over the years to try and give the concept of arousal more precision. I will enlarge on that particular theme later, noting in the meantime that it does illustrate one of the major difficulties in the field, namely that of defining "arousal" or, put another way, discovering what in the original idea can be usefully retained and incorporated into a more precise account of, to quote Hebb, the "conceptual nervous system".

Attempts to achieve that end have taken different forms, mainly because investigators working within an arousal framework have often had different sorts of data to explain. Consequently it is often difficult to discern anything but the most tenuous links between their theories, models, or points of emphasis. One thing they do have in common, however, is the opinion that the notion of arousal as a global, undifferentiated state is inadequate and that, even if satisfactorily defined more narrowly, it serves to explain only a small part of the total pattern of physiological response which parallels the individual's fluctuating level of consciousness and interaction with the environment.

One solution to the vagueness of theorizing in this area is to consider it more useful to distinguish different *types* of arousal, for example autonomic, cortical, behavioural and so on. Although not in itself furthering very much our understanding of the dynamic mechanisms involved, this approach does at least partly help towards operationalizing the definition of arousal as observed under given conditions and as measured by particular indices. It also has the merit of recognizing the complex relationships that exist between different types of index, such as those noted earlier between EEG and autonomic measures. Elaborating the idea recently Mangan (in press) considered that it may be most useful to distinguish three types of arousal: cortical, autonomic, and somatic. Differences in the pattern of correlation between these three components might then, he argues, help to define different organismic states and the strategies employed to deal with the environmental demands associated with them. For example, starting from an assumption that the somatic system acts to modulate autonomic function, Mangan suggests that under threat the resulting increase in muscle tension may cause autonomic arousal to decrease, thus acting partly as a protective device against excessive cortical excitation. The strategy of examining the significance of differences in the covariation between various types of arousal index is an interesting one and one which we shall come across again shortly in another context; it certainly merits further attention as a way of dissecting out different aspects of arousal.

Another approach to the problem, already mentioned, is the distinction made by Eysenck between "activation" and "arousal". We saw earlier that the necessity for this distinction arose out of Eysenck's need to account for the apparent "arousal" implications of both of his dimensions of neuroticism and introversion–extraversion. He argues that fluctuations in arousal—associated as an individual difference variable with introversion—can occur quite independently of changes in emotional activation. Thus, the person sitting quietly reading in a chair will vary in arousal level depending on a number of factors, such as the warmth of the room, the interest of the book, his degree of introversion and so on. But, so the argument goes, only if he is suddenly emotionally excited, and especially if he is high in neuroticism, will the second system controlling activation come into play. Eysenck's analysis clearly bears some resemblance to the suggested distinction, referred to a moment ago, between different types of arousal. Thus, it perhaps does not stretch the limits of the imagination too far to see some similarity between the notions of "cortical" and "autonomic" arousal and Eysenck's twin systems of "arousal" and "activation" Eysenck's formulation does differ, however, in the way in which he identifies the two systems physiologically. They are seen as separable in terms of their brain circuitry (reticular and limbic respectively) but the circuits in both cases involve neocortical connections and influences. In other words, the division of the nervous system is vertical rather than horizontal. One would guess that Eysenck's model corresponds more closely with the physiological reality, as indeed the evidence suggests. Thus, Routtenberg (1968), basing his views on neuro-physiological data from animal research, arrived at a very similar theory to that proposed by Eysenck, namely a two-process arousal model in which the reticular formation and limbic system were seen as separate but mutually inhibitory parts of a neocortical–subcortical circuit helping to maintain the ongoing behaviour of the organism. Unfortunately for the human worker the potential veracity of such models is double-edged. Psychophysiology has no direct access to the reticular formation or the limbic system. Instead, it relies on studying activity in the intact, integrated nervous system, the different parts of which may have similar effects on the measures it is forced to use; for instance, both "arousal" and "activation", as defined by Eysenck, have identical desynchronizing influences on the EEG. Since the two components of arousal opted for by Eysenck are difficult to define psychophysiologically, isolating their theoretically separable, but in practice interacting, influences presents a problem for the model, which is not easy to translate into an empirically testable form. On balance, and for certain purposes, the physiologically less real but operationally more precise division into "cortical', "autonomic" and other forms of arousal may have an advantage, as long as the quotation marks around such terms are kept constantly in mind.

The attempts to refine the arousal concept considered so far have had, as their main emphasis, the elaboration of those aspects of arousal theory concerned with the maintenance of, or variations in, the overall level of consciousness; in other words with the "energetics" or intensity aspect of behaviour which originally led Duffy to try and unify drive and emotion. However, much of the data which arousal theory is brought up against has to do with another aspect of behaviour. This can be variously, though perhaps not entirely synonymously, described as concerned with attentiveness, with the directional component in behaviour, with the responsiveness of the organism to discrete stimuli in its environment, or, to recall a distinction made several times in this paper, with the phasic as compared with the tonic aspects of arousal. The distinction has not always been clearly drawn or, sometimes, been too clearly drawn. Where the latter has been the case it is presumably because some workers have felt the term "arousal" should indeed be reserved as a description of its energetics component, leaving to other terminology and other theoretical models those aspects of psychological function which it mediates or with which it interacts, but from which it can be distinguished. However, such an argument becomes difficult to sustain when, as is increasingly the case, theorists in the field are seeking to underpin their ideas with neurophysiological evidence. "Arousal" as traditionally defined then becomes almost impossible to discuss except in the context of a total view of the nervous system, even though the term itself is best confined to one aspect of its activity.

When the distinction being considered has been recognized, it has often not been made very explicit, for two reasons. One is that arousal theory as such has not traditionally contained within it the necessary concepts with which to handle the distinction, having instead to borrow them from elsewhere. The second reason has to do with interpretation of the kinds of measurement used by arousal theorists. As we have seen, these are dimensionally rather complex, even one autonomic system often yielding several parameters that are highly interdependent. Yet they may all, wrongly perhaps, be interpreted as indicators of "arousal" in its energetics sense. To take an example, the tonic level of electrodermal activity almost certainly reflects a different central nervous process from that responsible for phasic GSRs (Sharpless and Jasper, 1956); yet research workers have often used them interchangeably as indices of "arousal" or been vague about their possibly different psychological and neurophysiological significance.

One notable exception to this has been Lacey (Lacey, 1959; Lacey *et al.*, 1963); he has consciously distinguished the intensity from the directional components of arousal. In doing so Lacey formulated the notion of "directional fractionation" which is essentially a statement of "stimulus specificity" discussed earlier; namely, that under arousal different parts of the total physiological response may alter in different ways depending on the situation. Lacey then elaborated this idea into the distinction between tasks or situations requiring "sensory intake" and those demanding "sensory rejection". Basing his hypothesis mainly on observations of changes in cardiovascular function, Lacey argued that where, as in thinking, the attention is directed inwards and information from the environment is rejected there is an increase in the phasic heart rate, whereas the reverse is the case where attention is being directed towards external events and there is a high rate of sensory intake. More recent studies of autonomic patterning have supported Lacey's hypothesis (Williams *et al.*, 1975; Bittker *et al.*, 1975) and, indeed, the general importance of distinguishing the intensity from the directional aspects of arousal (Eason and Dudley, 1971). The latter authors, for example, compared physiological responses across sessions differing in level of experimentally induced activation with changes occurring within sessions while subjects were performing a perceptual–motor task. They found that different degrees of activation produced the predicted uniform shifts in physiological activity, as measured by a variety of indices. However, changes within sessions, that is at any given intensity level of arousal, were more complex. One interesting feature, in view of an earlier comment about the interrelationship between the somatic and autonomic systems, was that several measures of the latter, including skin conductance, declined in association with increases in muscular tension.

The studies just considered are, of course, of rather narrow thrust, being concerned mainly with the functional significance of physiological patterning. However, other writers have been more ambitious in trying to construct models of the whole "conceptual nervous system". In those cases "arousal", in its intensity aspects, has formed only one part of their theorizing, which has also tried to take account of other processes, like attention, to which it is inextricably related. In order to handle the kinds of experimental data they are trying to explain such theorists have often had to go beyond the bounds of traditional arousal theory and, as noted earlier, borrow concepts from elsewhere. One such concept is that of inhibition. The term "inhibition" has been almost as much abused, if such is possible, as that of "arousal". Its usage has ranged from rather vague attempts to account for performance decrement to more precise analysis of its involvement in the development of visual function. Nevertheless, as Diamond *et al.* (1963) pointed out in their much neglected book "Inhibition and Choice", the role of inhibition at all levels of behaviour is too well-established for its importance to be ignored, a conclusion which has been further strengthened over the years since they wrote their review. There is now no doubt that many, perhaps all, psychological functions represent the end product of a mutual interaction between some excitatory or facilitatory determinant and a suppressor or inhibitory process; only in this way can the smoothness of thinking, learning, attention, motor activity—and arousal—be maintained.

Work carried out under the umbrella of Pavlovian "nervous type" theory has, of course, made considerable use of the concept of inhibition and since Eysenck's early takeover of certain ideas from that theory there has been continued convergence of Western and East European research (Nebylitsyn and Gray, 1972). This has resulted in the development, on both sides, of very similar models of the nervous system. All of these models contain, as a crucial feature, the notion of inhibitory feedback loops involved in the cortical–subcortical regulation of arousal. Thus Eysenck (1967) retained this idea of "excitation–inhibition balance" when revamping his theory in more neurophysiological form. Similarly, Nebylitsyn (1973), arriving at a model almost identical to that of Eysenck, postulated two brain systems—fronto-reticular and fronto-limbic—to account for temperamental differences in general activity and emotionality, traits clearly similar to those of extraversion and neuroticism. Finally, in a parallel exercise Gray (1972) has also tackled the possible neurophysiological basis of the Eysenckian dimensions of personality. Regarding extraversion Gray's suggestion is that differences there derive basically from variations in the activity of a negative feedback loop consisting of the ascending reticular formation (ARAS), the orbital frontal cortex, the medial septal area, and the hippocampus. According to Gray the state of arousal, and presumably the arousability, of the individual is dependent on ascending reticular influences more or less subject to the modulating control of the septo-hippocampal system, which he sees as having an inhibitory effect both directly on the ARAS and on sensory input, forming, in its latter function, part of a selective attention mechanism.

   The evolution of these ideas, out of Western arousal theory and Russian nervous type theory, is of considerable interest because of the way in which another area of research, proceeding to a large extent independently, has also converged on a similar view of the "conceptual nervous system". I am referring to the application of the arousal concept to the psychotic states. As previously mentioned, a disturbance of the intensity aspects of arousal alone has proved of very little explanatory value in the psychoses. Yet it is obvious that psychotic patients show very gross alterations in emotional arousal. However, it is also obvious, both from subjective (Chapman, 1966) and experimental accounts (McGhie, 1969), that they suffer too from a severe disorder of selective attention, or of the directional aspects of arousal. Indeed, it can be said that the psychoses—and here I am referring mainly to the schizophrenias—strongly highlight the inadequacies of a global view of arousal, since in those states the distinction, often blurred in the normal individual, between the intensity and the directional components of arousal, become clearly manifested. For that reason, pursuing an earlier theme, schizophrenia has proved to be an interesting "natural experiment" through which to explore and dissect the mechanisms of arousal.

One strategy for doing so—in fact, stumbled upon by accident—has been to examine, not the absolute *levels* found in schizophrenics on various measures of "arousal"; instead to look at the manner in which these different measures covary with each other in schizophrenics compared with other types of individual. The most interesting feature to emerge from work using this strategy is that, in schizophrenics, there is a tendency for some "arousal" measures to covary in a counter-intuitive fashion; that is the measures become relatively "dissociated" compared with the relationships observed in non-psychotic subjects. An example of this phenomenon comes from an early study in our own laboratory in which we examined the sedation threshold and Archimedes spiral after-effect in acute schizophrenics (Herrington and Claridge, 1965). In the latter the normally predicted positive correlation between those two measures was reversed, schizophrenics with high sedation thresholds (arousability) showing weak perceived after effects and vice versa. Most of the recent research in this area, however, has made use of two different types of measure, the two-flash threshold and electrodermal level, following Venables' (1963) demonstration that the correlation between them is inverted in schizophrenics compared with normal subjects. Venables' exact result subsequently proved difficult to replicate (Lykken and Maley, 1968; Gruzelier *et al.*, 1972; Gruzelier and Venables, 1975) but it now turns out that this was due to the use of medicated schizophrenics. The last and most recent study (Claridge and Clark, submitted for publication), using unmedicated patients, confirmed that there is indeed a very unusual relationship between two-flash threshold and skin conductance in schizophrenics. The form it takes is a curious U-function, perceptual discrimination being acute at very low and at very high levels of autonomic arousal. worsening towards the middle range—in other words, exactly the reverse of the *inverted*-U function normally expected. Interestingly enough the same relative dissociation between two-flash threshold and electrodermal activity found in psychotic patients has also been demonstrated in normal subjects under LSD-25 (Claridge, 1972) and in people with high scores on Eysenck's questionnaire scale of psychotocism (Claridge and Chappa, 1973; Claridge and Birchall, 1978).

What implication one considers these findings have for arousal theory depends to some extent on the interpretation that is put on the measure themselves. Venables, in his original studies of the two-flash threshold in schizophrenia supposed that the measure could be regarded as an index of "cortical arousal", following Lindsley's (1957) research on its neurophysiological basis. Pursuing that interpretation it

could be concluded that there are certain states of altered consciousness—found in schizophrenia, under drugs like LSD, and in some
normal individuals high in "psychotic" personality traits—where the
usually expected relationships between "cortical" and "autonomic"
arousal no longer hold, where, for example, high levels of cortical
activity are found in conjunction with low levels of autonomic response.[1] Although such an interpretation has operational value it tells us
little of the underlying mechanisms involved. Nor does it recognize the
limitations inherent in explanations which rely solely on modifying the
original concept of arousal by subdividing it into various components. An
alternative view is that the "dissociation" of psychophysiological
function observed in schizophrenia (and allied states) represents the
natural breakdown of the homeostasis of the CNS, the change in tonic
arousal being only one aspect of that breakdown. It was this kind of
model which I suggested some years ago (Claridge, 1967) to explain our
own data on schizophrenia. Two processes were postulated, one of tonic
arousal, and the other named the "arousal modulating system". The
latter was considered to have two properties, both mediated through its
twin properties of facilitation and inhibition. One function was directly
to maintain tonic arousal at an appropriate level. The other was to
regulate, through filtering, the individual's response to sensory input.

It was felt at the time that this model had several advantages. First, it
was parsimonious in explicity retaining the term "arousal" to refer to
those aspects of its intensity function which Duffy originally tried to
describe. Secondly, it nevertheless recognized the importance of the
phasic or attentional aspects of central nervous activity, aspects which
it was felt any model of the CNS had to take account of in explaining,
certainly schizophrenia, but normal behaviour as well. And, thirdly, it
incorporated the notion of inhibition, and hence homeostatic regula-

---

[1]It will be recalled from an earlier part of the discussion that a similar "dissociation"
between these two components of arousal was noted by Darrow and others who
examined differences in the direction in which, in their case, EEG measures of cortical
arousal varied as autonomic arousal altered. However, an interesting paradox which
should be noted in passing is that they considered that the two types of measure
covaried in opposite directions when the individual was in a resting, rather than in a
highly aroused, state. Yet there is good reason to believe (Claridge and Clark, submitted for publication.) that the "dissociation" observed in psychotic and psychotic-
like states occurs more commonly where the individual is anxious. A purely speculative,
but testable, solution to this discrepancy would recall Mangan's distinction, discussed
previously, between *three* types of arousal: cortical, autonomic and somatic. Thus, it is
possible that the negative relationship between the first two of these components
observed in anxious psychotics occurs because somatic arousal is so high that it leads to
an actual decrease in autonomic responsiveness. Clinical observation would certainly
support such a view.

tion, as an important process in the nervous system, of which arousal in its traditional sense forms only one part.

As originally presented the model was admittedly rather vague, but recent developments in theory and research have suggested that the distinctions it made were valid. Thus, some of the so-called "dual-process" arousal models already referred to, such as those of Eysenck and Routtenberg, bear some resemblance to it. However, the most obvious convergence is with Gray's attempt, described earlier, to account for the neurophysiological basis of introversion–extraversion. Thus, there is a clear similarity between our model and his notion of a feedback loop between the ascending reticular formation and the septo-hippocampal system, the latter corresponding well to our "arousal modulating system". We, of course, have been concerned with a rather different aspect of central nervous function—the possible breakdown or at least alteration in homeostatic feedback in certain psychological states—but the match with Gray's model is sufficiently good to suggest that these may be mediated through the same brain circuitry. That seems especially likely in view of the considerable amount of research which now suggests that dysfunction of the limbic system—and parti-cularly the hippocampus—may be involved in the peculiarities of arousal, orientation, and attention observed in schizophrenia (Vena-bles, 1973).

Another related though slightly different line of research, again in psychopathology, underlines the importance of embedding the arousal concept in a more elaborate homeostatic view of the central nervous function. Briefly referred to earlier were attempts to account for the sensation-seeking behaviour of people chronically low in arousal and to Buchsbaum's interpretation of the individual difference characteristic of "augmenting–reducing" as an indicator of sensory input regulation, a process distinct from, even though intimately concerned in, the control of arousal. Recently Buchsbaum and his colleagues (Haier *et al.*, 1980) elaborated this view following a study in which they examined persona-lity styles and degree of psychopathology in individuals subdivided simultaneously on two indices of central nervous function. One was the augmenting–reducing response—measured in the usual way as the slope of change in evoked response amplitude as a function of increasing stimulus intensity; the other was the level of platelet monoamine oxidase (MAO), a measure currently of interest as an indirect bio-chemical index of central nervous excitability. Their results led them to propose a model almost identical to that I have described earlier. They suggested that the two measures they used reflected two different central processes, corresponding, respectively, to our "tonic arousal" (MAO level) and to our "arousal modulating system" (augmenting–

reducing slope). Invoking the notion that the latter partly serves the inhibitory function of protecting against overstimulation they went on to explain their results. These showed evidence of greater psychopathology in individuals in whom the two systems were "out of balance"; that is to say where high tonic arousal (low platelet MAO) was found in association with poor inhibitory regulation of sensory input (augmenting), or where low arousal and over-regulation (reducing) were observed. The opposite combinations were considered to reflect nervous systems in a more balanced state of homeostasis.

Apart from its theoretical interest the study just described illustrates again the power of the research strategy used, of examining not absolute levels of behaviour, but, instead, the covariation between what are considered to be functionally different aspects of CNS activity. A similar conclusion was reached by Shagass *et al.* (1975) who used this same technique to demonstrate differences between patient and normal samples according to the correlation observed in the groups between augmenting–reducing slope and background EEG taken as a measure of tonic arousal.

To date the published work adopting this strategy has concentrated on its use in individual difference research, that is comparing within group correlations in samples defined according to clinical or personality trait criteria. However, another application, which promises to extend much more our insight into the dynamic mechanisms involved in arousal and its modulation, is to examine the fluctuations that can occur in any given individual when studied under different conditions. In, as far as we know, the first attempt to do that a study from our laboratory (Birchall and Claridge, 1979) has recently examined the way in which, for an individual subject, the augmenting–reducing slope of the visual evoked response varies as a function of changing tonic arousal, measured by level of skin conductance. Briefly, the results clearly show that an individual's tendency to augment or reduce as stimulus intensity increases is partly state-dependent, altering as a function of the tonic arousal obtaining at the time of measurement. Even more interesting was the finding that the *direction* of augmenting–reducing change was closely related to the subject's overall arousal level. Thus, individuals who on average were poorly aroused tended to augment more as their arousal level increased. The response of highly aroused subjects, on the other hand, was to augment less, or reduce more; in other words, their reaction to a combination of increasing arousal and stimulus intensity was to switch to a protective, reducing cortical response. Further, as yet unpublished, analysis of these data strongly suggests that there is indeed a systematic, albeit complex, relationship between skin conductance level, stimulus intensity, and the amplitude of individual sets of averaged evoked responses. We hope that by examining the interaction between these three parameters in more detail it will be possible to get a better understanding of the way in which the brain modulates its phasic response to sensory input according to the relative demands of the environment and of the internal state of tonic arousal.

In conclusion, drawing together the many threads that have run through this chapter is no easy task. The data to be explained are very disparate and the methodologies and theoretical viewpoints adopted correspondingly varied; so much so that the links between them are often tenuous, in some cases perhaps even illusory. The reader may therefore be forgiven if he concludes that he knows what arousal is when he sees it, but that he still cannot define it. Perhaps this does not matter since the term "arousal" has, in any case, been out-stripped as a precise explanatory concept, by itself, of anything other than the fact that people sometimes seem to be rather sleepy and sometimes rather excited. What is more important is that the idea has spawned a great deal of research which is slowly leading to some understanding of the central nervous mechanisms responsible for these observed variations in behaviour. As we have seen, the research in question has involved studies of the patterning of autonomic response under different conditions, attempts to differentiate tonic and phasic and intensity and directional aspects of "arousal", and a convergence of Western ideas about the nervous system with those of Eastern European workers, whose manipulation of concepts like "inhibition" has been usefully borrowed to extend the scope of otherwise rather limited explanatory models.

Particularly stressed here has been the contribution from research of individual differences and its extension into psychopathology. This has been deliberate since I believe—and I think results in the area discussed warrant that view—that the understanding of any phenomenon is facilitated by studying its natural variations. In this respect I have especially emphasized the relevance of the psychotic states because of the evidence that they involve an alteration in central nervous homeostasis of a peculiar form, which may make it possible to dissect out different aspects of arousal and sensory modulation that are otherwise difficult to examine. There is, however, another reason for this emphasis; namely the possibility that the psychotic states simply represent pathological variants on normal modes of behaviour and consciousness. That such may be the case is now coming, not only from formal experimental studies of personality structure (Eysenck and Eysenck, 1976) and cognitive style (Woody and Claridge, 1977) but also from phenomenological investigations of the "psychotic experience", in which there is currently a resurgence of interest (Fadiman and Newman, 1973). The latter is, or course, no coincidence, for it represents just one part of the growing concern with a number of related topics like the creative process, the meditative state, dreams, hallucinations, the paranormal and other aspects of consciousness which mainstream academic psychologists have been loth—indeed ashamed—to discuss openly for most of this century.

So far, attempts to relate such phenomena to models of the central nervous system vary in imaginativeness according to the extent to which authors have presumably broken away from their behaviourist upbringing, as witnessed, for example, in the range of viewpoints adopted in some recent excursions into the field (Ornstein, 1972; Siegel and West, 1975; Schwartz and Shapiro, 1976). In the more narrow context of this chapter's remit, which I have implicitly defined as research carried out within psychological arousal theory, there has been a conspicuous lack of reference to the real data of consciousness, the models described having been truly behaviourist in origin. In fact, arousal theory and its variations have failed dismally to come to grips with such data, despite the stance—talked glibly about, even by myself earlier in this chapter—of academic psychophysiology as an interface between brain and mind. It is now timely that psychophysiologists proceed more often to the other side of the interface and study in detail the experiential data of which their pen recording traces are an otherwise meaningless correlate. Arousal theory will then begin to come of age in making its contribution to our understanding of consciousness.

References

Andreassi, J. L. (1966). Skin-conductance and reaction-time in a continuous auditory monitoring task. *American Journal of Psychiatry*, **79**, 470–474.

Ax, A. F. (1953). The physiological differentiation between fear and anger in humans. *Psychosomatic Medicine*, **15**, 433–442.

Benjamin, L. S. (1963). Statistical treatment of the law of initial values (LIV) in autonomic research: a review and recommendation. *Psychosomatic Medicine* **25**, 556–566.

Berlyne, D. E. (1960). "Conflict, Arousal and Curiosity". McGraw-Hill, New York.

Birchall, P. M. A. and Claridge, G. S. (1979). Augmenting–reducing of visually evoked potential as a function of changes in skin conductance level. *Psychophysiology*, **16**, 482–490.

Bittker, T. E., Buchsbaum, M. S., Williams, R. B. and Wynne, L. C. (1975). Cardiovascular and neurophysiologic correlates of sensory intake and rejection. II. Interview behaviour. *Psychophysiology*, **12**, 434–438.

Buchsbaum, M. and Pfefferbaum, A. (1971). Individual differences in stimulus intensity response. *Psychophysiology*, **8**, 600–611.

Buchsbaum, M. and Silverman, J. (1968). Stimulus intensity control and the cortical evoked response. *Psychosomatic Medicine*, **30**, 12–22.

Callaway, E. III and Dembo, E. (1958). Narrowed attention: a psychological phenomenon that accompanies a certain physiological change. *Archives of Neurology and Psychiatry*, (Chicago), **79**, 74–90.

Cannon, W. B. (1929). "Bodily Changes in Pain, Hunger, Fear, and Rage". Branford, Boston.

Cattell, R. B. (1972). The interpretation of Pavlov's typology, and the arousal concept in replicated trait and state factors. *In* "Biological Bases of Individual Behaviour" (Eds V. D. Nebylitsyn, and J. A. Gray), Academic Press, New York and London.

Chapman, J. (1966). The early symptoms of schizophrenia. *British Journal of Psychiatry*, **12**, 225–253.

Cigánek, L. (1967). The effects of attention and distraction on the visual evoked potential: a preliminary report. *Electroencephalography and Clinical Neurophysiology, Supplement*, **26**, 70–73.

Claridge, G. S. (1960). The excitation–inhibition balance in neurotics. *In* "Experiments in Personality" (Ed. H. J. Eysenck), vol. 2. Routledge and Kegan Paul, London.

Claridge, G. S. (1967). "Personality and Arousal". Pergamon, Oxford.

Claridge, G. S. (1970). Psychophysiological techniques. *In* "The Psychological Assessment of Mental and Physical Handicaps" (Ed. P. Mittler), Methuen, London.

Claridge, G. S. (1972). The schizophrenias as nervous types. *British Journal of Psychiatry*, **121**, 1–17.

Claridge, G. S. and Birchall, P. M. A. (1978). Bishop, Eysenck, Block and psychoticism. *Journal of Abnormal Psychology*, **87**, 664–668.

Claridge G. S. and Chappa, H. J. (1973). Psychoticism: a study of its biological basis in normal subjects. *British Journal of Social and Clinical Psychology*, **12**, 175–187.

Claridge, G. S. and Clark, K. H. (submitted for publication). Covariation between two-flash threshold and skin conductance level in first breakdown schizophrenics. I. Relationships in drug-free patients.

Claridge, G. S. and Herrington, R. N. (1960). Sedation threshold, personality and the theory of neurosis. *Journal of Mental Science*, **106**, 1568–1583.

Claridge, G. S. and Ross, E. (1973). Sedative drug tolerance in twins. *In* "Personality Differences and Biological Variations" (Eds G. S. Claridge, S. Canter and W. I. Hume), Pergamon, Oxford.

Dardano, J. F. (1962). Relationships of intermittent noise, intersignal interval, and skin conductance to vigilance behaviour. *Journal of Applied Psychology*, **46**, 106–114.

Darrow, C. W., Pathman, J. and Kronenberg, G. (1946). Level of autonomic activity and electroencephalogram. *Journal of Experimental Psychology*, **36**, 355–365.

Davis, R. C., Buchwald, A. M. and Frankmann, R. W. (1955). Autonomic and muscular responses and their relation to simple stimuli. *Psychological Monographs*, **69**, 1–71.

Diamond, S., Balvin, R. S. and Diamond, F. R. (1963). "Inhibition and Choice". Harper and Row, New York.

Duffy, E. (1934). Emotion: an example of the need for reorientation in psychology, *Psychological Review*, **41**, 239–243.

Duffy, E. (1962). "Activation and Behaviour". Wiley, New York.

Eason, R. G. and Dudley, L. M. (1971). Physiological and behavioural indicants of activation. *Psychophysiology*, **7**, 223–232.

Easterbrook, J. A. (1959). The effect of emotion on cue utilization and the organisation of behaviour. *Psychological Review*, **66**, 183–201.

Engel, B. T. (1960). Stimulus–response and individual-response specificity. *Archives of General Psychiatry*, **2**, 305–313.

Eysenck, H. J. (1955). A dynamic theory of anxiety and hysteria. *Journal of Mental Science*, **101**, 28–51.

Eysenck, H. J. (1957). "The Dynamics of Anxiety and Hysteria". Routledge and Kegan Paul, London.

Eysenck, H. J. (1959). "Manual of the Maudsley Personality Inventory". University of London Press, London.

Eysenck, H. J. (1960). Levels of personality, constitutional factors, and social influences. *International Journal of Social Psychology*, **6**, 12–24.

Eysenck, H. J. (1967) *The Biological Basis of Personality*. Charles C. Thomas, Springfield, Ill.

Eysenck, H. J. and Eysenck, S. B. G. (1976). "Psychoticism as a Dimension of Personality". Hodder and Stoughton, London.

Fadiman, J. and Kewman, D. (Eds) (1973). "Exploring Madness". Brooks/Cole, Monterey.

Gray, J. A. (1964). "Pavlov's Typology". Pergamon, Oxford.

Gray, J. A. (1967). Strength of the nervous system, introversion–extraversion conditionability and arousal. *Behaviour Research and Therapy*, **5**, 151–169.

Gray, J. A. (1972). The psychophysiological nature of introversion–extraversion. *In* "Biological Bases of Individual Behaviour" (Eds V. D. Nebylitsyn, and J. A. Gray), Academic Press, New York and London.

Greenfield, N. S. and Sternbach, R. A. (1972). "Handbook of Psychophysiology". Holt, Rinehart and Winston, New York.

Gruzelier, J., Lykken, D. and Venables, P. (1972). Schizophrenia and arousal revisited. *Archives of General Psychiatry*, **26**, 427–432.

Gruzelier, J. and Venables, P. (1975). Relations between two-flash discrimination and electrodermal activity re-examined in schizophrenics and normals. *Journal of Psychiatric Research*, **12**, 73–85.

Gullickson, G. R. (1973). "The Psychophysiology of Darrow". Academic Press, New York and London.

Haider, M. (1967). Vigilance, attention, expectation and cortical evoked potentials. *Acta Psychologica*, **27**, 245–252.

Haider, M., Spong, P. and Lindsley, D. B. (1964). Attention, vigilance and cortical evoked-potentials in humans. *Science*, **145**, 180–181.

Haier, R. J., Buchsbaum, M. S., Murphy, D. L., Gottesman, I. I. and Coursey, R. D. (1980). Psychiatric vulnerability, monoamine oxidase and the average evoked potential. *Archives of General Psychiatry*, **37**, 340–345.

Hare, R. D. (1970). "Psychopathy, Theory and Research". Wiley, New York.

Hassett, J. (1978). "A Primer of Psychophysiology". Freeman, San Francisco.

Heath, H. A. and Oken, D. (1962). Change scores as related to initial and final levels. *Annals of the New York Academy of Sciences*, **98**, 1242–1256.

Hebb, D. O. (1955). Drives and the CNS (conceptual nervous system). *Psychological Review*, **62**, 243–254.

Herrington, R. N. and Claridge, G. S. (1965). Sedation threshold and Archimedes' spiral after-effect in early psychosis. *Journal of Psychiatric Research*, **3**, 159–171.

Lacey, J. I. (1956). The evaluation of autonomic responses: toward a general solution. *Annals of The New York Academy of Science*, **67**, 125–164.

Lacey, J. I. (1959). Psychophysiological approaches to the evaluation of psychotherapeutic process and outcome. *In* "Research in Psychotherapy" (Eds E. A. Rubenstein and M. D. Perloff), National Publishing, Washington.

Lacey, J. I., Bateman, D. E. and Van Lehn, R. (1953). Autonomic response specificity. An experimental study. *Psychosomatic Medicine*, **15**, 8–21.

Lacey, J. I., Kagan, J., Lacey, B. C. and Moss, H. A. (1963). The visceral level: situational determinants and behavioural correlates of autonomic response patterns. *In* "Expression of the Emotions in Man" (Ed. P. H. Knapp), International University Press, New York.

Lacey, J. I. and Lacey, B. C. (1958). Verification and extension of the principle of autonomic response-stereotypy. *American Journal of Psychology*, **71**, 50–73.

Lader, M. H. (1975). "The Psychophysiology of Mental Illness". Routledge and Kegan Paul, London.

Lader, M. H. and Wing, L. (1966). "Physiological Measures, Sedative Drugs and Morbid Anxiety". Oxford University Press. London.

Lapidus, L. B. and Schmolling, P. (1975). Anxiety, arousal and schizophrenia: a theoretical integration. *Psychological Bulletin*, **82**, 689–710.

Lindsley, D. B. (1951). Emotion. *In* "Handbook of Experimental Psychology" (Ed. S. S. Stevens), Chapman and Hall, London.

Lindsley, D. B. (1957). The reticular system and perceptual discrimination. *In* "Reticular Formation of the Brain" (Eds H. J. Jasper *et al*). Churchill, London.

Lykken, D. T. (1975). The role of individual differences in psychophysiological research, *In* "Research in Psychophysiology" (Eds P. H. Venables and M. J. Christie), Wiley, London.

Lykken, D. and Maley, M. (1968). Autonomic versus cortical arousal in schizophrenics and non-psychotics. *Journal of Psychiatric Research*, **6**, 21–32.

McGhie, A. (1969). "Pathlogy of Attention". Penguin, Harmondsworth.

Mackworth, J. F. (1969). "Vigilance and Habituation". Penguin, Harmondsworth.

Mackworth, N. H. (1950). Researches in the measurement of human performance. MRC Special Report No. 268, H.M.S.O., London.

Malmo, R. B. (1959). Activation: a neuropsychological dimension. *Psychological Review*, **66**, 367–386.

Mangan, G. (in press). "The Biology of Human Personality". Pergamon, Oxford.

Moruzzi, G. and Magoun, H. W. (1949). Brainstem reticular formation and activation of the EEG. *Electroencephalography and Clinical Neurophysiology*, **1**, 455–473.

Neary, R. S. and Zuckerman, M. (1973). Sensation seeking. trait and state anxiety, and the electrodermal orienting reflex. *Psychophysiology*, **10**, 211.

Nebylitsyn, V. D. (1973). Current problems in differential psychophysiology. *Soviet Psychology*, **9**, 47–70.

Nebylitsyn, V. D. and Gray, J. A. (Eds) (1972). "Biological Bases of Individual Behaviour". Academic Press, New York and London.

O'Hanlon, J. (1965). Adrenalin, noradrenalin and performance in a visual vigilance task, *Science*, **150**, 507–509.

Ornstein, R. E. (1972). "The Psychology of Consciousness". Freeman, San Francisco.

Pavlov, I. P. (1935). General types of animal and human higher nervous activity. *In* "Selected Works" (Translation, S. Belsky). Foreign Languages Publishing House, Moscow.

Regan, D. (1972). "Evoked Potentials in Psychology, Sensory Physiology and Clinical Medicine". Chapman and Hall, London.

Routtenberg, A. (1968). The two-arousal hypothesis: reticular formation and limbic system. *Psychological Review*, **75**, 51–80.

Samuel, I. (1959). Reticular mechanisms and behaviour. *Psychological Bulletin*, **56**, 1–25.

Schwartz, G. E. and Shapiro, D. (Eds) (1976). "Consciousness and Self-Regulation. Advances in Research", vol. I. Wiley, London.

Shagass, C. (1954). The sedation threshold. A measure for estimating tension in psychiatric patients. *Electroencephalography and Clinical Neurophysiology*, **6**, 221–233.

Shagass, C., Straumanis, S. J. J. and Overton, D. A. (1975). Psychiatric diagnosis and EEG evoked response relationships. *Neuropsychobiology*, **1**, 1–15.

Sharpless, S. and Jasper, H. (1956). Habituation of the arousal reaction. *Brain*, **76**, 655–666.

Siegel, R. H. and West, L. J. (Eds) (1975). "Hallucinations, Behaviour, Experience and Theory". Wiley, New York.

Stennett, R. G. (1957). The relationship of alpha amplitude to the level of palmar skin conductance. *Electroencephalography and Clinical Neurophysiology*, **9**, 131–138.

Stern, R. M. (1966). Performance and physiological arousal during two vigilance tasks varying in signal presentation rate. *Perceptual and Motor Skills*, **23**, 691–700.

Sternbach, R. A. (1960). Two independent indices of activation. *Electroencephalography and Clinical Neurophysiology*, **12**, 609–611.

Stevens, J. M. and Derbyshire, A. J. (1958). Shifts along the alert–repose continuum during remission of catatonic "stupor" with amobarbital. *Psychosomatic Medicine*, **20**, 99–107.

Surwillo, W. W. and Quilter, R. E. (1965). The relation of frequency of spontaneous skin potential responses to vigilance and to age. *Psychophysiology*, **1**, 272–276.

Venables, P. H. (1963). The relationship between level of skin potential and fusion of paired light flashes in schizophrenic and normal subjects. *Journal of Psychiatric Research*, **1**, 279–287.

Venables, P. H. (1964). Input dysfunction in schizophrenia. *In* "Progress in Experimental Personality Research" (Ed. B. A. Maher), vol. 1. Academic Press, New York.

Venables, P. H. (1973). Input regulation and psychopathology. *In* "Psychopathology: Contributions from the Social, Behavioural and Biological Sciences" (Eds M. Hammer, R. Salzinger and S. Sutton). Wiley, New York.

Wilder, J. (1957). The law of initial values in neurology and psychiatry. *Journal of Nervous and Mental Diseases*, **125**, 73–86.

Williams, R. B., Bittker, T. E., Buchsbaum, M. S. and Wynne, L. (1975). Cardiovascular and neurophysiologic correlates of sensory intake and rejection. I. Effect of cognitive tasks. *Psychophysiology*, **12**, 427–433.

Woody, E. Z. and Claridge, G. S. (1977). Psychoticism and thinking. *British Journal of Social and Clinical Psychology*, **16**, 241–248.

Yerkes, R. M. and Dodson, J. D. (1908). The relation of strength of stimulus to rapidity of habit formation. *Journal of Comparative Neurology and Psychology*, **18**, 459–482.

Zuckerman, M. (1971). Physiological measures of sexual arousal in the human. *Psychological Bulletin*, **75**, 297–329.

Zuckerman, M. (1972). Sensation seeking and habituation of the electrodermal orienting response. *Psychophysiology*, **9**, 267.

Zuckerman, M. (1974). The sensation seeking motive. *In* "Progress in Experimental Personality Research" (Ed. B. Maher), vol. 7. Academic Press, New York and London.

Zuckerman, M., Murtaugh, T. and Siegal, J. (1974). Sensation seeking and cortical augmenting-reducing. *Psychophysiology*, **11**, 535–542.

5 Schizophrenia: An Abnormality of Consciousness?

C. D. FRITH

CRC Division of Psychiatry, Harrow

Prologue

Oh, Oh dog biscuit. And when he is happy he doesn't get snappy. Please please to do this. Then Henry, Henry, Frankie, you didn't meet him. You didn't even meet me. The glove will fit, what I say. Oh! Kai-Yi, Kai-Yi. Sure, who cares when you are through? How do you know this? Well then, oh cocoa know, thinks he is a grandpa again. He is jumping around. No hoboe and phoboe I think he means the same thing. . . . Oh mamma I can't go on through with it. Please oh! And then he clips me. Come on. Cut that out. We don't owe a nickel. Hold it instead hold it against him. . . . How many good ones and how many bad ones? Please I had nothing with him. He was a cowboy in one of the seven days a week fights. No business no hangout no friends nothing. Just what you pick up and what you read. . . . This is a habit I get. Sometimes I give it up and sometimes I don't. . . . The sidewalk was in trouble and the bears were in trouble and I broke it up. Please put me in that room. Please keep him in control. . . . Please mother don't tear don't rip. That is something that shouldn't be spoken about. Please get me up, my friends, please look, the shooting is a bit wild and that kind of shooting saved a man's life. . . . Please mother you pick me up now. Do you know me? No, you don't scare me. They are Englishmen and they are a type I don't know who is best they or us. Oh sir get the doll a roofing. You can play jacks and girls do that with a soft ball and play tricks with it. No no and it is no. It is confused and it says no. A boy has never wept nor dashed a thousand kim. And you hear me?. . . All right look out look out. Oh my memory is all gone. A work relief. Police. Who gets it? I don't know and I don't want to know but look out. It can be traced. He changed for the worst. Please look out. My fortunes have changed and come back and went back since that. . . . They dyed my shoes. Open those shoes. . . . Police mamma Helen mother please take me out. I will settle the indictment. Come on open the soap duckets. The chimney sweeps. Talk to the sword. Shut up

you got a big mouth! Please help me get up. Henry Max come over here.
French Canadian bean soup. I want to pay. Let them leave me along.

Arthur Flegenheimer[1]

1 Abnormalities of conscious processes

The nature and purpose of conscious and unconscious processes have
been considered in great detail by both psychoanalytic and existential
psychiatrists. Distinctions between conscious and unconscious processing similar to those more recently recognized by experimental psychologists have also been described. It is therefore surprising that no
taxonomy of possible pathologies of consciousness has been constructed. Only one abnormality of consciousness seems to play any
major role in the description of psychiatric patients. This concerns the
relationship between type of processing and wakefulness which are
considered to be intimately related in normal states. Thus rather than a
dichotomy between conscious and unconscious processes, the continuum
from unconscious/sleep to conscious/wakeful is considered important.
Abnormalities of consciousness therefore result when a type of processing appears which is incompatible with the associated level of wakefulness.

1.1 Clouding of consciousness

The most commonly described symptom of this kind is "clouding of
consciousness". As the name graphically suggests, in this state conscious processing occurs in a kind of fog. In mild cases perceptions and
memories are dim, and thought is difficult and slow. In more serious
cases consciousness becomes fragmented with no consistent flow of
events. The patient performs a series of isolated, unconnected acts.
Introspection as to his state of mind becomes impossible. An extreme
pathology of consciousness of this type is found in amentia (or subacute
delirious state). This state is characterized by a total lack of thought,
haphazard associations, fragmentation of sequences and the random
performance of old habits.

[1]Alias "Dutch Schultz," who in the early thirties was the most powerful racketeer and
bootlegger in New York City. The above are some of his dying words after he was shot,
with three others of his gang, in a Newark bar on October 23, 1935. They were taken
down in the city hospital by F. J. Long, stenographer of the Newark Police Department,
and were later printed in *Gang Rule in New York*, by Grain Thompson and Allen Raymond
(Dial Press, 1940).

. . .the psychic life is, as it were, disintegrated into a host of fragments since particular acts of object-awareness appear haphazardly and follow the individual's old habits without any relation to previous and subsequent acts. The rules of association, perseveration and a haphazard bondage to sense perceptions alone prevail and govern the sequence of conscious contents mechanically. Chance objects that enter the field of vision are noted and named, but immediately another idea replaces them aroused by some meaningless association. Alliterations of words, rhymes and similar things dominate the contents of talk. The investigator's questions are thoughtlessly repeated without rhyme or reason and change abruptly.

Jaspers, 1972, p. 594

A famous example of the kind of rambling speech associated with this state are the last words of "Dutch Schultz" after he was shot in a Newark bar in 1935 (Thompson and Raymond, 1940). As with most of these states there is afterwards a lasting gap in memory for the period of abnormal consciousness. These states of altered consciousness can be associated with concussion, epilepsy and fever (delirium). The level of processing found in this abnormal state of consciousness is probably also found quite normally in the twilight period close to the onset of sleep. However here no actions are performed.

In terms of the distinctions between conscious and unconscious processing discussed elsewhere in this volume, a patient suffering from amentia appears to show unconscious processing in the absence of conscious processing. Thus automatic actions and associations seem to be occurring without the benefit of any higher-order controlling system to link them together. This abnormality is consistent with Rozin's (1976) characterization of cognitive processes as a hierarchical system in which consciousness at the top of the hierarchy enables the organism to make use of a large set of unconscious routines for novel and general purposes although they were originally developed for specific functions.

1.2 Consciousness as a monitor system

One may conceive of the various unconscious subroutines as having a goal-directed property so that once set in action they continue to function until their goal is reached (cf. TOTE systems). At this point the higher-level system that we assume is conscious must decide on the next course of action (subroutine) to set in train. (The higher-level system that we assume is conscious must decide on the next course of action (subroutine) to set in train.) The higher-level system must also take action if a subroutine fails. I would suggest that this failure occurs not because of overload, but because a stimulus configuration or context occurs which is not in the repertoire of the automatic routine. This could occur either as a result of a novel environmental event or as a result of a novel error on the part of the subject.) If this happens a more appropriate routine must be selected. In either case the higher-level controlling system equated with conscious processes is responsible for selecting and setting into action subroutines to deal with an ever changing environment. Mandler (1975) has suggested that consciousness is necessary both for selecting subroutines and for "trouble shooting" when they fail. Shallice (1972) has taken this particular aspect of consciousness somewhat further and suggested that it is in addition necessary for alternative and competing subroutines to be suppressed while the one originally selected is carried out. This property is necessary for an efficient executive system in order that once a choice of action has been made it will be carried out without prevarication until the goal is reached or the action fails. In amentia it appears that this higher level conscious controlling system has ceased to operate. As a result subroutines are selected at random and in addition other subroutines may interrupt the flow of action before a goal is reached. Thus old habits (automatized activities) are performed at random and sequences of behaviour are fragmented. The haphazard associations presumably reflect the uncontrolled action of automatized perceptual processes.

If we conceive of consciousness as a controlling and selecting mechanism for various specific subroutines then it has a number of similarities with the monitor system of a computer. Such a system "runs" the specified programs, calling in routines for operating keyboards, teletypes, etc. as required. With such a system it is relatively easy to find an error in one of the subroutines since the monitor can usually abandon the routine when it fails and probably give some indication as to the type of error that occurred. However it is extremely difficult to identify an error in the monitor system itself, since there is no higher-order controller to take over when it fails. Subroutines may continue to run without control giving a totally misleading impression as to the location and nature of the fault.

It seems very plausible to assume the same problems arise when we study cognitive deficits in people rather than computers. If the fault lies in the "cognitive unconscious" involving faculties such as short-term memory, language and motor skills, then the subject will very probably be aware of it and be able to to describe some of its manifestations. Even if he is not aware of the fault, as might be the case for example with a visual field defect, it will be relatively easy to identify by asking the subject to perform an appropriate task. If, however, it is the higher-order conscious monitoring system that is at fault then the subject's introspections are likely to be misleading. Furthermore it will be extremely difficult to interpret the results of any task given to the subject. The vast majority of tests used by clinical psychologists are designed to identify faults in the unconscious subroutines. Thus there are tests of short- and long-term memory, language comprehension and expression, manual dexterity, picture recognition, mental arithmetic and so on. If these cannot even be correctly called into action then effectively the task being performed by the subject is not that intended by the psychologist.

Clearly then it would be very difficult to define specific test results that could be interpreted as characteristic of a defect in the higher-order controlling system involving consciousness. On the contrary the resulting defects are likely to be multiple and diffuse. It is, no doubt, for this reason that disorders of consciousness play such a small role in psychiatric diagnosis and psychological testing. As far as I am aware no attempt has yet been made to devise tests for clinical use which reveal faults specific to the higher-order conscious controlling mechanism.

It might be more fruitful to approach the problem from the other direction. That is to propose a defect in the system involving consciousness and attempt to deduce what various cognitive disorders might result. The remainder of this essay will be devoted to such an attempt with particular reference to the various cognitive disorders associated with schizophrenia.

1.3 The problem of schizophrenia

Schizophrenia has remained among the most mysterious of mental disorders particularly in terms of its symptoms. These include *hallucinations* usually in the form of hearing voices (e.g. hearing one's own thoughts spoken aloud), *delusions* (e.g. believing that thoughts are being inserted or removed from one's mind) and *thought disorder* which is manifested in abnormal speech which is fluent, but makes little sense. It is striking that two of the most important symptoms from a diagnostic point of view (Feighner *et al.*, 1972; Wing *et al.*, 1974) are hallucinations and delusions which can only be revealed in the introspections of the patient. The difficulty we have in dealing with schizophrenic symptoms has been formally incorporated into a diagnostic system by Jaspers (1972). He proposed that the symptoms of schizophrenia (and other psychotic states) can be characterized as those which cannot be understood since they are entirely outside normal experience. This is in contrast with other symptoms (e.g. depression) which can be understood since they do occur in normal experience although rarely.

Problems of a different nature have arisen in psychological studies of schizophrenia. The literature is filled with failures to replicate and with claims that schizophrenic patients may show a particular pattern of results or else its opposite. For examples in investigations of size constancy some patients may show overconstancy while others show underconstancy (Price and Eriksen; 1966). Perhaps the safest claim for any investigator to make is the schizophrenic patients will show greater variations in performance than controls. Not surprisingly these confusions and difficulties have lead to the suggestion that the term schizophrenia covers a number of different entities. Nevertheless since the syndrome was first described by Kraepelin in 1919 (see Kraepelin, 1971) the diagnosis has continued to be widely used by psychiatrists. Recently various standardized diagnostic procedures have been developed (Wing *et al.*, 1974) and when these are rigorously applied it is found that the proportion of schizophrenics in the population remains remarkably constant in situations as different as New York and Agra (India) (World Health Organisation, 1973). In addition a large amount of evidence has accumulated showing that the symptoms of schizophrenia respond only to drugs with a very specific action on the central nervous system (blocking dopamine receptors) (Crow *et al.*, 1976).

I would like to suggest that the problems that have arisen in understanding the symptoms of this disease and in defining the underlying cognitive deficits result, not from an attempt to explain many different disorders as if they were one, but from the difficulties in characterizing a defect in the higher-order cognitive mechanisms that involve consciousness.

1.4 The "defective filter" theory of schizophrenia

The hypothetical deficit explaining the performance of schizophrenic patients on psychological tests that has best withstood the passage of time is the "defective filter" (Payne *et al.*, 1964; Cromwell, 1968). This notion very much stems from the claim by many patients that they are overwhelmed by stimulation.

"It was as if parts of my brain awoke which had been dormant, and I became interested in a wide assortment of people, events, places and ideas which normally would make no impression on me. . . The walk of a stranger in the street could be a 'sign' to me which I must interpret. Every face in the windows of a passing street car would be engraved on my mind, all of them concentrating on me and trying to pass me some sort of message. . . a hodge-podge of unrelated stimuli were distracting me from things which should have had my undivided attention. . . I had very little ability to sort the relevant from the irrelevant. . . Completely unrelated events became intricately connected in my mind."

MacDonald, 1960

Such experiences and abnormal performance in various test situations have been explained in terms of a defective filter which no longer separates relevant from irrelevant stimuli so that all stimuli impinge on the awareness of the patient. There are a number of difficulties with this explanation of the psychological aspects of schizophrenia.

Firstly little has been made of the relationship between the defective filter and the major symptoms (hallucinations, delusions and thought disorder). It is not at all clear how these symptoms would follow from such a deficit. Secondly the deficit does not account for the various difficulties with response selection (Broen and Storms, 1967) that are often found in schizophrenic patients. Thirdly, since it is clear that filtering of some sort has a major role at all stages of information processing, a general filtering deficit would lead to a severe reduction in cognitive abilities more akin to that found in subnormality than in schizophrenia. It is possible to find patients successfully carrying out demanding jobs (e.g. accountancy) while at the same time experiencing persistent hallucinations and delusions. It is cearly necessary to specify at which stage of information processing the filtering deficit occurs. Having made the distinction between conscious and unconscious processes perhaps it will be possible to specify more precisely the stage at which the breakdown in filtering might occur. I would like to suggest that it is not a general filtering deficit that underlies schizophrenia, but a specific deficit concerning the selection of information that enters awareness. There is thus no fault in the functioning of the various automatic routines that normally function below this level. As a result the sufferer can function fairly well in many situations. I shall now consider how this defect might result in the symptoms and the cognitive defects found in schizophrenia.

2 Awareness of automatic processes

Carr (1979) has reviewed some of the evidence that the learning of a skill involves a strategy from a conscious stringing together of a number of small units of action to the automatic unconscious performance of the skill as a whole unit. Once the skill has become automatic it can be carried out more smoothly and more rapidly. Furthermore once a skill has become automatic and needs little conscious attention for its performance it can be carried out at the same time as other skills. These automatic skills can be quite complex and include not only motor skills such as riding a bicycle and producing speech, but also perceptual skills such as reading and understanding speech. I hypothesize that in schizophrenia a defect occurs in the mechanism that allows these processes to operate below the level of awareness. Among other advantages automatic unconscious processes can be carried out quickly and fluently. If they become conscious these advantages are likely to be lost since the patient will experience difficulty in preventing himself from consciously interfering with the running of the routines. For example Underwood (1977) has shown in normal subjects that awareness of a process can materially alter that process. Thus we would expect schizophrenic patients to have difficulty with automatic processes performing them more slowly and less fluently than before the illness. Such problems have indeed been reported by patients.

"None of my movements come automatically now. I've been thinking too much about them, even walking properly, talking properly and smoking — doing anything. And if I do something like going for a drink of water, I've got to go over every detail — find cup, walk over, turn tap, turn tap off, drink it."

Chapman, 1966

"I can't move and hear things or move my eyes and talk at the same time. I can't move and do something else at the same time."

Chapman, 1963

A general slowness has for a long time been recognized as one of the characteristic features of schizophrenia (Babcock and Levy, 1940). More recently this has been confirmed in a number of studies of reaction time using an information processing paradigm (e.g. Marshall, 1973). On the basis of these studies Hemsley (1976) has concluded that the principal contribution to this slowness comes from response selection. This is what we would expect if the patients were trying to perform a normally automatic process consciously.

This difficulty with automatic processes should equally apply to perceptual routines. Such routines are essentially concerned with selecting and combining a large number of cues. If the subject becomes conscious of these processes he will not only be slowed down, but will also tend to overemphasize some cues at the expense of others since he cannot handle a large number of cues simultaneously with limited capacity conscious processes.

2.1 Size constancy

Inferring the absolute size of an object in various situations is a largely automatic skill requiring the selection and integration of many cues. A large number of studies have found schizophrenic patients to perform this task abnormally. However, there is no consensus as to whether they show under or overconstancy. Price and Eriksen (1966) have attempted to resolve this impasse by suggesting that schizophrenics are always inaccurate, but may make their errors in different directions. This is consistent with our expectations if the subjects are trying consciously to perform normally automatic perceptual processes. They overemphasize one cue (e.g. retinal size) at the expense of others. Which cue is selected could be largely a matter of chance, but the end result will be symstematically inaccurate processing.

2.2 Perceptual integration

Clearly if a subject is required to perform a task in which cues normally automatically integrated are to be considered separately then the schizophrenic patient should have an advantage. Some evidence for this has been found in a preliminary study (Frith and Frith, 1978) in which subjects were required to sort fifteen faces or abstract designs into three groups. The objects were constructed from five variable features which acted as cues for the sorting task. In the faces these cues were such things as the size of the eyes and the length of the chin. Normally these cues are integrated and the face is seen as a whole. For the abstract designs the cues were five black lines of varying thickness arranged in a column.

These cues tend to be seen separately. For both sets of objects 4 cues went together to form three distinct groups. In one condition the fifth cue was constant and therefore irrelevant to the grouping. In the other condition the fifth cue varied randomly. It was therefore also irrelevant to the grouping, but could act as a distractor. Examples of the sets are shown in Fig. 1. Clearly it should be more difficult to ignore the distracting cue when it is integrated with the others. On the other hand when there is no distracting cue it should be easier to find the underlying groupings when the relevant cues are integrated. This was indeed the case with the control subjects (neurotic outpatients matched for age and sex with the schizophrenics). With the distracting cue they recovered the groupings for the faces better than for the abstract designs. When the distracting cue was present performance with the faces was impaired, but performance with the abstract designs did not change. The schizophrenic patients on the other hand sorted the faces no better than the abstract designs when no distractor was present, but were not adversely affected by the presence of the distractor in terms of sorting errors. Interestingly in terms of time to complete the task of sorting faces the schizophrenics took significantly longer when the distractor was present while the control subjects were not affected. This suggests that the controls did not even notice that the task with the distractor was

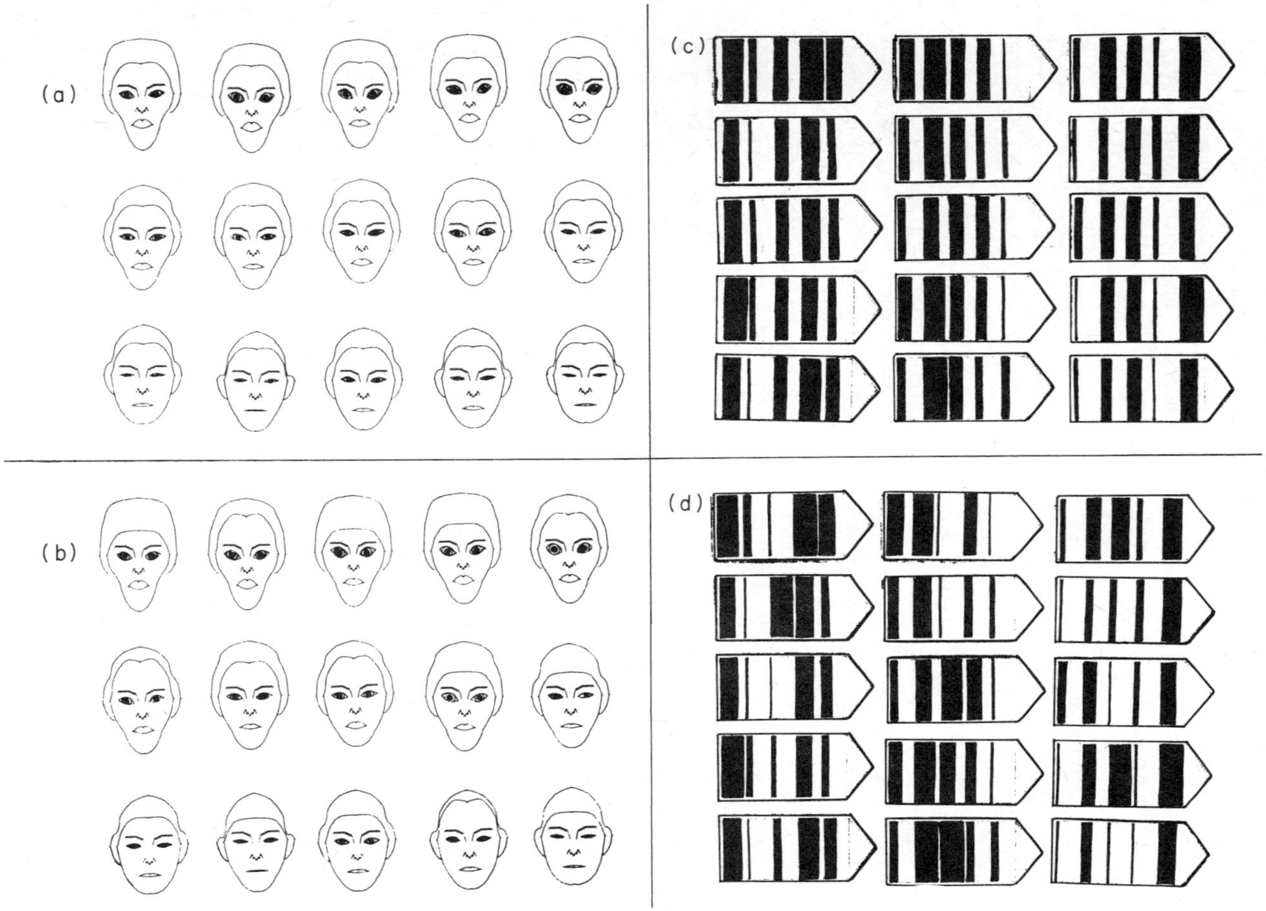

FIG. 1. (a) The three groups of five faces are defined by the states of the four features: hair, chin, eyes and mouth. The fifth feature, brow, remains constant. (b) The three groups are defined by the same 4 features as in (a), but the fifth feature varies randomly. (c) The three groups of five objects are defined by the thickness of the four outermost

somewhat more problematic so well integrated were the cues. Presumably their grouping was perfectly adequate given that the distractor was taken into account. The results of this experiment strongly suggest that the schizophrenic patients were failing to integrate the component cues of schematic faces when normally such cues are integrated. It is possible that this results from an awareness of the normally unconscious processes by which such cues are integrated.

2.3 Inner speech and thought

It is believed by some that thought is essentially internalized speech (Sokolov, 1972). It is assumed that thought develops rather like a motor skill. At first it is conscious and carried by audible speech, then this becomes subvocal and finally the process is carried out automatically and largely below the level of awareness. Becoming abnormally aware of these processes could clearly lead to the hallucination of "hearing one's thoughts spoken aloud".

The delusion of having thoughts "inserted into the mind" might also arise from an awareness of these normally unconscious thought processes. Hennell (1967) described vivid thoughts and images racing through his mind in a semidream stage: "Neither will nor thought of my own possessed my mind, but an urgent, continuous stream of thoughts and directions."

2.4 Delusions

The flooding of consciousness with stimuli not normally noticed is a common subjective experience of schizophrenic patients and the basis of the "defective filter" theory. Normally the stimuli that reach awareness do so because they are likely to be of some significance. Thus stimuli reaching awareness abnormally have to be explained by the subject in this light. This mechanism could underly certain delusions in which the patient not only notices and remembers many trivial stimuli, but believes that they have a special significance in relation to himself. Maher (1974) among others has suggested that delusions arise not from abnormal processes of deduction and logic, but from normal thinking processes applied to abnormal perceptions. Requiring normal people to notice and document trivial events, as in an information collecting agency, should also induce attempts to read the hidden significance of the events. This might be the origin of some of the more bizarre conspiracy theories that emanate from journalists and intelligence agencies from time to time.

3 Multiple meanings and actions

If processes normally carried out below the level of awareness become conscious then the simultaneity of activities possible in the unconscious will also become a feature of consciousness. This will of course be extremely distracting. Having chosen to attend to one task the sufferer will not be able to avoid noticing other things. Distractability is indeed a well-known feature of schizophrenia (Payne and Lairds, 1967; Rappaport, 1968).

"If I am talking to somebody they need only to cross their legs or stratch their heads and I am distracted and forget what I was saying."
                                             McGhie and Chapman, 1961

3.1 Dichotic listening

In a dichotic listening task for example, schizophrenic patients have considerable difficulty in shadowing one task while ignoring the second. They also show many intrusions from the secondary task (Richardson, 1976).

3.2 Habituation

Habituation provides an even simpler paradigm in which unconscious processing is implicated. In this task a series of stimuli are presented (pure tones, words, patterns, etc.). Initially the subject will show an orienting response to these stimuli (e.g. a skin conductance response), but after five or six stimuli such responding ceases and the subject is said to have habituated. If, however, a novel stimulus is presented (tone with different pitch, pattern with different symmetry, etc.) the response will be re-elicited. Clearly the subject must analyse the stimuli sufficiently to know what is novel and therefore needs to enter awareness (Sokolov, 1966). Deakin *et al.* (1979) and Frith *et al.* (1978) have found that a proportion of drug-free schizophrenic patients fail to habituate to a series of simple tones and that this failure relates to the severity of their symptoms. This result would be expected if the patients were failing to inhibit awareness of the unconscious processing by which the novelty of the stimulus is checked.

3.3 Multiple word meanings

Marcel (1976) has shown that while the many meanings of an ambiguous word are present simultaneously in the unconscious only one meaning arrives in consciousness. The same effect has been demonstrated by Underwood (1979) using an entirely different paradigm. Both these experiments also suggest that when the process of word association occurs below the level of awareness retrieval of other words can be facilitated, but is never inhibited. It seems likely that only conscious processing results in the inhibition of word retrieval. One of the more explicit statements of these two processes is given by Posner and Snyder (1975). The first process is called spreading activation and occurs below the level of awareness. It is assumed that a stimulus automatically activates its logogen (a representation of a word in long-term memory, Morton, 1969) and that this activation automatically spreads to adjacent semantically related logogens. The important properties of spreading activation are that it is fast acting, it occurs without awareness and it does not affect unrelated logogens. Hence it can only facilitate and never inhibit retrieval. The second process involves limited capacity conscious attention and has properties almost exactly the opposite of spreading activation. It is slow acting, it cannot operate without awareness and while it facilitates retrieval from logogens on which it is focused it inhibits retrieval from semantically unrelated logogens on which it is not focused. Many of the predictions that can be derived from these two processes have been confirmed by Neely (1977) using a primed lexical decision task. For the patients with the defect of consciousness I am hypothesizing the inhibition of spreading activation by conscious attention should fail.

There is much evidence that schizophrenic patients attach unlikely or inappropriate meanings to words.

For example, Ogden (1947), a factory foreman, said that whenever he heard the term "green gauges", he automatically thought of "green-gages" the fruit. Only when he realized that this meaning made no sense did he think of the other meaning of the sound "gauges". Oppenheimer (1975) placed a key and a book of matches before a patient and asked her to produce a sentence containing words for both objects. She replied, "This key matches a lock". Errors of this kind lead Broen and Storms (1967) to put forward the notion of "collapsed response hierarchies" by which the most appropriate meaning of a word in a particular context no longer had the highest probability of occurring. Often the patient seems to give the most frequent meaning rather than the one appropriate to the context. Allen, in an unpublished BSc project, presented subjects with word pairs to which a single word association was to be given. The second word of the stimulus pair was always ambiguous while the first either primed one of the two possible meanings or was neutral (e.g. tree-palm, hand-palm, cage-palm). It was found that schizophrenic patients, particularly those currently showing symptoms of hallucination, delusions or thought disorder, were significantly more likely than controls to give responses to the secondary, unprimed meaning of the ambiguous word.

De Silva and Hemsley (1977) used the cloze procedure in which subjects are presented with mutilated texts and have to fill in the missing words. Normally the more context there is available around each missing word the better the task is performed. Acute schizophrenic patients, however, showed an increase in errors when more context surrounded the missing word. This clearly would be expected if each word of context actually increased the number of multiple and irrelevant associations of which the patient was aware, rather than decreasing the number of alternatives for the missing word.

3.4 Thought disorder

This failure to inhibit alternative meanings of words so that multiple and inappropriate meanings are present in consciousness could well account for some aspects of the symptom of thought disorder. Patients with this disorder are unable to stick to a single thread of conversation, showing for example the phenomenon called "knight's move" in which they suddenly jump to a different, but remotely related topic. This and other features could clearly result from a failure to inhibit the awareness of alternative and irrelevant meanings and implications of words.

Critchley (1964) quotes an example of a patient whose speech begins perfectly normally, but then gets carried away on a string of loose associations.

"See the committee about me coming home for Easter on my 24th birthday. I hope all is well at home. How is father getting on? Never mind, there is hope, heaven will come, time heals all wounds, rise again glorious Greece and come to Hindoo Heavens. . ."

The same phenomenon seems to occur in reading.

"I try to read even a paragraph in a book, but it takes me ages because each bit I read starts me thinking in ten different directions at once."

McGhie and Chapman, 1961

3.5 Multiple task performance

The very distractability of schizophrenics might, in certain circumstances, be to their advantage. Many experiments mentioned in other chapters of this volume concern what happens when a person has to perform two tasks at once. In these circumstances performance of the secondary task is delayed especially when the primary task is making heavy demands of information processing, e.g. response selection (Posner and Keele, 1969; Posner and Boies, 1971). For the schizophrenic patient in these circumstances secondary perceptions and irrelevant responses will not so efficiently be inhibited from reaching awareness and they might therefore be able to perform such tasks better.

4 Premature activation of responses

Normally a percept reaches awareness when all the underlying information processing has been completed and the most plausible reconstruction of the original stimulus has been achieved. At this point the subject decides what to do about the stimulus and makes a response. Because of his abnormal awareness of unconscious processes the schizophrenic patient may make such an interpretation of stimuli and hence make the associated response prematurely. As a result the interpretation of the stimulus of which he is aware is likely to be an implausible one based more on prior expectations than the physical properties of the stimulus. This is particularly likely to happen with speech or speech-like sounds since the processing involved is particularly complex and there is no possibility of rechecking auditory stimuli as there usually is for visual stimuli. Such abnormal mechanisms could underly some schizophrenic hallucinations. If this is the case then some hallucinations should be associated with real sounds of some sort. This is usually considered by psychiatrists not to be the case. However some patients do describe both the real sound and the voice it carries. Thus, "When the door slams I hear some one say, 'Get out'." This is known as a functional hallucination (Hamilton, 1976) but is rare.

Hallucinations are obviously very difficult to study since the major source of information about them must come from the patients' introspections. If the patient himself is unaware that his hallucinations are being "carried" by real sounds then it will be extremely difficult for an observer to judge what is happening. In many cases he may not even notice many of the possible sound sources that might be influencing the patient. A very similar problem arises in the study of "spontaneous" retrieval from memory (see Underwood, this volume) where it is possible that priming events can always be found for the supposedly spontaneous retrievals). As a result most of the evidence for the contention that hallucinations are carried by real sounds must come from indirect sources.

Dixon (1971) has observed that normal subjects will make bizarre and remote responses, akin to those of schizophrenic patients, when they are forced to read words with insufficient information in a sub-liminal perception experiment. This is equivalent to the premature interpretation hypothesized to occur in schizophrenia.

If hallucinations are due to misinterpretations of sounds then they should be reduced by increasing the signal-to-noise ratio so that even a premature interpretation is likely to be correct. Slade (1974) has found that auditory hallucinations are reduced in intensity when patients have to perform an auditory information processing task. Such a task effectively increases the signal-to-noise ratio by providing a simple clear-cut and predictable signal.

Even normals sometimes experience hallucinations when the signal-to-noise ratio is dramatically reduced as in sensory deprivation experi-ments (Schulman, et al., 1967). Signal-to-noise ratio is also reduced in deafness and it is therefore interesting that Cooper et al. (1976) have observed a positive relationship between deafness and schizophrenic symptoms in the elderly.

In the Verbal Transformation Effect discovered by Warren and Gregory (1958) the same word is repeated over and over again. This produces a "satiation" of the true interpretation and changes to a number of alternative interpretations are heard. Thus the task induces the kind of misinterpretations hypothesized to occur in schizophrenia. Slade (1976) found that when people with auditory hallucinations were subjected to the verbal transformation task they heard more extreme changes than those heard by the normal controls.

If schizophrenic patients are prone to misinterpret sounds as words then they should also have difficulty in interpreting real speech. McGhie and Chapman (1961) found patients who claimed that it was exhausting to keep up with the flow of words and to perceive them as integrated, meaningful units rather than as a jumble or babble of unrelated sounds. Both Moon et al. (1968) and Bull and Venables (1974) found that schizophrenic patients were more likely to misinter-pret words than controls in the absence of any straightforward hearing loss.

4.1 Speech disorder

I have already discussed below how the awareness of unconscious processes might make it difficult for a patient to stick to the topic of his conversation. The premature activation of responses discussed above could lead to the more severe abnormalities of speech associated with thought disorder. The same process of guessing and checking involved in the understanding of speech also applies to its production. The subject must select the appropriate word from the many more or less likely possibilities that are activated by its context. He must then select the appropriate phonemes to voice that word. Awareness of this process before it is complete is likely to lead to the production of inappropriate words or even nonsense and neologisms, both features of the speech of thought-disordered patients.

Sechehaye's patient (Sechehaye, 1951) said that she replaced real words with meaningless syllables like "gao" and "gibastow" because she believed that she was denied the privilege of using words to label her feelings. She said that she did not deliberately create new words, but that they came to her of themselves. There are superficial similarities between schizophrenic speech and certain kinds of aphasia. However the mechanism I have postulated would predict that the pause before nonsense or inappropriate words in schizophrenic speech should be shorter than usual. This is exactly the opposite of what is found in Jargon Aphasia (Butterworth, 1977).

Lecours and Vernier-Clement (1976) have compared "schizo-aphasia" with other kinds of aphasia in terms of content and quality of language. They conclude that the various aphasias are characterized by poverty of production at all levels, phonemic, morphemic and semantic. Schizophrenic speech, on the other hand, is characterized by an excessive richness of production at all these levels. For example the production of a succession of puns may occur at a level most normal people would find difficult to maintain. Schizophrenic patients seem "excessively aware of the polysemous nature of words". All these observations are consistent with hypothesis that schizophrenic patients have an abnormal awareness of the processes underlying speech production.

5 Conclusions

Postulating an awareness of the "cognitive unconsciousness" leads to the expectation of many diverse abnormalities in behaviour and in psychological test situations many of which seem to be observed in schizophrenic patients. However nearly all the evidence for an abnormality of consciousness in schizophrenia is indirect. There is an urgent need for a methodology for studying defects in the conscious monitoring system. It is to be hoped that the burgeoning interest shown by experimental psychologists in the distinction between conscious and unconscious processes will lead to such methodologies. It may be that schizophrenic patients will prove a most useful group for developing theory and methodology in this area, just as amnesic patients have in the field of memory.

Acknowledgements

My understanding of much of the theoretical background of this contribution was greatly increased by discussions with Tony Marcel and Tim Shallice. I am grateful to Geoff Underwood and Uta Frith for their comments on an earlier draft of this paper. Most of the accounts of the subjective experience of schizophrenia were extracted from Freedom (1974).

References

Babcock, H. and Levy, L. (1940). "Manual of Directions for the Revised Examination of the Measurement of Efficiency of Mental Functioning". Stoelting, Chicago.

Broen, W.C. and Storms, L.H. (1966). Lawful disorganization: the process underlying a schizophrenic syndrome. *Psychological Review*, **73**, 265–279.

Bull, H.C. and Venables, P.H. (1974). Speech perception in schizophrenia. *British Journal of Psychiatry*, **125**, 350–354.

Butterworth, B (1977). Hesitation and the production of neologism in jargon aphasia. Paper presented to the Experimental Psychology Society, Sheffield meeting.

Carr, T.H. (1979). Consciousness in models of human information processing: primary memory executive control and input regulation. *In* "Aspects of Consciousness (Eds G. Underwood and R. Stevens), vol. 1, pp. 123–149. Academic Press, London and New York.

Chapman, J. (1966). The early symptoms of schizophrenia. *British Journal of Psychiatry*, **112**, 225–231.

Chapman, J., Freeman, T. and McGhie, A. (1963). Clinical research in schizophrenia: the psychotherapeutic approach. *In* "Contributions to Modern Psychology" (Ed. D.E. Dulay Jr.). Oxford University Press, New York.

Cooper, A.F., Garside, R.F. and Kay, D.W.K. (1976). A comparison of deaf and non-deaf patients with paranoid and affective psychoses. *British Journal of Psychiatry*, **129**, 532–538.

Critchley, M. (1964). The neurology of psychotic speech. *British Journal of Psychiatry*, **110**, 353–364.

Cromwell, R.L. (1968). Stimulus redundancy and schizophrenia. *Journal of Nervous and Mental Diseases*, **146**(5), 360–375.

Crow, T.J., Deakin, J.F.W., Johnstone, E.C. and Longden, A. (1976). Dopamine and schizophrenia. *Lancet*, **ii**, 563–566.

Deakin, J.F.W., Baker, H.F., Frith, C.D., Joseph, M.H. and Johnstone, E.C. (1979). Arousal related to excretion of noradrenaline metabolites and clinical aspects of unmedicated chronic schizophrenic patients. *Journal of Psychiatric Research*, **15**, 57–65.

Dixon, W.F. (1971). Subliminal perception: the nature of a controversy. McGraw-Hill, London.

Feighner, J.P., Robins, E., Gaze, J.B., Woodruff, R.A., Winokur, G. and Munoz, R. (1972). Diagnostic criteria for use in psychiatric research. *Archives of General Psychiatry*, **26**, 57–63.

Freedom, B.J. (1974). The subjective experience of perceptual cognitive disturbance in schizophrenia: a review of autobiographical accounts. *Archives of General Psychiatry*, **30**, 333–340.

Frith, C. D. and Frith, Uta (1978). How do we perceive features when they form a Gestalt? Proceedings of the Experimental Psychology Society, Marburg.

Frith, C. D., Stevens, M., Johnstone, E. C. and Crow, T. J. (1979). Skin conductance responsivity during acute episodes of schizophrenia as a predictor of symptomatic improvement. *Psychological Medicine*, **9**, 101–106.

Hamilton, M. (1976). "Fish's Schizophrenia". John Wright & Sons, Bristol.

Hemsley, D. R. (1976). Stimulus uncertainty, response uncertainty, and stimulus–response compatibility as determinants of schizophrenic reaction time performance. *Bulletin of the Psychonomic Society*, **8**(6), 425–427.

Hennell, T. (1967). "The Witnesses". University Books, New Hyde Park, New York.

Jaspers, K. (1972). "General Psychopathology". Manchester University Press.

Kraepelin, E. (1971). "Dementia Praecox and Paraphrenia". (Translated by Barclay, R.M. and Robertson, G.M.), N.E. Krieger, New York.

Lecours, A.R. and Vernier-Clement, M. (1976). Schizophrenia and jargon aphasia. *Brain and Language*, **3**, 516–565.

MacDonald, N. (1960). Living with schizophrenia. *Canadian Medical Journal*, **82**, 218–221.

McGhie, A. and Chapman, J. (1961). Disorders of attention and perception in early schizophrenia. *British Journal of Medical Psychology*, **34**, 103–116.

Maher, B.A. (1974). Delusional thinking and perceptual disorder. *Journal of Individual Psychology*, **30**, 98–113.

Mandler, G. (1975). "Mind and Emotion". Wiley, New York.

Marcel, A.J. (1976). Unconscious reading. Paper given to the British Association for the Advancement of Science, Lancaster.

Marshall, W.L. (1977). Cognitive functioning in schizophrenia. *British Journal of Psychiatry*, **123**, 413–433.

Moon, A.F., Mefferd, R.B., Wieland, B.A., Pokorny, A.D. and Falconer, G.A. (1968). Perceptual dysfunction as a determinant of schizophrenic word associations. *Journal of Nervous and Mental Diseases*, **146** (1), 80–84.

Morton, J. (1969). Interaction of information in word recognition. *Psychological Review*, **76**, 165–178.

Neely, J.H. (1977). Semantic priming and retrieval from lexical memory. *Journal of Experimental Psychology: General*, **106**, 226–254.

Ogdon, J.A.H. (1947). "The Kingdom of the Lost". Bodley Head, London.

Oppenheimer, H. (1975). On the applicability of Karl Jasper's "Verstehende" psychology to some forms of schizophrenic thought and language disorder. *In* "Annual Review of Schizophrenic Syndrome" (Ed. R. Cancro), vol. 4. Brunner/Mazel, New York.

Payne, R.W. and Caird, W.K. (1967). Reaction time, distractability and over-inclusive thinking in psychotics. *Journal of Abnormal Psychology*, **72**, 112–121.

Payne, R.W., Caird, W.K. and Laverty, S.G. (1964). Overinclusive thinking and delusions in schizophrenic patients. *Journal of Abnormal Social Psychology*, **68**, 562–566.

Posner, M. I. and Boies, S. J. (1971). Components of attention. *Psychological Review*, **78**, 391–408.

Posner, M. I. and Keele, S. W. (1969). Attention demands of movement. *In* "Proceedings of the 16th International Congress of Applied Psychology". Swetts & Zeitlinger, Amsterdam.

Posner, M. J. and Snyder, C. R. R. (1973). Attention and cognitive control. *In* "Information Processing and Cognition: The Loyola Symposium" (Ed. R. L. Solso). Erlbaum, Hillsdale, New Jersey.

Price, R. H. and Eriksen, C. W. (1966). Size constancy in schizophrenia: a reanalysis. *Journal of Abnormal Psychology*, **71**(3), 155–160.

Rappaport, M. (1968). Attention to competing voice messages by nonacute schizophrenic patients: effects of message load, drugs, dosage levels and patient background. *Journal of Nervous and Mental Diseases*, **146**, 404–411.

Richardson, P. (1976). An investigation of cognitive disturbance in schizophrenia. Unpublished PhD Thesis, London University.

Rozin, P. (1976). The evolution of intelligence and access to the cognitive unconscious. *In* "Progress in Psychobiology and Physiological Psychology" (Eds J. M. Sprague and A. N. Epstein). Academic Press, New York and London.

Schulman, C. A., Milton, R. and Weinstein, S. (1967). Hallucinations and disturbances of affect, cognition, and physical state as a function of memory deprivation. *Perception and Motor Skills*, **25**, 1001–1024.

Sechehaye, M. (1951). "Autobiography of a Schizophrenic Girl". Grune & Stratton, New York.

Shallice, T. (1972). Dual functions of consciousness. *Psychological Review*, **79**, 383–393.

Silva, W. P. de and Hemsley, D. R. (1977). The influence of context on language perception in schizophrenia. *British Journal of Social and Clinical Psychology*, **16**, 337–345.

Slade, P. D. (1974). The external control of auditory hallucinations: an information theory analysis. *British Journal of Social and Clinical Psychology*, **13**, 73–79.

Slade, P. D. (1976). An investigation of psychological factors involved in the predisposition to auditory hallucinations. *Psychological Medicine*, **6**, 123–132.

Sokolov, Y. N. (1966). Orienting reflex as information regulator. *In* "Psychological Research in the USSR" (Eds A. Leontyev, A. Luriya and A. Smirnov), vol. 1, Progress Publishers, Moscow.

Sokolov, A. N. (1972). "Inner Speech and Thought". Plenum Press, New York.

Thompson, C. and Raymond, A. (1940). "Gang Rule in New York". Dial Press, New York.

Underwood, G. (1979). Memory systems and conscious processes. *In* "Aspects of Consciousness" (Eds G. Underwood and R. Stevens), vol. 1, pp. 91–121. Academic Press, London and New York.

Warren, M. and Gregory, R.L. (1958). An auditory analogue of the visual reversible figure. *American Journal of Psychology*, **71**, 612–613.

Wing, J.K., Cooper, J.E. and Sartorius, N. (1974). "The Description and Classification of Psychiatric Symptoms. An Instruction Manual for the PSE and Catego System". Cambridge University Press, London.

World Health Organization (1973). Report of the International Pilot Study of Schizophrenia, WHO, Geneva.

6 Hallucinogenic Drugs and Altered States of Consciousness

G. G. SHAW and J. CROSSLAND

Department of Pharmacy
University of Nottingham

1 Hallucinogenic drugs

1.1 Introduction

The deliberate induction of changes in perception by the use of drugs has held a fascination for mankind since time immemorial and has long been associated with witchcraft and religious rites. Even today, primitive groups and obscure religious sects continue to use hallucinogens in their ceremonial. In these circumstances, the consumption of the hallucinogens is deeply enshrined in ritual and the precise composition of the hallucinogenic cocktail is often a jealously guarded secret. A more recent development has been the widespread use of hallucinogens as a form of escapism. The ease with which both information and drugs can now be disseminated has led to the wide availability of an experience that was previously restricted to the knowledgeable or privileged few.

Contemporary interest in hallucinogenic drugs has led to the coining of a variety of supposedly descriptive synonyms. Some of these—for example, "delirient" and "fantastica"—have lost their popularity while others in current use inadequately reflect current thinking. Thus, the terms "psychotogen" and "psychotomimetic", which carry the implication that the drugs may generate psychoses or be used as valid models of psychotic conditions, are inappropriate, most investigators having come to believe that the hallucinations induced by drugs bear little relationship to those experienced in the psychoses and that truly psychotic reactions are only rarely precipitated by the drugs. Chronic amphetamine abuse provides a much better example of a model psychosis whose symptomatology closely resembles that of schizophrenia (Woodrow *et al.*, 1978). Rivalry among the champions of the different synonyms has reportedly produced some amusing exchanges. Thus,

Aldous Huxley in advocating the use of the term "phanerothyme" wrote:

> To make this mundane world sublime,
> Take half a gram of phanerothyme

to which Humphrey Osmond is alleged to have replied:

> To sink in hell or soar angelic
> You'll need a pinch of psychedelic.

Osmond has now abandoned this term because of its narrowness (Hoffer and Osmond, 1967) and like most of us he now prefers hallucinogen. It should be pointed out that the use of the word does nothing to indicate the mood and thought changes that are important components of the drug experience. It might be also desirable to introduce a subdivision to include those drugs that produce perceptual distortion without delusion. "Illusionogen" has been suggested as a suitable name for such substances, although it is to be hoped, if only on aesthetic grounds, that a more euphonious synonym can be coined.

In the present discussion, only those drugs that induce changes in perception, mood and thought as a prime component of their action will be mentioned. Others, such as alcohol or quinine, which induce these effects only as part of a toxic syndrome, are excluded.

1.2 Classification

It is as difficult to provide a generally acceptable classification of the hallucinogens as it is to define their activity. A simple chemical classification is inadequate because compounds like LSD that possess larger ring systems could be viewed as having indole or phenylethylamine moieties. Moreover, for some substances the relationship between chemical structure and hallucinogenic action is inadequately defined. In a similar fashion, a pharmacological sub-division into, for example, sympathomimetic, parasympatholytic and anaesthetic substances leaves some compounds unplaced and gives undue emphasis to the importance of these classical pharmacological effects for the genesis of hallucinations.

Nevertheless, for the sake of convenience in discussion it is desirable to attempt some form of classication and a somewhat arbitrary chemical division, as shown in Table 1, has been adopted here.

The various compounds will be discussed in the order in which they appear in Table 1.

TABLE 1
Classification of hallucinogenic drugs

Phenylethylamines
> Mescaline
> 2,5-methoxy-4-methyl amphetamine
> myristicin

LSD and its congeners

Indole alkylamines and β carbolenes
> psilocyn and psilocybin
> bufotenine
> dimethyltryptamine, diethyltryptamine
> harmine and harmaline

Multicyclic compounds
> tetrahydrocannabinols
> acetylcholine antagonists
> phencyclidine and its congeners

Muscimol

1.2.1 *Phenylethylamines*

a. *Mescaline*

It is appropriate to begin a discussion of hallucinogenic drugs with mescaline. Mescaline is the classical hallucinogen. It is a naturally occurring plant product whose use in religious rites in Mexico has a history of several hundred years. The Mexican Indians were in the habit of chewing the dried crowns or drinking an aqueous extract of a cactus indigenous to the Rio Grande region. This plant is characterized by the possession of white hairs that grow in clusters in the crown, which give the plant its native name "peyotl" or "peyote" (white fuzz). Modern knowledge of the drug is due to Louis Lewin who, in 1887, obtained some dried crowns for the Parke-Davis Laboratories in America and initiated the study of their actions. In recognition of this the cactus has been given the botanical name Anhalonium (or Lophophora) Lewini, though it is also referred to as A. Williamsi. Lewin's work inspired Heffter who successfully isolated the active phenylethylamine alkaloid (mescaline, Fig. 1) in 1896. More recent studies have shown that mescaline is also a constituent of Trichocereus pachanoi, a Peruvian cactus.

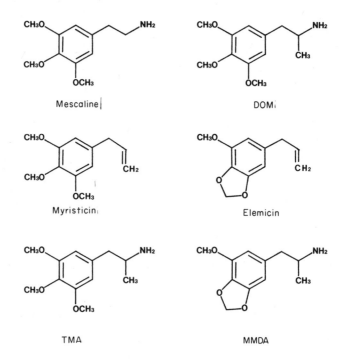

Mescaline

DOM

Myristicin

Elemicin

TMA

MMDA

FIG. 1. Phenylethylamine hallucinogens.

Hallucinogenic effects are produced by a minimum of three dried crowns (mescal buttons) or by 200–500 mg of the purified alkaloid. Based partly on his own experiences and partly on an analysis of the descriptions provided by others, Kluver (1926, 1928) produced the most complete accounts of the hallucinatory events provoked by mescaline. His accounts have never been bettered. They emphasize the fact that mescaline commonly gives rise to particularly vivid colour hallucinations accompanied by a marked increase in the perception of brightness. The colours may burst into life or may adopt symmetrical or richly patterned designs. Subjects are able to exert little influence on the forms they experience and the effects are observed whether the eyes are closed or open. Auditory hallucinations are uncommon, though external noises may provoke a coloured display. The colour intensity of objects in the visual field is also increased and these objects sometimes appear to move or be transformed into illusory images. Alterations in the perception of body images are also observed so that, for example, the digits of a hand may be perceived as being altered in size. The mood is not euphoric but there is awareness of an awesome experience.

It should be pointed out that the ingestion of mescaline is also accompanied by rather less pleasant somatic symptoms. These are those associated with autonomic disturbance and include slowing of the heart, nausea, dilatation of the pupil, headache and sweating. These somatic effects are more marked if the vegetable drug rather than mescaline itself is taken and some subjects have been discouraged from further experimentation by the unpleasant somatic effects produced by the intake of a single button, which provided an insufficient amount of mescaline to provoke hallucinations. Other isoquinoline alkaloids such as lophophorine and anhalonidine which are present in the plant may contribute to these unpleasant effects. These latter alkaloids are not hallucinogenic.

The effects of mescaline can be readily antagonized by the administration of major tranquillizers such as chlorpromazine. Thus, Schwarz *et al.* (1955) were able to antagonize the effects of 400 mg of mescaline sulphate within 5 mins by means of an intramuscular injection of 25 mg chlorpromazine. Prior to the advent of phenothiazines, barbiturates were also successfully employed to this end.

b. 2,5-Methoxy-4-methyl amphetamine (DOM)

This drug is a synthetic mescaline-like compound (Fig. 1) which was probably first consumed in the San Francisco Bay area. It has an amphetamine-like structure and it is not, therefore, surprising that its intake causes a markedly euphoric or excitatory state. Low doses of the drug produce an amphetamine-like state without hallucinations. The street name for this drug is STP. The origin of this name is a matter of conjecture and several versions are proposed. It has, for instance, been suggested that it arises because the "pep" produced by the drug is comparable to that allegedly induced in motor vehicle engines by the petroleum product that bears the same initials. Other plausible translations include "serenity, tranquillity and peace", "super terrific psychedelic" and the rather less likely "stop the police".

Although DOM is more potent than mescaline in that a 10–15 mg dose is sufficient to induce hallucinations which may last up to 3 days, it is also undoubtedly more toxic. Small does are associated with classical sympathomimetic effects such as stimulated respiration, dilatation of the pupils, an accelerated heart rate and increased blood pressure, whereas overdosage produces convulsions and sometimes death. Chlorpromazine is unsuccessful in antagonizing the toxic effects associated with overdosage although it may ameliorate the sympathomimetic effects seen with lower doses.

The 4-ethyl analogue (DOET) is equipotent with DOM (Snyder *et al.*, 1971) and its use is associated with more controllable mood changes.

c. Myristicin

Perhaps the most strange example of a hallucinogen in use today and certainly the most readily available is myristicin, the main constituent of the volatile oil which is extractable from the seed kernel of Myristica fragrans, the culinary nutmeg. The nutmeg is freely available in commerce and contains 5–15% by weight of the oil. Nutmeg is a favoured substance among alcoholics and other drug takers confined in penal institutions that deny them ready access to their more usual drugs. The fact that the oil was the source of the active constituent was first recognized in 1909 by H. H. Dale, that most illustrious English pharmacologist.

The unpalatability of nutmeg undoubtedly acts as a deterrent to any but the resolute. It is necessary to consume some six to eight spoonfuls of ground nutmeg taken as a suspension in water. Intake is associated with dry mouth, pupillary constriction with reddened, dry eyes and intense nausea which may provoke vomiting and thus nullify the exercise. Intense vasodilatation, manifested by flushing, may also occur. Eventually lethargy sets in and visual hallucinations occur. Consumers are aware of their environment and may be roused to communication. The effects may last for 24–36 hours and are likely to be followed by an unpleasant hangover with abdominal and muscle pains and an inability to concentrate or work. Myristicin is not an alkaloid since there is no nitrogen atom in the molecule. However, Shulgin (1966) has suggested that it may be metabolized *in vivo* to 3,4,5-trimethoxyamphetamine (TMA), a mescaline analogue (Fig. 1) which has been shown to be an active hallucinogen in a dose of 175 mg and is therefore about twice as potent as mescaline. Elemicin (Fig. 1), another natural constituent of nutmeg oil, may also be responsible for the hallucinogenic effect in that it may be converted *in vivo* to 3-methoxy-4,5-methylene dioxyamphetamine (MMDA) which is even more active than TMA.

1.2.2 *Lysergic acid diethylamide (LSD) and Ololiuqui*

Lysergic acid derivatives occur naturally in Claviceps purpurea, the ergot fungus that causes ergotism (St Anthony's fire). In 1938 Stoll and Hofmann at the Sandoz Laboratories in Basle, Switzerland, were using lysergic acid obtained by alkaline hydrolysis of the ergot alkaloid mixture as a starting material for the synthesis of ergometrine. The realization that the diethylamide derivative of lysergic acid (Fig. 2) would have a similar structure to nikethamide, a respiratory stimulant, led to

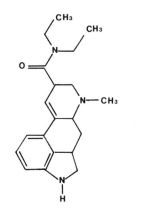

Lysergic acid diethylamide
LSD

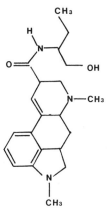

Methysergide

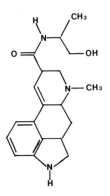

Ergometrine

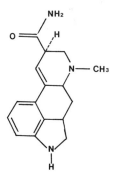

Lysergic acid amide
(in isolysergic acid amide the
planes of the amide and the
hydrogen are reversed)

FIG. 2. Lysergic acid diethylamide and some congeners.

the production of the diethylamide, using synthetic processes analogous to those used for nikethamide. Pharmacological testing of LSD demonstrated pronounced oxytoxic and weak vasoconstrictor actions but the hallucinogenic effects were not discovered until some years later when Hofmann accidentally ingested a minute quantity of the drug. Realizing that his hallucinatory state might have been brought about the LSD, Hofmann deliberately ingested what must have seemed the modest dose of 0.25 mg. The circumstances of that 1943 experiment are now well known and have been well described by Hofmann himself (Hofmann, 1970).

The effective dose of LSD is between 50 and 100 μg, though some individuals are sensitive to as little as 25 μg. Of the four possible isomers, only one form is active. This has the configuration found in the naturally occurring ergot alkaloids.

Within about 15 min of taking a dose of LSD, the consumer experiences autonomic effects. These include feelings of cold, sweating, dilatation of the pupil, headache and dry mouth but these peripheral effects are relatively slight unless milligram doses are consumed. With these larger doses nausea and vomiting are likely.

The effects of LSD are in many ways similar to those of mescaline. Colour perception is enhanced and the patterning associated with mescaline intake is also present. Proprioceptive perception is again altered and body images, particularly facial images, may be distorted. Although many skilled artists have made attempts to draw the images they have seen under the influence of LSD, few have subsequently been satisfied with the result. The imagery is very much dependent on the presence of external stimuli and focusing the subject's attention on a painting can be an effective way of producing imagery. Objects may develop unusual movements, changes in size or shape or they may pulsate. Hallucinations involving animals, people or scenes occur less frequently.

An effect which is quite commonly noted is the prolongation of after images so that rapid arm movement may be perceived as several arms in an arc, just as might be seen in a series of superimposed still photographs. Present and past perceptions may overlap and the sense of time is disturbed. Intellectual performance is impaired and there is difficulty in reasoning and concentration so that subjects perform poorly in tests. The subjects may experience bizarre ideas or ideas of reference.

One difference between LSD and mescaline is that the mood changes occurring under LSD cover the whole spectrum. Euphoria or a transcendental state of supreme happiness and peace are common but reactions of fear or anxiety may also occur. Phases of depression or acute paranoia are also often seen and these can lead to aggression or suicide. The unpredictable nature of the mood changes that might occur is a deterrent to some potential LSD users.

The effects of a moderate dose of LSD persist for some six to eight hours and they are often followed by a period of insomnia. Tolerance to LSD develops extremely rapidly so that repetition of the dose on successive days leads to a diminution of response on the first occasion and to its abolition on the second repetition. However, recovery is almost equally rapid so that a three to five days' period of abstinence is sufficient to fully restore sensitivity.

The effects of LSD, like those of mescaline, can be antagonized by barbiturates or major tranquillizers. It has also been reported that large doses of nicotinic acid effectively reverse the drug's effects.

Congeners of LSD tend to have a shorter duration of action and are often weaker than LSD itself. For example, the monoethylamide has only about five per cent of the activity of LSD. Methysergide (Sansert), which is used therapeutically in the prophylaxis of migraine, has only 0·5 % of the potency of LSD but even it has been subjected to abuse by those in search of the psychedelic experience.

The small round seeds of Rivea corymbosa known as ololiuqui (round object) which have long been used in ritual by the South American Indians, contain lysergide derivatives. These same substances are found in even greater quantity in the seeds of Ipomoea violacea, a violet flowered plant of the morning glory variety. Another recently discovered botanical source is the Hawaian baby woodrose Argyeia nervosa. The principal alkaloid constituents of these plants are lysergic acid amide (ergine) and isolysergic acid amide (isoergine) which occur in an admixture with other ergot alkaloids. Abuse of morning glory seeds, dates from an article in the New York Times of 11 July, 1963, which was subsequently reproduced in other journals and thus rapidly disseminated. Strangely enough, controlled laboratory studies have failed to substantiate the hallucinogenic effects of the seeds. Osmond, for example, has ingested a powder made from 100 seeds (Osmond, 1955). He reported apathy, withdrawal, listlessness and sedation but no hallucinations. Even more telling is the report of Isbell and Gorodetzky (1966) that the ingestion of 5 mg of an alkaloid mixture produced no hallucinations and little perceptual distortion. It may be that other components of the mixture is ololiuqui may have a synergistic action with the lysergide derivatives.

1.2.3 *Indole alkylamines and β carbolenes*

  a. *Psilocybin and psilocyn*

Psilocybin (Fig. 3) is the most potent member of the indole alkylamine group. It is present in a concentration of 0·2 to 0·4 % of the dry weight of the Southern Mexican mushroom Psilocybe mexicana. The use of this drug dates back to the Aztec civilization and the trivial name of "teonanacatl" (God's flesh) reflects the veneration in which tribal users held the plant. The effects of psilocybin are chronicled by Hoffer and Osmond (1967). The somatic and psychic effects of psilocybin are similar to those of LSD but are of a shorter duration. The maximum effect is exerted about one hour after intake and recovery is often complete within three hours. According to Heim and Wasson, the mood changes produced are pleasant, consisting of increased sociability

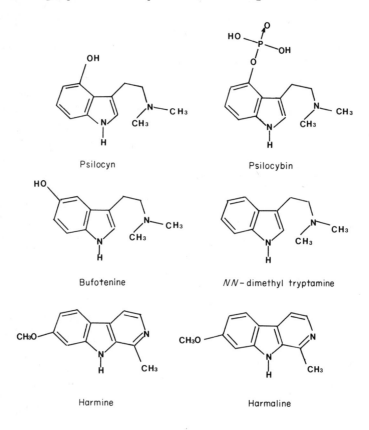

FIG. 3. Indole alkylamine and β-carbolene hallucinogens.

and confidence. The effective dose varies from 5 to 15 μg of pure alkaloid or 2 g or more of dried plant extract equivalent to 30 or more plants.

Psylocin (Fig. 3) is a minor constituent of P. mexicana but the pure alkaloid produces quantitatively similar effects to those of psilocybin. Cross tolerance is reported between psilocybin and mescaline or LSD.

b. Bufotenine

As its name implies, bufotenine (Fig. 3) was originally isolated from the skin glands of the toad (Bufo). It also occurs in the seeds of Adenanthera peregrina which grows in Haiti and South America. These seeds form the basis of a snuff, "cohoba snuff", which is used as an intoxicant. Inhalation of the snuff produces vasomotor effects such as swelling and reddening of the face and extremities and intense perspiration as well as nausea and vomiting. Ataxia and extreme excitation consisting of vocalization, tremors or convulsions then follow and finally there is stupor and sleep. Hallucinations are only infrequently reported, whether the powder or bufotenine itself is administered and they may be limited to simple changes in colour vision and the appearance of spots or squares. Side effects are predominant and disturbing.

c. NN-dimethyltryptamine (DMT) and its analogues

DMT is another constituent of A. peregrina and it is also found in the Brazilian plant Mimosa hostilis from which a decoction is made (vinho de Jurema). Szara (1956) reported that intravenous doses of between 50 and 100 μg produced an LSD like syndrome which had a rapid onset (3 to 5 min) but a short duration (1 hour). Autonomic disturbances, compulsive movements and peculiar motor disturbances are also described. The observation that oral dosage with DMT fails to produce hallucinations even when up to 1 gram is taken, raises doubts about the validity of the suggestion that DMT is the active constituent of the decoctions used in native ritual. However, the observation that methysergide can potentiate the action of DMT (Sai-Halasz, 1962) suggests the possibility that natural synergists which can render oral dosage with DMT effective might exist in the plant material used to make the decoction.

Szara (1957) has reported that NN-diethyltryptamine is active in oral doses of 300 mg or more. It has a slower onset (45 min) and a longer duration of action (3 hours) than DMT itself. The diisopropyl derivative is alleged to be particularly active when taken by mouth.

d. Harmine and harmaline

Harmine may be derived from the seeds of Peganum harmala (Harmel) or from the tropical vine Banisteriopsis caapi. Chemically it is a β carbolene but it can be regarded as a cyclized phenylethylamine (Fig. 3). Intoxication takes the form of vertigo and vomiting followed by psychomotor excitement and, finally, somnolence. Western writers have reported hallucinations in the form of colour flashes. Feelings of body numbness and convulsions may also occur under its influence.

Harmaline, the dihydro analogue of harmine (Fig. 3), is also present in some Banisteriopsis species. The effects of the pure alkaloid are described by Naranjo (1967). Physical and psychic symptoms appear simultaneously. The drug is active both orally and intravenously and more often produces hallucinations than does harmine. There was little distortion of sensory perception but vivid colour hallucinations occurred, particularly when the subject's eyes were closed. The subjects became withdrawn and absorbed in their visions. Somatic symptoms included paraesthesiae, numbness, vomiting and headache.

e. Ibogaine

Although this substance has a reputation as a hallucinogen and is placed on the American listings as such, recent studies fail to substantiate its reputation. It is merely reported to produce alcohol-like intoxication and mild stimulation followed by sedation.

1.2.4 Multicyclic compounds

a. Cannabis

The use of the flowering tops of the hemp plant, Cannabis indica, as an intoxicant dates from antiquity. Cannabis is available either in the form of a compressed block of the dried tops or in the active form of the resin which exudes from the flowers at certain periods in the plant's life. The almost universal use of cannabis has resulted in the appearance in common usage of several trivial names, including marihuana, hashish, kif and pot. The substance may be eaten, drunk in an alcoholic cocktail or, as commonly occurs in the Western world, smoked. Inhalation produces a more speedy onset of intoxication, though irritation of the respiratory tract with bronchospasm and coughing is a frequent consequence. Whereas in the East the consumption of hashish is generally undertaken under circumstances of isolation, Western consumers tend to use it at social gatherings.

Individuals show a great deal of variation in their reaction to cannabis but a convivial atmosphere influences the outcome so that grouped participants are more demonstrative of their feelings and more inclined to humour than are isolated individuals. There is generally a feeling of well-being and in the early phase of intoxication locomotor activity may be increased though this gives way to torpor as the dream-like visual images intensify. A common sensation is that of swimming or flying. There may be sexual arousal and a feeling of hunger. Hunger often remains prominent after the major visual component has disappeared. Participants have an altered perception of space and time and sensory inputs including proprioception and pain are diminished. Nevertheless it is usually possible to rouse the consumer and communicate with him. The occurrence of antisocial behaviour may depend upon the predisposition of the individual concerned and on the predilections of the group in which he finds himself. Peripheral effects are common and include acceleration of the heart and a dry mouth. Ptosis is commonly observed. Tolerance to repeated exposure is not marked.

Intense interest in cannabis has led to the characterization of the active constituents that may be extracted from the plant or resin by organic solvents. The tetrahydrocannabinol isomers (Fig. 4) are the

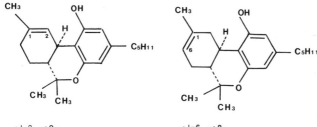

Δ^{1-2} (Δ^9) trans THC Δ^{1-6} (Δ^8) trans THC

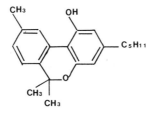

Cannabinol

FIG. 4. Active constituents of cannabis.

most active constituents, particularly the Δ^{1-2} (Δ^9) and Δ^{1-6} (Δ^8) trans isomers. Cannabinol is slightly active. Cannabidiol, cannabinolic acid and cannabigerol are inactive but the possibility remains that they may be converted to active compounds during smoking.

b. Acetylcholine antagonists

Hyoscine, a naturally occurring alkaloid, is widely distributed botanically and it might be cited as the principal hallucinogenic constituent of witches brew. Plants rich in hyoscine include belladonna, mandrake and henbane, all traditional ingredients of such concoctions. The capacity to induce hallucinations is shared by most acetylcholine antagonists, though in all cases signs of intoxication are accompanied by the classical symptoms of parasympathetic blockade including acceleration of the heart, dry mouth, slurred speech, disturbed accommodation and blurred vision. With some substances, for example atropine, hallucinations appear only as part of the toxic syndrome that is precipitated by large doses of drug. Such symptoms of toxicity include disorientation, confusion, apprehension and anxiety, impaired memory and motor performance, drowsiness and coma. On the other hand, benactyzine and benzilic acid derivatives such as Ditran seem particularly likely to produce hallucinations and have appeared as drugs of misuse. Figure 5 depicts the formulae of active drugs.

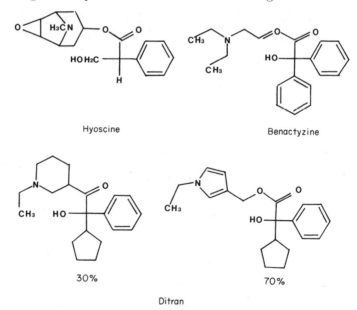

Hyoscine

Benactyzine

30%

70%

Ditran

F IG. 5. Acetylcholine antagonists with hallucinogenic activity.

The anticholinergic action of cannabis derivatives does not account for their hallucinogenic action.

c. *Phenyclidine and its congeners*

As evidenced by ether frolics held in Europe and the USA in the early nineteenth century and the term "Laughing gas" adopted for nitrous oxide, many general anaesthetics can produce a delirious or euphoric state during the induction of and recovery from anaesthesia. This property is particularly evident in phencyclidine, an orally active agent that was studied clinically in 1957. Although a dose of 10 to 20 mg given intravenously produced satisfactory anaesthesia, recovery was often eventful and patients displayed manic behaviour with agitation and disorientation. They reported that they experienced vivid dreams and hallucinations. Although the use of phencyclidine for human anaesthesia was abandoned in 1965, it was marketed as a veterinary anaesthetic in 1967. Since that time phencyclidine and its congeners have become drugs of abuse and are distributed as "PCP" (phenyl cyclohexhyl piperidine) which has been distorted to "peace pill". Sub-anaesthetic oral doses of 3 to 10 mg of phencyclidine produces a feeling of isolation and separation from the environment, social withdrawl, depersonalization, anxiety or depression and hallucinations. Somatic effects include ataxia, numbness, sweating and flushing. The overall experience may be unpleasant and frightening rather than satisfying.

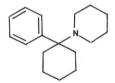

Phencyclidine (Sernyl)

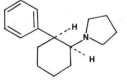

N–ethyl–l–phenylcyclohexylamine

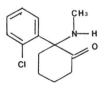

Ketamine

RX 67668

FIG. 6. Phencyclidine and its analogues.

Phencyclidine and its congeners have been used to adulterate LSD and marihuana mixtures.

The compound RX 67668 (Fig. 6) which underwent clinical trial as an anticholinesterase, was withdrawn because of the hallucinogenic effect it exerted in high intravenous doses (Wray and Cowan, 1973).

d. *Muscimol*

The mushroom Amanita muscaria is widely distributed in nature and may be recognised by its red crown which carries white spots. It is known by the trivial name of fly agaric because of its reputation as a fly killer. The fungus is a rich source of biologically active compounds which include muscimol, acetylcholine, muscarine, choline, atropine, hyoscyamine and bufotenine. It should be added that the last three substances are present in quantities much too small to exert any hallucinogenic effects. Intoxication with fly agaric produces transient depression and a sleep-like state with illusory images, which is followed within 15 to 20 minutes by elation and excitement accompanied by distortion of real images and auditory and visual hallucinations. The alkaloid that is the most likely candidate for the role of hallucinogen is muscimol which is structurally analogous to muscarine (Fig. 7). According to Waser (1967), ingestion of 10 to 15 mg of muscimol produces dilated pupils, central excitation, accelerated respiration and visual disturbances such as echo picture. These disturbances are less severe than those experienced when the mushroom itself is ingested.

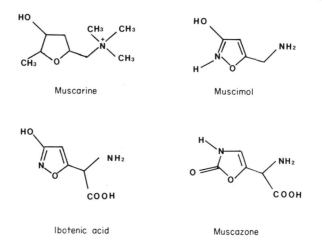

FIG. 7. Muscimol and related compounds.

Muscimol analogues such as ibotenic acid and muscazone which are also constituents of the mushroom, do not themselves produce dramatic changes in perception but they may exert a synergistic action. The possibility also remains that as yet undiscovered active constituents may be present in the mushroom and may contribute their own hallucinogenic effects.

2 Organic causes of hallucinations

2.1 Sleep deprivation

Hallucinations are a regular finding in subjects that have been deprived of sleep for periods of at least 72 hours. They coincide with the period in which the subjects have the most difficulty in remaining awake. The hallucinations are predominantly visual and consist largely of flashing lights and distortion or pulsation of real images. Dream-like visual experiences and auditory hallucinations are rather more rare.

2.2 Perceptual deprivation or monotony

Whereas in producing sleep deprivation experimenters have subjected their victims to vigorous sensory bombardment, an equally effective means of producing hallucinations is to reduce or monotonize the perceptual input as much as possible. It seems that in many subjects isolation from normal communications with other human beings is sufficient to elicit hallucinatory experiences as the tales of Antarctic explorers (Byrd, 1938) and lone yachtsmen (Bombard, 1953) testify. One might also speculate that the various Biblical visions associated with isolation in the wilderness might have arisen in the same way. In the study reported by Freedman *et al.* (1962) the subjects wore headphones which played white noise and gloves and cuffs to reduce sensory input from the limbs. Visual imagery was experienced by 40% of the subjects during a single eight-hour session. A mask which allowed the passage of diffuse unpatterned light was just as effective as a complete blackout. The images were of short duration and were largely unrelated to the subject's thought so that he was unable to control their appearance or content. Colours were vivid and details striking so that subjects compared the images to a rapidly appearing and disappearing slide show.

2.3 Metabolic and dietary deprivation

Hallucinations are common occurrences amongst prisoners of war. The occurrence of hallucinations in pellagra in vitamin deficient alcoholics has led to the suggestion that dietary deficiency of B vitamin may be a contributory factor. Visions certainly occur in ritual fasting.

2.4 Change in body temperature

As every schoolboy knows, hallucinations and delirium are likely to occur during hyperthermia, whether the origin is the febrile episodes of disease or exposure to a desert climate. Although hyperthermia usually produces somnolence, hallucinations may be produced when the brain is cooled during surgery (Fay, 1959).

2.5 Brain disease

It is not surprising that hallucinations are a feature of brain disease. They are produced as part of the central nervous manifestations of syphilis and are also often associated with cerebral abcess, tumour or trauma. A hallucinogenic component often occurs in psychomotor epilepsy. Such ictal hallucinations often take the form of involuntary recollections of past experience.

3 Physiological mechanisms

At a time when lysergic acid diethylamide was attracting a good deal of attention by reason of its striking hallucinogenic activity, it was found that the drug acted as a serotonin (5-hydroxy-tryptamine) antagonist on isolated tissue preparations. This observation provided grounds for believing that a similar antagonist action, exerted at serotonin receptors in the brain, might lie at the root of the drug's ability to provoke hallucinations. It certainly focused attention on the likelihood that serotonin plays an important functional role in the central nervous system. Structural similarities between serotonin and a number of other hallucinogenic substances reinforced the belief that interference with serotonin-regulated processes in the brain led to hallucinatory distortions of consciousness. Noradrenaline received almost as much attention as serotonin in this context: mescaline has obvious structural affinities with noradrenaline while some of the actions of lysergide, almost the prototypical serotonin antagonist, arise from an intervention in processes that depend on noradrenaline rather than on serotonin. The fact that many hallucinogenic drugs seemed to be related to serotonin or noradrenaline harmonized well with the then prevailing view that these two monoamines were pre-eminently important in the regulation of affective processes. But the idea that the actions of hallucinogenic agents were confined to processes controlled by the two monoamines had soon to be abandoned. As we have seen, atropine can cause hallucinatory activity, as can *N*-methyl-3-piperidyl benzoate. Both these substances are acetylcholine antagonists and the piperidyl benzoate more often than any other hallucinogen produces true hallucinations—sensory experiences, that is, that arise in the absence of any physiological stimulation of the corresponding sense organs. Yet other hallucinogens are not obviously related to any known neuro-humoral substance so that it is not possible to devise a unitary neuro-chemical hypothesis of hallucinatory activity.

The fact that perceptual deprivation, hyperthermia and general anaesthesia can all produce hallucinations strongly suggests that hallucinatory activity is to be regarded as the result of a generally disorganized neuronal activity. As far as anaesthesia and perceptual deprivation are concerned it may well be that the exclusion of meaning-ful sensory information from the brain releases restraints and precipi-tates distorted thought processes. A similar result would be expected to follow interference with any of the neurohumoral substances that are involved in the chemical regulation of cerebral activity. Such a hypo-thesis does not demand the participation (or exclusion) of a particular transmission system.

References

Bombard, A. (1953). "The Voyage of the Heretique". Simon & Schuster, New York.

Byrd, R. E. (1938). "Alone". G. P. Putnams & Sons, New York.

Fay, T. (1959). Early experiences with local and generalised refrigeration of the human brain. *Journal of Neurosurgery*, **16**, 239–260.

Freedman, S. J., Gunebaum, H. U., State, B. A. and Greenblatt, M. (1962). Imagery in sensory deprivation. *In* "Hallucinations" (Ed. L. J. West), pp. 108–117. Grune & Stratton, New York.

Heim, R. and Wasson, R. G. (1958). "Les Champignons Hallucinogènes du Mexique" Edit. Mus. Nat. Hist. Nat. Paris.

Hoffer, A. and Osmond, H. (1967). "The Hallucinogens". Academic Press, New York and London.

Hofmann, A (1970). Notes and documents concerning the discovery of LSD. *Agents and Actions*, **1**, 148–150.

Isbell, H. and Gorodetsky, C. W. (1966). Effect of alkaoids of ololiuqui in man. *Psychopharmacologia*, **8**, 331–339.

Kluver, H. (1926). Mescal visions and eidetic vision. *American Journal of Psychology*, **37**, 502–515.

Kluver, H. (1928). "Mescal—the Divine Plant and its Psychological Effects". Kegan-Paul, London.

Naranjo, C. (1967). Psychotropic properties of the harmala alkaloids. *In* "Ethnopharmacologic Search for Psychoactive Drugs" (Eds D. H. Effron, B. O. Holmstedt and N. S. Kline), pp. 385–391. U.S. Dept. of Health Education and Welfare, Washington DC.

Osmond, H. (1955). Ololiuqui: The ancient Aztec narcotic. *Journal of Mental Science*, **101**, 526–537.

Sai-Halasz, A. (1962). The effect of antiserotonin on the experimental psychosis induced by dimethyltryptamine. *Experientia*, **18**, 137–138.

Schwarz, B. E., Bickford, R. G. and Rome, H. P. (1955). Reversibility of induced psychosis with chlorpromazine. *Proceedings of Staff Meetings of the Mayo Clinic*, **30**, 407–417.

Shulgin, A. T. (1966). Possible implication of myristicin as a psychotropic substance. *Nature, London*, **210**, 380–384.

Snyder, S. H., Weingartner, H. and Faillace, L. A. (1971). DOET (2,5-Dimethoxy-4-ethylamphetamine), a new psychotropic drug. *Archives of General Psychiatry*, **24**, 50–55.

Szara, S. (1956). Dimethyltryptamin: Its metabolism in man; The relation of its psychotic effects to serotonin metabolism. *Experientia*, **12**, 441–442.

Szara, S. (1957). The comparison of the psychotic effect of tryptamine derivatives with the effects of mescaline and LSD-25 and self-experiments. *In* "Psychotropic Drugs" (Eds S. Garattini and V. Ghetti), pp. 460–467. Elsevier, Amsterdam.

Waser, P. G. (1967). The pharmacology of Amanita muscaria. *In* "Ethnopharmacologic Search for Psychoactive Drugs" (Eds D. H. Effron, B. O. Holmstedt and N. S. Kline), pp. 419–439. U.S. Dept. of Health Education and Welfare, Washington, DC.

Woodrow, K. M., Reifman, A. and Wyatt, R. J. (1978). Amphetamine psychosis—a model for paranoid schizophrenia? *In* "Neuropharmacology and Behaviour" (Eds B. Haber and M. H. Aprison), pp. 1–22. Plenum Press, New York and London.

Wray, S. R. and Cowan, A. (1973). Correlation between animal and clinical findings with a psychotomimetic anticholinesterase. *Neuropharmacology*, **12**, 397–400.

7 Split Brain Studies and the Duality of Consciousness

J. G. BEAUMONT

Department of Psychology
The University, Leicester

Cerebral commissurotomy, the "split brain" operation, besides being the key to the development of techniques upon which the new field of experimental neuropsychology is based, has been widely considered to provide a unique opportunity for the study of cerebral substrates of human consciousness. The operation was introduced by Van Wagenen in 1940 (Van Wagenen and Herren, 1940), but its significance was not fully realized until Sperry, together with Gazzaniga and a number of other workers, undertook studies from about 1960 on a later series of patients operated upon by Vogel and Bogen (Bogen and Vogel, 1962). The surgical procedure, undertaken for the treatment of intractible epilepsy, involves complete section of the corpus callosum, the anterior and hippocampal commissures, and the massa intermedia when present. There is also a group of patients who have undergone partial commissurotomy, with incomplete section of the corpus callosum, but these patients will not be considered in the following review. Commissurotomy therefore divides all direct cortical links between the two cerebral hemispheres, isolating the cortex of each hemisphere, hence the "split brain".

I am reluctant to summarize the deficits in performance shown by these patients because I shall argue below that part of the disagreement about the implications of this operation can be seen to arise from the overextension of descriptions of the behaviour of split brain patients which are too summary to be accurate. However, for readers unfamiliar with the field, the most striking finding has been the absence of any apparent disability in everyday behaviour. Nevertheless, under appropriate testing conditions, it can be shown that split brain patients have a deficit in the cross-integration of information. Patients cannot point to a stimulus source on the opposite side of the body, and cannot respond to stimuli projected in the visual field contralateral to the hand of response. They cannot respond with speech to information presented to the right hemisphere via the left hand or the left visual field. Cross-modal and intramodal integration between stimuli which are presented on opposite sides of the body midline are impossible. The general conclusion has been that these patients exhibit "two independent streams of conscious awareness" (Sperry, 1968a, p. 724) which are out of contact with each other, and each with its own "separate and private sensations; its own perceptions; its own concepts; and its own impulses to act" (Sperry, 1968a). In other words that the consciousness of these patients has been doubled, divided or in some way transformed, and that this hold implications for normal processes underlying consciousness.

Rather fuller introductory reviews of the deficits shown by these patients are given by Sperry *et al.* (1969), Gazzaniga (1967, 1970) and Dimond (1972).

1 Historical development

A scholarly account of the speculation about the effects of commissurotomy on consciousness which antedates the introduction of the operation has been provided by Zangwill (1974, 1976). Despite these early discussions, the findings with the earlier Van Wagenen series, studied by Akelaitis and Smith (Akelaitis, 1944; and references cited therein) argued against any major functions for the corpus callosum. The largely negative findings have been attributed to the lesser degree of sophistication of the testing procedures (Preilowski, in discussion of Preilowski, 1975), although differences in the patients treated, and the surgical procedures, have also been outlined (Bogen and Bogen, 1969; Sperry, 1968b). Gazzaniga (in discussion of Preilowski, 1975) has, however, replicated Akelaitis' procedures on the later series of patients, and Goldstein and Joynt (1969) confirmed the results on one of the original cases. Geschwind (1964) has also pointed out that Smith's results were not entirely negative but positive although statistically non-significant.

Theoretical proposals related specifically to consciousness date from Sperry (1964a), and his writings (1964b, 1966, 1968a, b, 1969, 1970, 1973, 1974, 1976) have formed the main theme running through discussion in this area. While there is insufficient space here to treat the development of Sperry's ideas, they make a fascinating study in themselves. Sperry was clearly strongly influenced by the early cases, especially the first, as Dimond (1972) has pointed out, and his subsequent accounts have shown a slow but clear change from early dogmatic statements about the complete independence of the two spheres of consciousness, generalizable to some extent to intact subjects, towards a more cautious appraisal of the degree to which the two split brains are really independent, except under particular circumstances.

Sperry's account has been reinterpreted and re-presented by a number of other writers in the last few years (Bogen, 1969; Bogen and Bogen, 1969; Critchley, 1972; Dimond, 1972; Gazzaniga, 1967, 1970, 1972; Kinsbourne, 1974, Nebes, 1974; Trevarthen, 1972, 1974a, b; Zangwill, 1974, 1976). These accounts have ranged from almost direct reiteration of Sperry's position to other variations which have considerably altered the emphasis and the scope of the interpretation. All, however, have in common the operation of two relatively independent spheres of consciousness, at least under certain circumstances, which may have different qualities or be associated with different abilities, and which are to some extent in competition for executive control. Both hemispheres are seen however, as "conscious".

The only major independent line of argument has been that of Eccles (1965; 1970; 1974; 1976; 1977; Popper and Eccles, 1977), who has maintained through the development of a series of models that while the two hemispheres become independent following commissurotomy, only the left hemisphere is truly "conscious" and that the right operates only in an automatic fashion, resembling but surpassing a non-human primate brain.

There has been little direct criticism of any of these accounts. MacKay (in discussion of Sperry, 1966) has made some discussion of Sperry's views, as has Zangwill (1974, 1976) who also provides a fuller critique of Eccles' position. Savage (1976) has discussed and assessed both positions. A reassessment of the current status of these various positions will be attempted after an examination of certain areas of the evidence.

2 The patients

It should constantly be borne in mind that the fairly considerable literature on split brain humans is derived from a very small number of subjects. At the last published count (Sperry, 1974) patients in the Vogel and Bogen series who had undergone total commissurotomy numbered 16, to which may be added 2 patients from the more recent series operated upon by Wilson (Gazzaniga *et al.*, 1975), and one or two surviving cases of the Akelaitis series (whose lesions were, in any case, serial).[1] The relative unpopularity of the operation outside the United States, and the relative success of partial commissurotomy, mean that these numbers are unlikely to increase significantly within the near future.

---

[1]Since the preparation of this chapter in 1978, studies of a number of additional patients in the Wilson series have been published.

Even within the group of operated patients, the numbers suitable for study, and from whom behavioural data has been derived, are a minority. The early papers of Sperry (1964a, b, 1966, 1968a) concentrated on the first three cases, and the reviews of Gazzaniga (1967, 1970) described 4 and 3 respectively out of a population of 10 cases available at that date. Later discussions by Sperry (1968b, Sperry *et al.*, 1969) where it has been possible to identify the subjects have tended to concentrate on the two patients LB and NG. These patients have been deliberately selected because they seem to have suffered least cerebral damage before or during the operation, and are regarded as being both most amenable to testing and producing evidence which may be more validly generalized to normal intact subjects. Nevertheless, as pointed out by Oxbury (1975), care must be exercised in generalizing even from LB and NG. LB was 12 years old at the time of operation and has suffered epilepsy from the age of 3, raising at least the suspicion that normal cerebral dominance might not have been established within his brain. NG had a relatively low pre-operative I.Q., an epileptogenic focus in the anterior left temporal lobe and intracerebral calcification in the right hemisphere. Again the development of cerebral laterality for psychological functions is likely to have been abnormal, producing, in particular, bilateralization of language representation. This must be considered when assessing the important question of the language abilities of the right hemisphere as demonstrated in split brain patients. (Searleman, 1977).

Ettlinger and Blakemore (1969) have also suggested that the effects of commissurotomy may be to reveal deficits which are in fact due to specific functional lateral lesions of the hemispheres, but which are only apparent when alternative systems, dependent on the callosum, are deprived of input or output connections. They also point out that additional pathology might be incurred during the surgical procedures, which, as the right hemisphere is conventionally retracted, would presumably be more likely to be to that hemisphere.

All these factors, the small number of patients, their different pre-operative histories and neurological status, their individual response to the operation, and current anticonvulsive medication suggest caution in treating split brain patients as a single group. Kinsbourne (1974) has in fact recommended that the data from the patients be analysed and reported individually. While this seems desirable it is not always possible to relate published results to specific cases for retrospective review, and the remedy lies with those who have published the primary studies. To be fair, many writers (*e.g.* Sperry, 1973, 1974) have pointed to these difficulties, but it bears repetition that the data are derived from a very small and specially selected group of patients, about whom it is extremely difficult to generalize, even without considering the problems of generalization to the normal intact population.

3 "Consciousness"

Few writers have paid careful attention to the term "consciousness", and in particular to the distinction between "consciousness" and "conscious awareness". As a result, much of the debate about a possible duality of consciousness in the brain could be resolved by clarifying this definition. The range of behaviour and of psychological processes which are taken to be relevant to the demonstration of consciousness is very wide. At one extreme, Trevarthen lists "attention, perceptual selection, spatial coordination, and patterning of voluntary performance" (1974a, p. 256) as indicating consciousness, while Kinsbourne refers to "a particular cognitive style, a manner of attending and responding selectively" (1974, p. 288), and Gazzaniga (1967) seems to imply that any cognitive activity can be equated with consciousness.

By contrast, Eccles (1977; Popper and Eccles, 1977) is clearly concerned with conscious awareness, or the *experience* of consciousness. He, as others, tends to use "consciousness" flexibly so that sometimes it indicates conscious awareness, as a subjective definition, and sometimes attentional responsive behaviour, which is an objective behavioural definition, thus confusing two forms of evidence which, as Burt (1969) has pointed out, cannot be reconciled.

Sperry (1969, 1970, 1976) has, exceptionally, described in detail his definition of "consciousness" and discussed the theoretical position upon which it is based. He takes conscious awareness to be a dynamic emergent property of brain activity, able to influence neural processes, and therefore different from and more than the elements from which it emerges. This view has been discussed by Bindra (1970) who points out that "emergence" is generally applied to patterns rather than to structures and questions how the higher-order "consciousness" and lower-order "non-conscious" can be distinguished without resort to extra-neural mentalistic influences; and by Wimsatt (1976) who also raises the problems expounded by the configurational properties of Sperry's model, and questions whether it fundamentally differs from a dualist position. It seems that Sperry has not satisfactorily resolved the problem of the identity of the higher-level process involved. If it has emerged from, and is entirely determined by, lower levels then it is difficult to see how it is not an epiphenomenon (although not a "mere epiphenomenon" Sperry, 1969). As Sperry (1970) accepts, it is incumbent on him to define in concrete terms the exact organizational process responsible for the conscious effects, which he seems as yet unable to do.

Savage (1976) has made a significant contribution by analysing the use of "consciousness" by Sperry and Eccles, and extracting three forms: consciousness$_1$ in the sense that we see; consciousness$_2$, self-consciousness of the actions and perceptions of oneself; consciousness$_3$, self-consciousness "in the ordinary sense of the term" of what one is doing and what one's situation is. Even this seems insufficient, for if "consciousness" is extended to cover all attentional processes, as it has been, then none of the above definitions seem to describe a situation in which stimuli are perceived and processed as evidenced by later behaviour, but in which they are not "seen" at the time and are not the subject of directed attention. In what sense is the latent or incidental learner conscious? These distinctions are crucial for in that Eccles adopts a much more restricted definition of consciousness he demands different evidence to support the demonstration of consciousness.

In any normally accepted meaning of "consciousness" of an event, then conscious awareness of that event, normally but not necessarily expressed in speech or writing, either at the time or later, must be demonstrated. The problem undoubtedly lies in the definition of the test of consciousness, and whether, when it is not reasonable to expect the subject to indicate awareness by a verbal report, intelligent rational behaviour constitutes a sufficient test. Eccles' requirement of verbal introspective report of awareness is undoubtedly too strict, while any intelligent activity without any evidence of conscious awareness that it is reasonable to expect is probably too lax, as evidence for consciousness, in the normal sense. For the purposes of this chapter I shall accept that introspective report of awareness is the normal requirement to demonstrate consciousness, but that if the subject is prevented from producing such a report, then intelligent, adaptive, responsive and rational behaviour may be cautiously accepted as providing such a demonstration.

It is also important to distinguish between consciousness as a process and consciousness as related to structural properties of the brain. This has been pointed out by Nagel (1971), Dimond (1972) and Bell (1975) but has hardly influenced current debate. Sperry, Eccles and the associated writers seem at least partly to assume a location for consciousness, Eccles in association with the dominant hemisphere, Sperry in relation to neural events at various levels of the nervous system, thereby linking it to structural properties of the cerebrum. It is alternatively possible to see consciousness entirely as a process, which, if it is a dynamic process, cannot be considered to have an essential structure which is capable of description in the terms which are currently employed.

Finally, the debate among philosophers about the problem of enumerating minds should be noted. Nagel (1971), having considered a range of possible interpretations, has argued persuasively that there is no number of minds that an individual can be considered to have. Our sense of the normal unity of consciousness and our concept of a single mental person is perhaps an illusion, which we should be prepared to reject for some more sophisticated concept. This view was foreshadowed by the discussion of Geschwind (1965), sadly before the current evidence was available. Parfit (1971) and Puccetti (1973) have discussed the problem for personal identity of separating the hemispheres, transplanting them into separate bodies, and later recombining them. While a fascinating question, not yet open to empirical investigation, it raises relevant problems about identity. Parfit argues that following transplantation of the hemispheres into two separate bodies it would be possible to survive as two different people, but without implying identity with both of those people. Puccetti agrees that neither would be really continuous with the original person. These writers also find defects in the language used for discussion of identity and suggest that psychological continuity is the most important variable to be associated with personal identity. If we link this with a process, rather than with a structural view of consciousness then we have at least the possibility of flexible rearrangements of the process of consciousness within different physical forms, associated with psychological continuity, but not embroiled in the problem of the number of minds, or any association with identity of specific physical forms. Unfortunately, pressure of space precludes a proper discussion of these topics.

4 The evidence

The intention here is not to summarize the evidence, but to demonstrate that with respect to certain key questions, the summary conclusions which are often presented do not accurately distil the available evidence. Excessive generalization and premature conclusions have distorted the picture and encouraged the production of quite wild and certainly unfounded views of the nature and function of cerebral specialization. For illustrations, and a proper criticism of the "faddism" of split brain psychology, see Goleman (1977). Even more sober commentaries have summarized excessively. Sperry (1973) describes the right hemisphere as "alexic, agraphic" (p. 212), "lacking language" (p. 213) and (1974, p. 11) "unable to respond . . . in writing". Ornstein (1972, p. 57) states "the left(hand). . .could not copy a written word".[1] However,

[1]Omited in the second edition (Ornstein, 1977).

there was at that time evidence (Dimond, 1972) that some patients could carry out verbal commands and write with the left hand, and much additional evidence for language abilities, if not speech, in the right hemisphere. The problem is simply one of a neglect of the fine detail of the results, so that writers in allied fields have taken the summaries as a valid representation of the findings and gained the erroneous impression that statements such as "there is general agreement that an individual with a severed corpus callosum has *two* minds which are not acquainted with each other" (Globus, 1976, p. 280) are entirely supported by the evidence.

4.1 Does the right hemisphere possess language?

There is a common and quite inexcusable confusion of "speech" and "language" (Bell, 1975) which perhaps accounts for Sperry's (1973) extraordinary statement that the minor hemisphere lacks language. There is no disagreement about speech, the minor hemisphere does appear mute except for exclamations and "automatic" utterances such as are known from clinical lesion studies, but there has been a trend, which originated early, to recognize linguistic abilities in the right hemisphere. Gazzaniga and Sperry (1967) described writing with the left hand; Sperry (1968b), Ettlinger and Blakemore (1969) and Gazzaniga (1970) presented evidence for simple reading and more advanced auditory comprehension; Levy *et al.* (1971) reported left hand language expression through writing and arranging letters to form words, although associated with a relative inferiority in dealing with verbs against nouns, and words against pictures; Zaidel (1973) concluded that the disconnected right hemisphere could comprehend abstract words and a variety of syntactic structures including verbs, sentential transformations, and long non-redundant and semantically abstract references; Bogen (1976) has again described writing by the non-speaking hemisphere. Zaidel (1976) assessed the auditory vocabulary of the right hemisphere performing alone, and rated it at an "average aphasic" level, but found parameters, such as a frequency function, which suggested truly linguistic behaviour, while its picture vocabulary and auditory comprehension were at the 11- and 4-year-old level respectively, but not absent from the right hemisphere (Zaidel, 1977). Levy and Trevarthen (1977) showed that the right hemisphere is competent at semantic matching, and can perform rhyme matches, although at a more restricted level. Recently Gott *et al.* (1975, 1977) have reported both behavioural and evoked potential evidence that while the left hemisphere was superior for detecting rhyming words (mean correct 80.3%), the right hemisphere also possessed real ability on the task (mean correct 65·6%). Finally, Sugishita (1978) has examined mental association to objects presented tactually to the left hand of one split brain patient, the response being selection by the left hand from an array of visually presented words the word semantically related to the object. The patient was able to select words coordinate, contingent and superordinate to the object as well as words representing occupations related to the object. Some difficulty was, however, experienced with abstract conceptual words, although the results still point to considerable ability for semantic association by the right hemisphere.

Against these findings must stand the report of Gazzaniga and Hillyard (1971) that "little or no syntactic capability exists in the right hemisphere" (p. 273) and although their data were derived from the earlier patients, they emphasize the opportunity for cross-cuing in many of the testing situations (see section 4.3 below). Zaidel and Sperry (1977) give the results of a 5–10 year post-operative follow-up on 8 patients which suggest that the quality of their motor performance is essentially unimpaired, but they did note the persistance of marked dysgraphia with the left hand.

Reviews and more extended discussion of the findings can be found in Benson (1976), Ettlinger (1972), Galin (1974), Nebes (1974), Oxbury (1975) and Searleman (1977).

Anomia for objects palpated by the left hand has also been much discussed as indicating a right hemisphere deficiency in linguistic abilities. However, as Bogen (1976) in his detailed account of the post-operative course in several patients has shown most clearly, while there may be a persistent left hand anomia, it is only an *anomia*. The absence of speech behaviour is at it were "absence in the test, and *not in cognition*" (Brown, 1976, p. 78).

The right hemisphere may be effectively mute; it is probably also less proficient at most linguistic abilities, considerably so with respect to some, but it does possess a remarkable (in view of early reports) variety of linguistic abilities. The disconnected right half brains of commissurotomy patients cannot be considered to lack language—although in view of their preoperative neurological status, it is always possible that they have an abnormal bilateralization of language, which is not typical of the normal intact brain.

4.2 Are there non-linguistic abilities the right hemisphere does not possess?

It is worth enquiring whether the right hemisphere has been shown to be deficient in any non-linguistic cognitive ability, allowing of course for response other than by speech. Partly to counter the impression given by the term "minor" hemisphere and to avoid association with an outmoded neuropsychological position (I take it that its retention is, for most neuropsychologists, as short hand for "minor hemisphere for speech"), as well as to emphasize their opposition to Eccles' position linking consciousness to the major, left, hemisphere of the brain, most writers have been rather at pains to emphasize the abilities of the right hemisphere. Sperry (1968b) does this, and Sperry *et al.* (1969, p. 286) credit the right hemisphere with "fairly high-order mental processes including abstract thinking and reasoning". Gazzaniga (1972) presents evidence, both from commissurotomy patients and also from the training of global aphasics to perform linguistic operations by the language scheme originally developed for chimpanzees, for the right hemisphere's cognitive powers and Dimond (1972) places particular emphasis upon them.

Even where differences have been found in the abilities of the two hemispheres, it is important to distinguish between a significant difference in the level of ability and an absolute difference which indicates that the right hemisphere lacks a particular ability. For example, Levy and Trevarthen (1976) discuss their elegant studies of metacontrol of hemispheric function employing chimaeric figures, which shows the right hemisphere to be relatively proficient at, and to assume control for, appearance matches, while relatively deficient at function matches which were under left hemisphere control. However, these authors properly point out the significant number of dissociations between controlling hemisphere and strategy of matching. The right hemisphere did not generally assume control of function matches, but it occasionally did so and was therefore capable of doing so. There is therefore no experimental evidence that the right hemisphere entirely lacks any non-linguistic ability.

4.3 Is there any cross-integration between the disconnected hemispheres?

It is often assumed that commissurotomy patients are unable to integrate stimulus material presented on opposite sides of the body midline, or to make responses across the body midline. Even from early reports (Gazzaniga *et al.*, 1965) it has been clear, however, that while it is difficult, it is not impossible for all split brain patients to, for instance, indicate with the contralateral hand, points of the body stimulated, or to respond with either hand to verbal instructions or to signals directed to a single hemisphere. This is partly explained by the availability of ipsilateral motor control for at least all but fine finger movements, for which there is growing evidence. Ettlinger and Blakemore (1969) pointed out that this availability grows with increasing time from surgery, and Ettlinger (1972) discusses whether it is a special phenomenon of motor learning or a long-standing adaptation to epilepsy. Preilowski's (1975) studies of bimanual motor performance have most clearly demonstrated the preservation of old bimanual skills, although with an inability to learn new tasks, and illustrated the role of ipsilateral innervation in performance of these skills. He also argues that ipsilateral control plays an important role in normal function by controlling the contralateral, and dominant, motor outflow. Zaidel and Sperry's (1977) follow-up study reported qualitative and quantitative impairment in certain bimanual tasks up to ten years after operation.

There is other evidence of cross-integrational abilities. Gazzaniga (1970) reports complete intermanual transfer of stylus maze problems, and Trevarthen in particular (1972, 1974a, b) has demonstrated integration occurring across the midline. He has shown that vision for space relations and of motion in space around the body ("ambient vision") is not divided, nor is information about the relative displacement of objects and their rates of motion (Trevarthen and Sperry, 1973). Patients are reported as able to synthesize percepts occurring in both visual fields in peripheral vision, and able to respond to both verbally. Active reaching by either arm for moving objects or lights was also little affected by commissurotomy. Visual completion across the midline was reported for incomplete geometric figures, pictures or words, even to the extent of completion to the right of the vertical meridian by the right hemisphere with *right* hand drawing.

Gazzaniga in particular has always argued that many of these effects can be shown to be the result of subtle cooperative and cross-cuing strategies (1970; Gazzaniga and Hillyard, 1971). Focusing the eyes out of the plane in which the stimuli are projected may allow stimuli to cross the midline; eye movements in the vertical plane might communicate the height of stimuli, or in following the track of a maze communicate its form by feedback in the bilateral system which controls gaze direction; the use of a restricted stimulus set may allow positive or negative valency to be transmitted by affective pathways across the brain. These more subtle mechanisms, besides the more obvious cross-modal cues and external feedback by vocalization, undoubtedly explain some of the bilateral integration which occurs. However, in at least one case (Trevarthen, 1974a) target-directed reaching across the midline has been shown to be possible without eye movement, in a carefully controlled experimental situation, without verbal cues available and with a sufficiently large stimulus set. Even if we allow for ipsilateral motor control, a unified perception of space is clearly implied.

In less experimentally constrained tasks involving complex integrated functions, such as anagram solving and facial description among others (Gazzaniga *et al.*, 1975), deficits have not been found, and rather an improvement demonstrated on a hypothesis testing task (Ledoux *et al.*, 1977). All allow maximum utilization of cross-cuing strategies, but still it is argued must need some exchange between the hemispheres. The conclusion must be, not that we underestimate the ability or potential for integration of a single hemisphere, but that our assumption about cross-integration is at fault. It may be possible in the most rigorous experimental situation, with a particular restricted task, to demonstrate a complete absence of cross-integration, but for most cognitive activities, and certainly for the unconstrained commissurotomy patient, there are mechanisms which do allow for substantial cross-integration.

4.4 Does conflict arise between the activity of the disconnected hemispheres?

The problem about assessing evidence relevant to this question is that it is largely anecdotal and relies on a few, much repeated, reports. In early writings, Gazzaniga and Sperry (Gazzaniga *et al.*, 1962; Sperry, 1964a, 1966) reported conflicts of will between the two hands in the first six months following surgery, the left hand pulling trousers on while the right tried to remove them, the right untying a belt just tied by both hands, or the right hand pushing the patient's wife away whilst the left sought help with some task (this is reported more dramatically in Gazzaniga, 1970). Also "the left hand usually cooperates with the right, but not always. At times the left hand may go off in a distracted way on independent and even antagonistic activities of its own. . ." (Sperry, 1964b, p. 46). "These minor differences of opinion . . . are seen rather commonly. . ." (Sperry, 1966, p. 302), although this seems to refer to situations in which the left hemisphere is ignorant of the stimulus and the spoken response is therefore a guess, while the left hand responds differently and correctly. Gazzaniga *et al.* (1965) report the intervention of the left hand trying to correct errors made by the right in a block design task, and a similar form of conflict is shown by Levy *et al.* (1971) in the right hand's attempt to write the name of a pipe presented to the right hemisphere, beginning uncertainly PI, but then converting the response to PENCIL. Aggressive intent of the left hand is also described by Gazzaniga (1970) in the context of antagonistic behaviour between the two hands, the left hand grabbing and shaking his wife while the right tried to come to her aid, but the incident refers to the same patient as the early papers (Gazzaniga *et al.*, 1962; Sperry, 1964a, 1966). Galin (1974) repeats these incidents, but comments "how often this occurs is questionnable" (p. 574).

MacKay (in discussion of Sperry, 1966) reports an anecdote of "automatically" donning pyjama trousers instead of the appropriate change of trousers while dressing for dinner and simultaneously holding a conversation. He presents this as parallel to the above incidents, and yet not implying the operation of two minds, but rather a special state or capability which is not normally present. Whether this analogy is accurate or not, the incidents of conflict described appear to be partly due to independent (but not conflicting) responses by the two body sides in an experimental situation where one side is informed about the correct response and the other bound to guess. The remaining incidents, entirely anecdotal and relating principally to a single patient, "may on rare occasions occur" (Kinsbourne, 1974, p. 287), but do not necessarily imply concurrent streams of consciousness.

The only relevant experimental evidence has been the studies of double function undertaken in humans following an animal analogue (Gazzaniga, 1970). Split brain subjects showed consistent mean reaction times for the right hand when a second simultaneous left field discrimination was demanded, in contrast to a significant increase shown by all normal control subjects, although it should be noted that the reaction times of the patients were far slower than those of the controls. Trevarthen (1974a) is critical of this evidence, and presents findings in visual search tasks with bilateral finger responses to show that patients cannot be "coaxed to perform like two separate individuals" (p. 249). A more recent report (Franco, 1977), studying a range of tasks, has suggested that the two disconnected hemispheres are capable of effective concurrent processing of entirely unrelated information, which within the same hemisphere would cause severe interference. However, the commissurotomy patients' performance in no way exceeded that of normals, who were able to perform all the tasks, unlike the patients. This demonstration relies on using tasks which are known to interfere within a hemisphere in normals, but to a lesser degree across the hemispheres, and therefore the result seems unsurprising. It appears as though similar or dissimilar tasks under certain conditions which minimize mutual interference, may proceed in parallel in split brain patients, but that this cannot be considered to be an expansion of their abilities in relation to intact normals.

Sperry (1966, 1968a) has argued for the operation of two independent wills in the two hemispheres, which is at least partly dependent on the possibility of the generation of conflicting, or at least parallel, responses. The evidence to suggest this is, however, sparse. Eccles by contrast (1974, 1976) has denied the operation of a volitional system within the right hemisphere altogether, even to the extent of claiming that the split brain patient "has no volitional control of the left hand" (1974, p. 91).

This is on the basis, presumably, that actions of which there is no conscious awareness cannot be willed, although the evidence for, and the validity of, this conclusion have both been criticized (Savage, 1976). We must conclude, with Lishman (1971) that the evidence is insufficient for firm conclusions, but that at present there is no evidence for distinct volitional systems.

4.5 Do patients lack awareness of right hemisphere processes?

Once again the evidence is difficult to assess because it is essentially anecdotal. The detailed post-operative case histories given by Bogen (1976) report no suggestion of any subjective lack of awareness, nor behavioural evidence of, for example, neglect. Sperry also reports that there is no evidence of a subjective splitting of conscious awareness (1968a, 1973) and has indeed made the assertion that commissurotomy patients could easily pass through a routine medical check-up without anything abnormal being noted (1973, 1974).

There are four pieces of evidence which are quoted to support independent awareness. The most repeated is the report of an emotional generalized response, for which the patient could not verbally account, to a female pin-up presented to the right hemisphere in a set of neutral stimuli (Gazzaniga, 1967, 1970; Lishman, 1971; Dimond, 1972; Ornstein, 1977[1]; Galin, 1974; Galin and Ornstein, 1975). The influence of this single instance may be attributed to its inclusion in a film of this patient made by Sperry and Gazzaniga, but its general validity, and the interpretation of the patient's response, "What a funny machine you have there, Dr. Sperry" (Ornstein, 1972, p. 60, although accounts differ), in a situation in which interpersonal variables in the laboratory must play a part (compare experiments in perceptual defence), must be in question.

Secondly there is the denial of actions carried out by the left hand: that it cannot be used to feel or to act, feels "numb", or that "[I] don't get the message from that hand" (Sperry, 1968a, p. 726; also Sperry, 1968b, 1973; Galin, 1974). This again is a single report, repeated, from one patient.

Thirdly there is the evidence from the chimaeric figures (for example, Sperry, 1973) that patients are not aware of the apparent discrepancy between the two lateral portions of the stimulus. Zangwill (1974) in particular places considerable stress on this evidence. However, in a recent investigation of normal subjects (Milner and Dunne, 1977) with similar chimaeric faces, when the central join was hidden by a narrow

[1]Significantly inserting that she "looked uncomfortable and confused".

vertical strip, seven out of twelve subjects did not realize that the stimulus was anomalous, implying perhaps that consciousness can be equally divided in normal subjects, but at least that this cannot be crucial evidence for an abnormal duplication of consciousness, with non-awareness of right hemisphere stimulation, in split brain patients.

Finally, there is the evidence (Johnson and Gazzaniga, 1969; Gazzaniga, 1972) that the effects of reward in a learning task can remain isolated and separate in the split brain, and that each hemisphere may assign different response probabilities to the same stimulus.

Despite the paucity of this evidence, Gazzaniga (1972, p. 317) is prepared to conclude that "the private experiences of the right hemisphere go on outside the awareness of the left"; Sperry (1973, p. 212) that "each hemisphere has its own inner visual world, cut off from the conscious awareness of the other" and Globus (1976, p. 280) that "there is general agreement that an individual with a severed corpus callosum has *two* minds which are not acquainted with each other". This seems no more sensible than to say we see two visual worlds, which are distinct, because we see through two eyes. It certainly goes beyond the available evidence.

4.6 Are there qualitative changes in the thinking of commissurotomy patients?

The most intriguing reports, but again hardly supported by empirical evidence, concern qualitative differences in the cognition of the disconnected hemispheres, leading to subtle general changes in behaviour. Sperry (1968a, p. 727) has given his "impression . . . that their intellect is nevertheless handicapped in ways that are probably not revealed in the ordinary tests", and Zangwill (1974, p. 273) finds it "difficult to avoid the impression that there has been some subtle change in the *quality* of the subject's consciousness". This has been partly formalized by Kinsbourne (1974) in line with his view of the corpus callosum as a "regulator" of attention and the interplay of the two processing modes which can be associated with the two hemispheres. The split brain person is seen therefore as "handicapped in his ability to select strategies" and "at the mercy of uncontrollable surges of hemispheric preponderance" (p. 288). In particular Kinsbourne believes the deficit to be most acute when fast fine lateral shifts of attention are required (Kinsbourne, 1975). It is interesting in this context that Dimond (1976) in a vigilance paradigm showed that the performance of the disconnected left hemisphere was characterized by "gaps" and "the 'black holes' of consciousness", illustrating a failure in the mechanisms maintaining the continuity of mental actions.

Other qualitative differences in the performance of the two hemispheres have been discussed by Sperry (1973, 1974). The evidence is contained in reports by Kumar (1971) that efficiency of category attainment in blind tactual sorting of either blocks or meaningful forms differed between the hemispheres, infering differences in high-level cognitive performance; and by Zaidel and Sperry (1973) that different strategies were adopted by the two hemispheres when each alone solved a modified Raven's Progressive Matrices task, although this is not supported by firm empirical evidence.

The absence of dreams in some split brain patients has been reported and discussed (Bogen, 1969; Ornstein, 1977) although the best conducted study (Greenwood et al., 1977) does report dreams for the single complete commissurotomy subject, and Bogen and Bogen argue for a loss in creativity following commissurotomy (1969) although again without the support of direct evidence. It should also be recalled that there appears to be no demonstration of any difference in the nature or extent of emotional responsiveness of the hemispheres (Gazzaniga, 1967; Lishman, 1971). The evidence for qualitative differences in cognitive strategies, or in supervision of cognitive performance at the highest level, seems not to be present, at least in commissurotomy patients.

While strictly outside the scope of this chapter, it is worth noting that comparable evidence from hemispherectomy patients (for reviews and discussion see Austin et al., 1974; Zangwill, 1976), especially in the rare case of adult left hemispherectomy, and from the effects of the Wada test using intracarotid sodium amytal administration (Rosadini and Rossi, 1967; Gazzaniga, 1972; Galin, 1974) suggest no disturbances of consciousness, no differences in the emotional behaviour of the two hemispheres, nor absolute differences between the hemispheres in high-level abilities, speech apart. This evidence, however, is not without its own peculiar difficulties for interpretation.

5 The current position

It now seems appropriate to review current models of consciousness following commissurotomy in the light of present evidence, some key features of which have been reviewed above.

The discussions of Galin (1974) and Galin and Ornstein (1975) draw the most extreme conclusions about the division of consciousness and the different qualities of consciousness associated with the two hemispheres. There is no doubt that their model goes far beyond the available evidence, but in that their intention is to be speculative, this is perhaps allowable. Nevertheless, it must be said that the trend of the evidence as it accumulates is not towards such an extreme position.

Eccles (1976, 1977; Popper and Eccles, 1977) in viewing conscious experience as an unique property of the left hemisphere, alone mediating will, has come under persuasive criticism (Zangwill, 1974; Savage, 1976). Eccles (1977) has responded to this by admitting that he may have made "too radical an inference" (p. 218, and see Fig. 6–17) and that the minor hemisphere in normals may have some liaison with the self-conscious mind, but has not altered his overall conclusions in any other way. It should, however, be recognized that his summary of the deficits shown by split brain patients is occasionally inaccurate (for instance, with respect to right hemisphere language and cross-transfer) and not supported by the general evidence. It is certainly too extreme to conclude that all the "goings on in the right hemisphere . . . are unknown to the speaking subject" (1977, p. 213), or "all of the actions programmed from the right cerebral hemisphere . . . are not recognized by the conscious subject as being instituted by him" (1976, p. 118; and see Popper and Eccles, 1977, p. 316). However, if we allow that Eccles is using the term "consciousness" interchangeably with "conscious awareness", and that he insists that evidence for this must be derived through speech, then surely the conclusion must be that we cannot *know* about the conscious awareness of the right hemisphere. Eccles appears to accept this, and yet if we are to be "agnostic" (p. 281) about it, given that all other writers agree that the behaviour generated by the right hemisphere is characteristically human and compatible with conscious awareness, it seems unreasonable to conclude that "originally the self had a brain with two hemispheres, but now it has only one" (p. 213), or that "the minor hemisphere is always *per se* an unconscious part of the brain and that linkage through the corpus callosum is necessary for it to receive from and give information to the conscious self" (p. 218). It is further misleading to state (Popper and Eccles, 1977, p. 329) that the "conscious (commissurotomized) subject has voluntary control of the right forearm and hand, but not of the left". Eccles cannot remain "agnostic" about the possibility of conscious experience in the separated right hemisphere, and yet re-assert that a "fundamental difference" exists between the hemispheres is that one is in liaison with and controlled by the self-conscious mind, and another which is not so controlled.

Sperry (1974) and Gazzaniga (1972) may be considered together because they adopt very similar positions, that there may be a duplication of conscious experience. While maintaining that the separate hemispheres are each capable of mediating conscious experience independently and concurrently, neither wishes to conclude that this happens under normal conditions. The disconnected hemispheres are seen to "function independently in most conscious mental activities", each "has its own chain of private memories", and each has "a separate 'mind of its own'" (Sperry, 1974, p. 7). While abilities are credited to the right hemisphere, it is still "carried along much as a passive, silent passenger" (p. 11). Gazzaniga accepts the presence of some central "metaorganizing system", and Sperry, particularly in recent papers, has stressed the unifying factors present in most normal situations. "It is easy to underemphasize the many components of behaviour that remain unified" (p. 10). Further, Sperry acknowledges the existence of lower structures that assist in mediating conscious unity, but that it is not possible at present to distinguish between this factor and the factor of bilateral duplication of abilities. In view of the evidence it seems too extreme to describe the split brain deficit as a "profound left-right separation in conscious awareness" (p. 18) without emphasizing the very limited conditions under which such a statement could be considered to apply.

The remaining models, which adopt the broadest definitions of consciousness are Kinsbourne (1974), Trevarthen (1974a, b) and Zangwill (1974, 1976). Kinsbourne equates consciousness with attention and concludes that the unity and continuity of consciousness is unchanged, while its content is more variable as a result of the lack of integration between the left and right hemispheric systems. This is a novel approach, but it is not clear how the corpus callosum can alone perform as a "regulator", and if there are systems which continue to preserve the continuity and content of consciousness, why these should not continue, in most situations, to regulate consciousness also.

Zangwill, also, while adopting a position rather closer to Sperry, maintains the notion of a unified person, but that this masks a genuine duality of consciousness in which the right hemisphere proceeds like an "automatic writer" (1974, p. 275). Zangwill is willing to concede that rare dissociated experiences of the right hemisphere are the "product of special experimental conditions" (p. 276) and that separate conscious states may result under appropriate conditions of lateralized input, but not to conclude that the phenomena reported in split brain patients might generally be attributed to such special conditions.

Trevarthen also invokes an hierarchical system involving midbrain circuits and concludes that "complete surgical duplication of consciousness in man (is) an impossibility" (1974a, p. 257). Nevertheless, in discussing the separate strategies and differences of functions of the hemispheres he does not make clear whether these are entirely dependent on particular experimental testing situations, or whether they in some degree apply to more general split brain behaviour.

Sperry himself has employed the image of a Y to characterize the mind of the split brain patient (1976). Each limb, a hemisphere, contains representation of both sides of the body, although with unequal power, each holding an anatomical substrate for a unified self and bound into intact brain stem mechanisms. I think this might be extended by a further analogy. The split brain is like a table, the top of which has been divided by cutting across its width. We would still regard this as a single table for all general purposes. The special experimental situation in which patients are placed can be represented by an upright screen inserted into the groove, and behavioural response by an observer carefully placed so that he only sees the table top to one side of the screen. This observer can only accurately report objects on that side of the screen, but can gain some information about objects placed on the other side by sensing vibrations, or by lifting the table to assess the weight of objects placed upon it, transmitted through the body of the table. Unrestricted, what the observer will sensibly do is shift his position so that he can see as much as possible on both sides of the screen. Some of the strategies employed for "cross-cuing", or for that matter the strategies which commissurotomy patients must develop to cope with everyday tasks, must be similar to this manoeuver. Even if we allow for hemispheric specialization, have one side of the table surfaced with plastic laminate, and the other with green baize, we still have a single table, and one which will still support hot dishes on both sides, even if, providing we are not burning our fingers, we will choose to place them on the plastic laminate. In no sense, other than a very restricted one, can we consider that by dividing the top of the table we have produced two tables. It is just a rather unusual table, with some special properties, but bound to one physical location, and with much the same function as previously.

The confusion between "consciousness" and "conscious awareness", especially as expressed in spoken reports and introspections, has led writers to rely excessively on high-level *cognitive* functions to draw inferences about broader conscious awareness. Further, a concern to relate brain structure to function has led to an excessive emphasis on structural conceptions of consciousness (including my analogy of the table). If we accept some version of the emergence view, and especially if it may be a dynamic emergence, then the form of consciousness will likewise be adaptive and flexible in response to cognitive, affective, attentional, physiological and other variables. This dynamic mutability will respond to the split brain condition, certainly producing occasional anomalous states, but not necessarily changed in any way in its fundamental characteristics. Without criticizing in general the inspired and rightly influential work on cognitive function which has come from the split brain studies, the very special experimental conditions employed have revealed only a limited anomaly (for which the evidence is not as powerful or unambiguous as we are sometimes led to believe) which is peculiar to these highly artificial and restricted conditions which inhibit all the normal mechanisms and strategies which individuals employ in response to their environment. The important finding for consciousness, which the dramatic nature of split brain cognitive deficits has tended to mask, is the continuing normal and human behaviour of the patients, and the almost total absence of verbal reports of objective behaviour which would support any fundamental change in either their level of consciousness or conscious awareness.

In conclusion, the studies of commissurotomy patients with specific reference to consciousness have not provided evidence of the importance often attributed to it. This evidence is less than unanimous, derived in a very selective way from a subgroup of a small number of patients, and attended by difficulties for interpretation which are often ignored. The brain operation results in a state which can, under certain highly artificial conditions, be shown to produce difficulties in dealing with a very restricted range of tasks. Within these conditions, there may be a special duality of cognitive processes, but this cannot be extended to a duality of consciousness. Split brain patients continue to be regarded, in general behaviour, as single actors with a single mind whose behaviour, verbal and non-verbal, continues to be unified and identifiably human. It is unsound to draw the dramatic conclusions which have been drawn about these patients, and certainly unsafe to amend our conception of consciousness in normal intact subjects from what we know about the split brain.

References

Akelaitis, A. J. (1944). Study of gnosis, praxis and language following section of corpus callosum and anterior commissure. *Journal of Neurosurgery*, **1**, 94–102.

Austin, G., Hayward, W. and Rouhe, S. (1974). A note on the problem of conscious man and cerebral disconnection by hemispherectomy. *In* "Hemispheric Disconnection and Cerebral Function" (Eds M. Kinsbourne and W. L. Smith), pp. 95–114. C. C. Thomas, Springfield, Illinois.

Bell, G. A. (1975). The double brain and mind brain relationship. *Journal of Behavioural Science*, **2**, 161–167.

Benson, D. F. (1976). Alexia. *In* "Aspects of Reading Acquisition" (Ed. J. T. Guthrie), pp. 7–36. Johns Hopkins University Press, Baltimore and London.

Bindra, D. (1970). The problem of subjective experience: puzzlement on reading R. W. Sperry's "A modified concept of consciousness". *Psychological Review*, **77**, 581–584.

Bogen, J. E. (1969). The other side of the brain, II: An appositional mind. *Bulletin of the Los Angeles Neurological Societies*, **34**, 135–162.

Bogen, J. E. (1976). Linguistic performance in the short-term following cerebral commissurotomy. *In* "Studies in Neurolinguistics" (Eds H. Whitaker and H. A. Whitaker), vol. 2, pp. 193–224. Academic Press, New York and London.

Bogen, J. E. and Bogen, G. M. (1969). The other side of the brain. III: The corpus callosum and creativity. *Bulletin of the Los Angeles Neurological Societies*, **34**, 191–220.

Bogen, J. E. and Vogel, P. J. (1962). Cerebral commissurotomy in man: Preliminary case report. *Bulletin of the Los Angeles Neurological Societies*, **27**, 169–172.

Brown, J. W. (1976). Consciousness and pathology of language. *In* "Neuropsychology of Language" (Ed. R. W. Rieber), pp. 67–93. Plenum Press, New York.

Burt, C. (1969). Brain and consciousness. *Bulletin of the British Psychological Society*, **22**, 29–36.

Critchley, M. (1972). Interhemispheric partnership and interhemispheric rivalry. *In* "Scientific Foundations of Neurology" (Eds M. Critchley, J. L. O'Leary and B. Jennett), pp. 216–221. Heinemann, London.

Dimond, S. J. (1972). "The Double Brain". Churchill–Livingstone, Edinburgh.

Dimond, S. J. (1976). Depletion of attentional capacity after total commissurotomy in man. *Brain*, **99**, 347–356.

Eccles, J. (1965). "The Brain and the Unity of Conscious Experience". Cambridge University Press, Cambridge.

Eccles, J. C. (1970). "Facing Reality". Springer–Verlag, Basel and New York.

Eccles, J. C. (1974). Cerebral activity and consciousness. *In* "Studies in the Philosophy of Biology: Reduction and Related Problems" (Eds F. J. Ayala and T. Dobzhansky), pp. 87–107. University of California Press. Berkeley, California.

Eccles, J. C. (1976). Brain and free will. *In* "Consciousness and the Brain: A Scientific and Philosophic Enquiry" (Eds G. G. Globus, G. Maxwell and I. Savodnik), pp. 101–121. Plenum Press, New York.

Eccles, J. C. (1977). "The Understanding of the Brain". Second edition. McGraw-Hill, New York.

Ettlinger, G. (1972). Brain bisection: Some unsolved problems. *In* "Cerebral Interhemispheric Relations" (Eds J. Cernácek and F. Podivinsky), pp. 369–377. Slovak Academy of Sciences, Bratislava.

Ettlinger, G. and Blakemore, C. B. (1969). The behavioural effects of commissural section. *In* "Contributions to Clinical Neuropsychology" (Ed. A. L. Benton), pp. 30–72, Aldine Publishing Company, Chicago.

Franco, L. (1977). Hemispheric interaction in the processing of concurrent tasks in commissurotomy subjects. *Neuropsychologia*, **15**, 707–710.

Galin, D. (1974). Implications for psychiatry of left and right cerebral specialization. *Archives of General Psychiatry*, **31**, 572–583.

Galin, D. and Ornstein, R. E. (1975). Hemispheric specialization and the duality of consciousness. *In* "Human Behaviour and Brain Function" (Ed. H. J. Widroe), pp. 3–23. C. C. Thomas, Springfield, Illinois.

Gazzaniga, M. S. (1967). The split-brain in man. *Scientific American*, **217**, 24–29.

Gazzaniga, M. S. (1970). "The Bisected Brain". Appleton–Century–Crofts, New York.

Gazzaniga, M. S. (1972). One brain—two minds. *American Scientist*, **60**, 311–317.

Gazzaniga, M. S. and Hillyard, S. A. (1971). Language and speech capacity of the right hemisphere. *Neuropsychologia*, **9**, 273–280.

Gazzaniga, M. S. and Sperry, R. W. (1967). Language after section of the cerebral commissures. *Brain*, **90**, 131–148.

Gazzaniga, M. S., Bogen, J. E., and Sperry, R. W. (1962). Some functional effects of sectioning the corpus callosum in man. *Proceedings of the National Academy of Science of the USA*, **48**, 1765–1769.

Gazzaniga, M. S., Bogen, J. E. and Sperry, R. W. (1965). Observations on visual perception after disconnection of the cerebral hemispheres in man. *Brain*, **88**, 221–236.

Gazzaniga, M. S., Risse, G. L., Springer, S. P., Clark, E. and Wilson, D. H. (1975). Psychologic and neurologic consequences of partial and complete commissurotomy. *Neurology (Minneapolis)*, **25**, 10–15.

Geschwind, N. (1964). Alexia and colour-naming disturbance. *In* "Functions of the Corpus Callosum" (Ed. G. Ettlinger), pp. 101–103. Churchill, London.

Geschwind, N. (1965). Disconnexion syndromes in animals and man. I, II. *Brain*, **88**, 585–644.

Globus, G. G. (1976). Mind, structure and contradiction. *In* "Consciousness and the Brain: A Scientific and Philosophic Enquiry" (Eds G. G. Globus, G. Maxwell and I. Savodnik), pp. 271–293. Plenum Press, New York.

Goldstein, M. N. and Joynt, R. J. (1969). Long term follow-up of a callosal-sectioned patient. *Archives of Neurology*, **20**, 96–102.

Goleman, D. (1977). Split brain psychology: Fad of the year. *Psychology Today*, **11**, 89–90, 149, 151.

Gott, P. S., Rossiter, V. S., Galbraith, G. C. and Saul, R. E. (1975). Visual evoked response in commissurotomy patients. *In* "Cerebral Localization" (Eds K. J. Zulch, O. Creutzfeldt, and G. C. Galbraith), pp. 144–149. Springer-Verlag, Berlin.

Gott, P. S., Rossiter, V. S., Galbraith, G. C. and Saul, R. E. (1977). Visual evoked response correlates of cerebral specialization after human commissurotomy. *Biological Psychology*, **5**, 245–255.

Greenwood, P., Wilson, D. H. and Gazzaniga, M. S. (1977). Dream report following commissurotomy. *Cortex*, **13**, 311–316.

Johnson, J. D. and Gazzaniga, M. S. (1969). Cortical–cortical pathways involved in reinforcement. *Nature*, **223**, 71.

Kinsbourne, M. (1974). Mechanisms of hemispheric interaction in man; Cerebral control and mental evolution. *In* "Hemispheric Disconnection and Cerebral Function" (Eds M. Kinsbourne and W. L. Smith), pp. 260–289. C. C. Thomas, Springfield, Illinois.

Kinsbourne, M. (1975). The mechanism of hemispheric control of the lateral gradient of attention. *In* "Attention and Performance V" (Eds P. M. A. Rabbitt and S. Dornic), pp. 81–97. Academic Press, London.

Kumar, S. (1971). Lateralization of concept formation in human cerebral hemispheres. *Biological Annual Reports, California Institute of Technology*, No. 136, 118.

Ledoux, J. E., Risse, G. L., Springer, S. P., Wilson, D. H. and Gazzaniga, M. S. (1977). Cognition and commissurotomy. *Brain*, **100**, 87–104.

Levy, J. and Trevarthen, C. (1976). Metacontrol of hemispheric function in human split brain patients. *Journal of Experimental Psychology: Human Perception and Performance*, **2**, 299–312.

Levy, J. and Trevarthen, C. (1977). Perceptual, semantic and phonetic aspects of elementary language processes in split-brain patients. *Brain*, **100**, 105–118.

Levy, J., Nebes, R. D. and Sperry, R. W. (1971). Expressive language in the surgically separated minor hemisphere. *Cortex*, **7**, 49–58.

Lishman, W. A. (1971). Emotion, consciousness and will after brain-bisection in man. *Cortex*, **7**, 181–192.

Milner, A. D. and Dunne, J. J. (1977). Lateralized perception of bilateral chimaeric faces by normal subjects. *Nature*, **268**, 175–176.

Nagel, T. (1971). Brain bisection and the unity of consciousness. *Synthese*, **22**, 396–413.

Nebes, R. D. (1974). Hemispheric specialization in commissurotomized man. *Psychological Bulletin*, **81**, 1–14.

Ornstein, R. E. (1972). "The Psychology of Consciousness". W. H. Freeman, San Francisco.

Ornstein, R. E. (1977). "The Psychology of Consciousness". Second edition. Harcourt, Brace Jovanovich, New York.

Oxbury, J. M. (1975). The right hemisphere and hemispheric disconnection. *In* "Recent Advances in Clinical Neurology" (Ed. W. B. Matthews), No. 1, pp. 1–22. Churchill-Livingstone, Edinburgh.

Parfit, D. (1971). Personal identity. *Philosophical Review*, **80**, 3–27.

Popper, K. R. and Eccles, J. C. (1977). "The Self and its Brain". Springer-Verlag, Berlin.

Preilowski, B. (1975). Bilateral motor interaction: perceptual-motor performance of partial and complete "split-brain" patients. *In* "Cerebral Localization" (Eds K. J. Zulch, O. Creutzfeldt and G. C. Galbraith), pp. 115–132. Springer–Verlag, Berlin.

Puccetti, R. (1973). Multiple identity. *The Personalist*, **54**, 203–215.

Rosadini, G. and Rossi, G. F. (1967). On the suggested cerebral dominance for consciousness. *Brain*, **90**, 101–112.

Savage, C. W. (1976). An old ghost in a new body. *In* "Consciousness and the Brain: A Scientific and Philosophic Enquiry" (Eds G. G. Globus, G. Maxwell, and I. Savodnik), pp. 125–153. Plenum Press, New York.'

Searleman, A. (1977). A review of right hemisphere linguistic capabilities. *Psychological Bulletin*, **84**, 503–528.

Sperry, R. W. (1964a). "Problems Outstanding in the Evolution of Brain Function". American Museum of Natural History, New York.

Sperry, R. W. (1964b). The great cerebral commissure. *Scientific American*, **210**, 42–52.

Sperry, R. W. (1966). Brain bisection and mechanisms of consciousness. *In* "Brain and Conscious Experience" (Ed. J. C. Eccles), pp. 298–313. Springer–Verlag, Berlin.

Sperry, R. W. (1968a). Hemisphere deconnection and unity in conscious awareness. *American Psychologist*, **23**, 723–733.

Sperry, R. W. (1968b). Mental unity following surgical disconnection of the cerebral hemispheres. *The Harvey Lectures*, **62**, 293–323.

Sperry, R. W. (1969) A modified concept of consciousness. *Psychological Review*, **76**, 532–536.

Sperry, R. W. (1970). An objective approach to subjective experience: further explanation of a hypothesis. *Psychological Review*, **77**, 585–590.

Sperry, R. W. (1973). Lateral specialization of cerebral function in the surgically separated hemispheres. *In* "The Psychophysiology of Thinking" (Eds F. J. McGuigan and R. A. Schoonover), pp. 209–229. Academic Press, New York and London.

Sperry, R. W. (1974). Lateral specialization in the surgically separated hemispheres. *In* "The Neurosciences. Third Study Program" (Eds F. O. Schmitt and F. G. Worden), pp. 5–19. M.I.T. Press, Cambridge, Massachusetts.

Sperry, R. W. (1976). Mental phenomena as causal determinants in brain function. *In* "Consciousness and the Brain: A Scientific and Philosophic Enquiry" (Eds G. G. Globus, G. Maxwell and I. Savodnik), pp. 163–177. Plenum Press, New York.

Sperry, R. W., Gazzaniga, M. S. and Bogen, J. E. (1969). Interhemispheric relationships: the neocortical commissures; syndromes of hemisphere disconnection. *In* "Handbook of Clinical Neurology" (Eds P. K. Vinkin and G. W. Bruyn), vol. IV, pp. 273–290. New Holland, Amsterdam.

Sugishita, M. (1978). Mental association in the minor hemisphere of a commissurotomy patient. *Neuropsychologia*, **16**, 229–232.

Trevarthen, C. (1972). Brain bisymmetry and the role of the corpus callosum in behaviour and conscious experience. *In* "Cerebral Interhemispheric Relations" (Eds J. Cernácek and F. Podivinsky), pp. 321–333. Slovak Academy of Sciences, Bratislava.

Trevarthen, C. (1974a). Analysis of cerebral activities that generate and regulate consciousness in commissurotomy patients. *In* "Hemisphere Function in the Human Brain" (Eds S. J. Dimond and J. G. Beaumont), pp. 235–263. Elek Science, London.

Trevarthen, C. (1974b). Functional relations of disconnected hemispheres with the brain stem and with each other: monkey and man. *In* "Hemispheric Disconnection and Cerebral Function" (Eds M. Kinsbourne and W. L. Smith), pp. 187–207. C. C. Thomas, Springfield, Illinois.

Trevarthen, C. and Sperry, R. W. (1973). Perceptual unity of the ambient visual field in human commissurotomy patients. *Brain*, **96**, 547–570.

Van Wagenen, W. P. and Herren, R. Y. (1940). Surgical division of commisural pathways in the corpus collosum. *Archives of Neurology and Psychiatry*, **44**, 740–759.

Wimsatt, W. C. (1976). Reductionism, levels of organization and the mind–body problem. *In* "Consciousness and the Brain: A Scientific and Philosophic Enquiry" (Eds G. G. Globus, G. Maxwell and I. Savodnik), pp. 205–267. Plenum Press, New York.

Zaidel, D. and Sperry, R. W. (1973). Performance on the Raven's Coloured Progressive Matrices Test by subjects with cerebral commissurotomy. *Cortex*, **9**, 34–39.

Zaidel, D. and Sperry, R. W. (1977). Some long term motor effects of cerebral commissurotomy in man. *Neuropsychologia*, **15**, 193–204.

Zaidel, E. (1973). Linguistic competance and related functions in the right hemisphere of Man following cerebral commissurotomy and hemispherectomy. Unpublished doctoral dissertation. California Institute of Technology.

Zaidel, E. (1976). Auditory vocabulary of the right hemisphere following brain bisection or hemidecortication. *Cortex*, **12**, 191–211.

Zaidel, E. (1977). Unilateral auditory language comprehension on the Token Test following cerebral commissurotomy and hemispherectomy. *Neuropsychologia*, **15**, 1–18.

Zangwill, O. L. (1974). Consciousness and the cerebral hemispheres. *In* "Hemisphere Function in the Human Brain" (Eds S. J. Dimond and J. G. Beaumont), pp. 264–278, Eleck Science, London.

Zangwill, O. L. (1976). Thought and the brain. *British Journal of Psychology*, **67**, 301–314.

8 Consciousness, Emotion, and the Right Hemisphere[1]

R. G. LEY and M. P. BRYDEN

Department of Psychology
University of Waterloo

In his very provocative book on the origins of human consciousness, Jaynes (1976) has argued that consciousness is characterized by *narratization, spatialization,* and *metaphor.* In consciousness, we *excerpt* particular items from our memory or from the sensory input, so that our consciousness of an object or thing is necessarily incomplete. William James, whose work is a fecund area for the researcher of consciousness, articulates his "excerption process" in the following: "Mind is at every stage a theater of simultaneous possibilities. Consciousness consists in the comparison of these with each other, the selection of some, and the suppression of the rest by the reinforcing and inhibiting agency of attention" (James, 1890, p. 288). The conscious process which James describes may be enacted at a variety of different levels. In particular, language has a very important role to play in ordinary consciousness. Much of our daily consciousness consists of a verbal description of events past, present, or imagined. The attribution of causes to our behaviour or of the explanation of our experiences is what James means by narratization.

In a somewhat similar vein, Ornstein (1972) has argued that ordinary consciousness is active, selective, and analytic, and that it depends on linear time, a concept of causality, and language. While Ornstein proposes that other modes of consciousness are possible, the emphasis on language is obvious in what he describes as "ordinary" consciousness.

We have cited these few examples to indicate that language, description, and narratization are necessary for what we normally consider to be human consciousness. In saying this, we are not attempting to arrive

[1]This work was supported by a Fellowship from the Canada Council to R.G.L. and a grant from the National Research Council of Canada to M.P.B.

at a definition of consciousness.[2] Nor are we attempting to deny that one can be consciously aware of visual or auditory images (Paivio, 1971). Rather, we are only emphasizing the important verbal component in much of consciousness.

Stimulated by Sperry's (1974) work on callosal section in man, there has been a recent surge of interest in the differential functions of the two cerebral hemispheres (cf. Corballis and Beale, 1976; Harnad *et al.*, 1977). The current general view describes the left hemisphere as being specialized for language and for analytic and sequential functions, while the right hemisphere is more concerned with spatial abilities, and is more holistic and integrative in its functions. Given this description, one may legitimately ask how the two hemispheres interact in normal consciousness. For example, Gazzaniga *et al.* (1977) have argued that the mechanisms of consciousness are split and doubled following brain bisection—affirming Wigan's (1844) conception of "two minds". Beaumont (this volume) however, has persuasively argued for discarding the notion that callosal section leads to a divided consciousness.

As mentioned above, the narrative properties of ordinary consciousness make it heavily dependent upon language. Thus, it follows that many of the processes that we normally ascribe to ordinary consciousness are carried out in the left hemisphere. However, despite this possible "hegemony" of the left hemisphere for ordinary consciousness, the right hemisphere is not merely a "weak sister". Ornstein (1972) and Bogen (1969) in particular, have emphasized the right hemisphere's role in a variety of states of consciousness. Recent experimental work (Ley and Bryden, 1979) has also suggested that the right hemisphere has a greater involvement than the left in emotional experience. Izard (1977), in his authoritative text on emotion, postulates that ordinary consciousness is characterized by some degree of emotion. He argues further that affects or "affective–cognitive orientations" are in fact the "most fundamental contents of consciousness and. . . provide it with its essential organization and directiveness" (p. 139). Gray (1973) also has proposed a theory of mind which maintains that all cognition is coded by emotion. Given this convergence, an issue of interest is the role of the right hemisphere in ordinary consciousness. While there may very well be important spatial components to ordinary consciousness (cf. Paivio, 1971; Jaynes, 1976), the present chapter is concerned with the role of the right hemisphere in emotion.

Current experimental evidence (e.g. Ley and Bryden, 1979) suggests that the right hemisphere is superior to the left in the identification of

[2]When discussing "personal consciousness" James said: "Its meaning we know so long as no one asks us to define it, but to give an adequate account of it is the most difficult of philosophic tasks. . ." (James, 1890, p. 225.)

emotional stimuli. One of the consequences of this is that emotional information from the right hemisphere may serve to modulate the narrative description given by the left hemisphere and thus alter the emotional content of what comes into conscious awareness.

1 Differential recognition of emotional stimuli

The work of Kimura (1961, 1967) has suggested a variety of experimental procedures for the investigation of hemispheric asymmetries in the normal intact human brain. Most common among these are the dichotic listening procedure, in which competing messages are delivered to the two ears simultaneously (Kimura, 1961), and visual half-field presentation techniques, whereby briefly exposed visual stimuli are presented to one visual field or the other. With both procedures, stimuli presented to the right side of the body have more ready access to the left hemisphere, and vice versa. Thus, it has generally been found that there is a right ear or right visual field superiority for the identification of language-related material, and a left ear or left visual field superiority for musical or spatial information (Kimura, 1966, 1967). More recently, these procedures have been applied to the identification of emotional material, with results indicating a right hemispheric superiority for the identification of emotion.

2 Auditory studies

Three dichotic listening studies have been carried out which suggest an asymmetry of emotions. In a study by King and Kimura (1971) where non-verbal human sounds such as laughing and coughing were identified from dichotic presentation, a slight left ear (right hemisphere) advantage (LEA) was found. Haggard and Parkinson (1971) asked subjects to identify both the emotional intonation and the verbal content of sentences which were dichotically presented, in competition with a continuous babble. The stimuli consisted of six sentences read in four emotional tones: anger, boredom, happiness and distress. They also found a slight LEA in identifying the emotional tone of the sentence. Carmon and Nachshon (1973) also investigated hemispheric asymmetry for perception of non-verbal sounds: the cries, shrieks and laughter of a child, of an adult female and of an adult male. They minimized verbal mediation in the task by having subjects manually indicate their responses. As in former experiments a slight but significant LEA was demonstrated.

Safer and Leventhal (1977) had subjects listen to taped monaural passages that had three levels of content (positive, negative and neutral). These passages were then read in three tones of voice (positive, negative and neutral). The positive tone passages were read in an exuberant, happy "almost laughing" fashion. The negative tone passages were read in a strong "angry sounding" voice and the neutral passages were read in an objective manner. Subjects listened on either the left or right ear.

Although this experiment did not involve a dichotic listening procedure, the results again indicate the right hemisphere's superiority for processing emotional information. They found that although subjects were not instructed about which cue to use, 29 of 36 subjects who listened on the left ear used the tone of voice cues to rate the passages. Conversely, 21 of 36 subjects who listened on the right ear used the content cues to evaluate the passages.

Although these studies provide the strongest support for differential hemispheric specialization for emotions, emotional sounds in particular, methodological and artifactual problems create some difficulties in interpretation. Often the experimental designs of dichotic studies do not permit a separate assessment of the contribution of stimulus and task factors. It often remains unclear whether the observed ear superiority occurs with a specific task, such as the verbal or linguistic decoding of the material. In the above studies one cannot unequivocally determine whether the LEA is due to the emotional aspects of the sound, as hypothesized, or to other sound features such as intonation, rhythm or simply to the lack of encoded auditory features in the stimuli.

Numerous subject factors also obfuscate the results of dichotic studies (Kinsbourne, 1976; Bryden, 1978). The individual's attention, motivation, task strategy or personal style, energy level, familiarity with the stimuli and even such traditional experimental bugaboos as the subject's intelligence or socioeconomic standing may be involved in producing the observed asymmetries, rather than the stimulus characteristics *per se*. For example, the person's mental set or task strategy (verbal versus non-verbal) may bias attention and result in a more efficient processing of material from that side. In Haggard and Parkinson's study (1971) for instance, the recognition errors for sentences and emotions may be due to such attentional factors and not differential hemispheric efficiency in processing. The correlation between accuracy in sentences and emotions suggests the possibility of fluctuations in the subject's attention or in the audibility of the sentences.

3 Tachistoscopic studies of emotionality

Although clinical and dichotic evidence suggests that the hemispheres differ in processing emotional information, a more reliable procedure is needed to examine this possibility in normal adults. Tachistoscopic paradigms afford this opportunity, although such investigations of brain laterality and emotions are few in number (Suberi and McKeever, 1977; Ley and Bryden, 1979). Despite the infrequency of these studies, the procedure avoids many of the methodological pitfalls inherent in dichotic listening paradigms. Most significantly, visual, as opposed to auditory, presentation of stimuli permits a greater number and variety of different emotions to be employed. Dichotic listening procedures have severe limitations on the extensity and intensity of emotions that can be recognized by the subject.

The strongest support for a right hemispheric specialization for emotionally laden stimuli is offered by Ley and Bryden in studies investigating visual field differences in recognizing emotional expressions. Their first study employed cartoon line drawings of human faces with definite emotional expressions. Three characters, a man, woman and child, were drawn with three different emotional expressions: positive, negative and neutral. The faces were unilaterally presented. Subjects were asked to compare the target face to a second, centrally presented face and decide whether the emotional expressions of the two faces were the same or different. A significant LVF (right hemisphere) superiority for emotional expression recognition was found. However, because something about the face must obviously be recognized in order to evaluate the expression, it is possible that this effect is some manifestation of the well established right hemispheric superiority for face recognition (Geffen *et al.*, 1971; Bradshaw *et al.*, 1972; Hilliard, 1973).

Ley and Bryden (1979) extended the range of characters and emotions in a second study, designed to dissociate emotional expression recognition effects from face recognition effects. The stimuli were five adult male cartoon characters, each with five emotional expressions: extremely positive, mildly positive, neutral, mildly negative and extremely negative. The procedure was identical to the first study except that subjects were required to judge the similarity or difference of *both* the emotional expressions and the characters. Significant LVF superiorities for both emotional expressions and face recognition were found, thereby replicating the results of their first study, as well as corroborating the finding of a left visual field effect for face recognition. Subsequent correlational and covariance analyses demonstrated the independence of these effects. Recognition of emotional expressions was not a manifestation or component of face recognition. In fact, primary analyses indicated that the character (or face recognition) effect was smaller than the emotion effect.

Suberi and McKeever (1977) have also demonstrated a LVF superiority for emotional expression recognition. Subjects were asked to study and memorize either emotional or non-emotional faces and to judge whether a unilaterally presented face was a target face or not. Although their original hypothesis that the correspondence of emotional and neutral expressions to target and non-target stimuli would augment LVF superiorities was not born out, regrouping of the data and subsequent analyses demonstrated results similar to Ley and Bryden. They found faster manual reaction times for emotional stimuli presented in the left, as opposed to the right visual field. Additionally, LVF superiorities were larger for subjects memorizing emotional as opposed to non-emotional faces. Suberi and McKeever's procedure does not permit a separate assessment of emotional expression and face recognition effects.

In Ley and Bryden's study, these two separate processes were apparent. However, it would seem that the constituents and/or mechanisms of these effects differ. Their demonstration of a LVF superiority for emotional expression recognition may actually have two somewhat different and slightly contrary underlying processes. The most obvious effect was the pronounced visual field difference for the extreme emotional expressions. From this it might follow that the greater the degree of expressed affect, the greater the left visual field superiority. The validity of this assumption is bolstered by the fact that this relationship appears in other experiments: for example, Carmon and Nachshon's (1973) dichotic listening data showed the greatest left ear advantage for crying as a stimulus. Again, this difference was about one-third larger than that observed with the other two stimulus sounds: laughing and shrieking.

The preceding studies suggest that the right hemisphere is more sensitive than the left to emotional stimuli. If this incoming information is incorporated into the stream of consciousness, it would suggest that the emotional tone of our normal consciousness will be more heavily influenced by right hemisphere activity. Thus, minor cues of emotional tone may be picked up by the right hemisphere and transmitted to the left, where they can be manifested in a verbal expression of emotion, and integrated into one's ongoing thought processes. One expectation from such a notion would be that perceptual defence effects would be more readily observed in the left visual field than in the right. Such a finding has, in fact, been reported (Jean and Reynolds, 1974).

4 Research on hysterical neuroses

If the right hemisphere is more sensitive to emotional stimuli, represen-tation of emotion should be more fully developed in the right hemis-phere than the left. Thus, instances of extreme emotional upset should lead to symptoms that would reveal this greater involvement of the right hemisphere. One such example of intense emotional upset occurs in the conversion type of hysterical neurosis. Here, symptoms of some physi-cal illness appear in the absence of underlying organic pathology. The manifest physical symptoms serve a defensive or symbolic function enabling the individual to paradoxically avoid and/or express fantasy in stressful experiences. Conversion hysteria may be manifest in sensory symptoms, as with hysterical blindness or deafness; in motor symp-toms, as with hysterical paralyses of the extremities; or in visceral symptoms, as with nausea or respiratory difficulties. Within these general categories symptomatic expressions of hysteria are many and varied, and may "mimic" most physical diseases. Engel (1970) for instance, has generated a list of 119 conversion symptoms.

Discernable physical representations of neurotic disorders might reveal hemispheric differences in emotionality. To sustain the hypothesis one would expect differences in the sidedness of hysterical symptoms.

Although never systematically reported or tallied, sidedness diff-erences in hysterical symptoms have been clinically observed for some time. Pierre Janet, in his 1901 book the "Mental State of Hystericals", refers to the French psychiatrist Briquet, who had observed fifty years earlier (1859) that three left-sided hysterical anaesthesias existed for every right-sided one. Dubois, writing in 1909 on the "Psychiatric Treatment of Nervous Disorders", noted that "it is striking to see so many hysterics avow that they feel less on the left side" (p. 179). Ferenczi stated that "in general, the hemianaesthetic stigma occurs more frequently on the left than on the right" (1926, p. 115), explaining that the left half of the body is more accessible to unconscious impulses. Likewise, Fenichel (1945) in his classic psychoanalytic work on neurosis reports that hysterical motor disturbances appear more frequently on the left. Remembering the contralateral innervation of the human body, such left-sided complaints clearly implicate the right hemisphere. Although the clinical observations are compelling, their infrequency in the clinical lore and the lack of quantitative support render them anecdotal as evidence. However, three recent studies have now documented the prevalence of left-sided hysterical symptoms. Employing exemplary diagnostic and subject selection criteria, Galin *et al.* (1977) and Stern (1977) found a 2:1 ratio of left- to right-sided symptoms among hospitalized, hysterical, psychiatric patients. Similar results are reported by Ley (1978) following a retrospective, archival examination of case studies in the hysteria literature between 1881 and 1945. Twice as many left-sided as right-sided symptoms existed in the case descriptions of hysterical conversion reactions.

One could argue that the prevalence of left-side disturbances reflects the greater number of right-handed people in the population, who have achieved some sort of "neurotic compromise" and not totally debilitated themselves by rendering their dominant hands useless. This argument is attenuated somewhat as Ley's data show that only a moderate number of patients had discrete hand or arm paralyses (19 right hand/arm disorders versus 13 left hand/arm disorders: 16%:11%). Many of the disorders were hemiplegias, anesthesias, foot and leg paralyses, limb twitches or tremors, muscular tics or sensory disturbances. Lateral preference has minimal significance for many of these complaints. Hysterical symptoms such as these would present equal difficulties for the individual, regardless of the side of the location. Even accepting an argument for preserving preferred hand functions, one would still expect a more even distribution of non-hand or arm conversion symptoms. The present data contradict such a prediction. In fact, of the 16 left-handed hysterics in Galin *et al.*'s (1977) and Stern's (1977) samples, 15 (94%) presented left-sided symptoms. However, it is a powerful refutation to a preservation of dominant hand function explanation for the frequency of left-sided symptoms.

An even stronger case can be made if one looks at the distribution of symptoms not involving the hand or arm. Of 68 such cases in Ley's study, 47 (69%) show left-sided symptoms. This figure substantially exceeds the left-side incidence shown for arm and hand symptoms (59%). The very fact that left-sided conversion reactions are more frequent when they do not involve the hand or arm is contrary to a preferred hand preservation hypothesis.

The results of these three studies offer robust confirmatory evidence for historical observations of a prevalence of left-sided hysterical symptoms. Additionally, these findings support a hypothesis of right hemispheric involvement in emotional experience and are consistent with experimental demonstrations of a predominant right hemisphere mediation of emotional stimuli (Ley and Bryden, 1979).

5 Research on anosognosia

Hysterical conversion symptoms would seem to have an exclusively psychological aetiology or basis, despite the reality of overt physical disability. Anosognosia is a somewhat different disorder which, like hysteria, seems to have a strong psychological component and specific sidedness differences in its manifestations, but unlike hysteria has a definite neurological basis. Also referred to as *la belle indifference*, anosognosia is a condition in which a patient with a severe neurological deficit, such as a hemiplegia or a hemianopia, is unaware of, indifferent to or simply denies the disability. An interesting aspect to this disorder is that sidedness differences and corresponding emotional reactions are apparent. Critchley (1953), for instance, concludes that anosognosics frequently display a disability of the non-dominant (right) hemisphere. It also seems that anosognosia for hemiplegia is found with left but not right paralysis. Similarly, Flor-Henry (1976) avers that it is an old neurological observation that euphoric indifference is a feature of cerebral tumours of the non-dominant hemisphere. According to Hecaen's (1962) statistics, the right hemisphere is affected seven times more frequently than the left.

The term "anosognosia" was introduced by Babinski in 1914 and specifically referred to unawareness or denial of *left hemiplegia*. Since then it has also been used to denote unawareness of other aspects of disease or disability. Although cases of denial of right-sided hemiplegia and disabilities are reported, Weinstein and Kahn (1955) state that there is a preponderance of cases of left hemiplegia and agree that anosognosia is much more common following right hemisphere damage than left.

Prior to Weinstein and Kahn's work, reports of anosognosia are methodologically suspect. Anosognosia seemed to be a "kinetic" concept, largely determined by the types of cases seen and the methods of examination used. The literature consists almost exclusively of case studies without control observations. For instance, those studies which describe associations between anosognosia and certain lesions have not observed individuals with similar lesions who do not show denial of illness. The technology of the time also did not permit exact statements about the diffuseness, specificity or severity of the brain disturbance. Damage was frequently ascertained at autopsy, which further weakens the association between right hemisphere disturbance and anosognosia. Furthermore, premorbid abilities were seldom evaluated.

Weinstein and Kahn's account of anosognosics is a more comprehensive and rigorous study. Longitudinal in nature, interviews were made over long periods of time to evaluate the patients' behaviour and brain function, at different stages in the disease process. A control group of patients with similar brain lesions was compared with the anosognosics. Premorbid personality and abilities were evaluated, psychological testing was carried out and attempts were made to experimentally produce anosognia. With these safeguards, Weinstein and Kahn's association of right hemisphere disturbance, denial of illness for left-sided disabilities and euphoric reactions is an acceptable one. Similarly, the relative absence of denial of illness for right-sided disabilities and left hemisphere damage is equally respectable.

Critchley (1953) explains the indifference as a denial reaction, as an extension of the brain lesion and unilateral spatial neglect. Weinstein and Kahn, however, attribute anosognosia to psycho-social factors. They believe that the indifference or denial is a motivated emotional reaction to the deficit, which may be due to the individual's personality, social attitudes toward illness, or to symbolic aspects of the disability. They view the euphoria as another type of the denial reaction, the variety depending on the premorbid personality. Weinstein and Kahn are careful to point out the potential danger of strictly attributing the emotional display to the intact hemisphere, in this case, the right. It is possible that the greater incidence of denial after right-sided lesions is due to language disturbance masking this symptom with left hemispheric injury.

For the purposes of the present chapter, however, the important point to be taken from the anosognosia literature is that one sees a characteristic emotional reaction to a right hemisphere lesion. Striking parallels exist between the emotional presentation of the anosognosic and the hysteric. In both cases, one of the most characteristic behavioural features is *la belle indifference* (Nemiah, 1976). Despite seemingly disabling disturbances in function (physically based in the anosognosic and psychologically based in the hysteric), each individual may be completely unaware of, blandly indifferent to, or spontaneously not mention their disability. In his discussion of anosognosia, Galin (1974) concludes that denial of illness is a way for the intact left hemisphere to cope with a right hemisphere lesion. Although this may be an over-interpretation of the available data, the essence of the statement is consistent with the current argument for hemispheric differences in emotional reactions.

6 The expression of emotion following unilateral disturbance

To this point, cases have been considered in which the intact brain has been found to be more sensitive to emotional stimuli coming to the right hemisphere, and has manifested a greater involvement of the right hemisphere in hysteria. Anosognosia, which shares many affective and physical features with hysteria, has also been evaluated. The critical difference between the two disorders is that anosognosia is directly linked with right hemisphere dysfunction, while a functional right hemispheric mediation of hysteria has been hypothesized.

However, as Weinstein and Kahn's caveat suggests, activation or disturbance of the brain leads to responses from both hemispheres. Thus, unilateral brain damage leads to an expression of emotion that is characteristic of the hemisphere damaged. Similar results can be found with unilateral electroconvulsive shock (ECT) or sodium amytal injection.

7 Research on patients with unilateral brain lesions

In the thirties clinicians were reporting observations on the emotional behaviour of patients affected by dominant (left) and non-dominant (right) hemisphere lesions. Alford (1933) published observations of 55 cases of right hemiplegia, 27 of whom had "definite and permanent confusion of consciousness and emotional instability". The emotional behaviour which was exhibited has a striking pattern. Goldstein (1939) also noted the consistency of the emotional reaction among left brain damaged patients and described it as a catastrophic reaction. The catastrophic reaction type of emotional instability was commonly associated with right, but not left hemiplegia, in other words with lesions of the dominant left hemisphere. This reaction contrasts with indifference reactions of subjects affected with left hemiplegia and lesions of the minor hemisphere cited earlier.

Gainotti (1969) compared the incidence of the indifference reaction and the catastrophic reaction in 150 cases of unilateral cerebral lesions. The incidence of catastrophic reactions was 62% with left hemisphere lesions and only 10% with right lesions. Conversely the incidence of the indifference reaction was 38% with right lesions and 11% with left lesions. Catastrophic reactions included such emotional behaviours as crying, swearing, anxiety reactions, and aggressive behaviour. Indifferent reactions included explicit indifference, jokes, anosognosia and minimization. In a subsequent study of 160 lateralized cerebrovascular lesions, 80 to the left and 80 to the right, Gainotti (1972) again found a strong association between catastrophic reactions and dominant lesions, as well as between indifferent reactions and non-dominant lesions.

Hecaen (1962) also found a greater incidence of catastrophic reactions in left-sided lesions (55 of 206 cases, 25.7%) when compared to right-sided lesions (20 of 154 cases, 12.9%). Indifference to failure was found in only 16.5% (34 of 206 cases) of left-sided lesions, versus 33% (51 of 154 cases) of right-sided lesions. These differences were significant for both the catastrophic and indifference reactions.

Clinical observations of patients with unilateral brain lesions thus suggest that there may be a particular emotional reaction which is characteristic of injury to each hemisphere. Other evidence also points to this asymmetry of affective response.

8 Research on patients following sodium amobarbytal injections

Terzian (1964) demonstrated that intracarotid injection of sodium amytal produces different behaviour in patients when injected on the dominant as opposed to the non-dominant side. The procedure is typically used prior to surgery to assess hemispheric dominance for language. The injection serves to "block" the ipsilateral hemisphere and to produce a contralateral hemiplegia; and if the dominant speech side is anesthetized, a complete aphasia results. The symptoms are transitory, lasting a few minutes. However, Terzian observed that severe emotional reactions often accompanied the dissipation of the anesthetic and that specific emotional responses typified siddedness of the injections. Dominant hemisphere injections were distinguished from non-dominant injections by the appearance of characteristic emotional reactions of the depressive–catastrophic type. Injections of the contralateral, non-dominant side evidenced emotional reactions of the opposite type, euphoric–maniacal.

Terzian's descriptions of the emotional reactions are markedly similar to the behaviours Gainotti described as characterizing left and right brain damaged patients. Terzian (1964) writes of the dominant injection:

> . . .amytal on the left side provokes. . . a catastrophic reaction. . . the patient especially when spoken to despairs and expresses a sense of guilt, of nothingness, of indignity and worries about his own future or that of his relatives, without referring to the language disturbances overcome and to the hemiplegia just resolved and ignored.

About the non-dominant injection he writes:

> [It] produces a complete opposite emotional reaction, an euphoric reaction that in some cases may reach the intensity of a maniacal reaction. The patient appears without apprehension, smiles and laughs and both with mimicry and words expresses considerable liveliness and sense of well being,   p. 235.

One is struck by the similarity of Terzian's description of the behaviour of patients with non-dominant injections, and Gainotti's right hemisphere lesion patients, Critchley's description of anosognosics and Weinstein and Kahn's description of patients who deny their illness.

Terzian's extraordinary findings have been confirmed by Rossi and Rosadini (1967) and Alema *et al.* (1961). Alema *et al.* (1961) reported that the lateralized affective response was seen most clearly in patients without brain damage. These reactions were not seen in patients with bilateral or diffuse damage, suggesting that an intact hemisphere is important for their generation.

Given the characteristic euphoric–depressive reactions following amobarbital injections, further information on a possible asymmetry could result from studying the emotional reactions of pathologically depressed patients receiving similar amobarbital injections. An intriguing, but methodologically weak study (Hommes and Panhuysen, 1971) reports on such effects. The authors found that in depressed patients both dominant and non-dominant injections induced euphoric responses. This contrasts with previous findings in normals that dominant injections produced depression. The authors suggest that further depressed reactions may not have been noticed in the already depressed patients.

Hommes and Panhuysen also found a negative correlation between speech laterality and depression (pre-amobarbital); the more depressed the patient the lesser was the left dominance for speech. In other words the more depressed the patient the more he appeared to show the organization of the non-dominant hemisphere in both hemispheres. The authors speculate that the process which leads to depression also reduces the level of functional dominance of the left hemisphere.

Although this study corroborates the hypothesis of hemispheric differences in organization of functional aspects subserving emotions, its credibility is minimal. There was tremendous individual variability amongst the 11 patients in response to unilateral injections, and many of the authors' conclusions are based on the emotional reactions of one patient. Artifacts because of failure to account for pre-morbid personality also intrude. Pre-test mood scores were based on a psychiatrist's rating of depth of depression while post-test mood scores were based on two psychologists' ratings of verbatim protocols of the patients' utterances to attendants during the ninety minutes following the injections. Finally the dominance measure on which the authors' most substantive statements are founded is rather crude. Differential durations, following left and right side injection, in which the patient was unable to perform all the tests correctly (i.e. calculation, counting backwards, etc.), was taken as the left dysphasia dominance measure, This measure also does not account for the task difficulty, patient's motivation, pre-test abilities, etc.

Generally, it is difficult to interpret the meaning of the different affective reactions following unilateral amobarbital injection. For example, depression may be seen and expected as a natural reaction to loss of speech or it may simply be that a mute patient seems more depressed. Similarly, the recurrence of speech following aphasia may be scored as mood increase, because of greater verbal productivity. Other interpretative difficulties arise because the affective reaction occurs as the anaesthetic is wearing off, rather than at the peak of the disability. The size of the dosage also fails to produce EEG changes or obvious neurological signs which could afford cleaner interpretations. Most importantly, one cannot definitely conclude whether the observed affect is resulting from the injected side in response to the drug, or from the non-injected side as the cerebral balance shifts. However, given the replication of results and the similarity between the amobarbital emotional asymmetry and the asymmetry following unilateral lesions, further support is provided for the argument that the two hemispheres are differentially involved in emotional reactions.

9 Research on patients receiving ECT

Additional support for the possible asymmetry of affective responses comes from research on the efficacy of electroconvulsive shock treatment. If there are hemispheric differences in emotionality, one would expect that therapeutic outcomes might differ depending on which side receives the shock. Evidence exists which confirms such a prediction.

It now seems to be accepted that unilateral non-dominant ECT is as effective in remitting pathological depressions as the more traditional bilateral ECT. Recent studies (Halliday et al., 1968; Cronin et al., 1970; Cohen et al., 1973) and extensive reviews of the literature (Galin, 1974; Robertson and Inglis, 1977) suggest that unilateral non-dominant induction is therapeutically more effective than bilateral, and also minimizes the memory disturbances and confusion following conventional bilateral ECT.

Substantial differences in treatment techniques, patient population, and means of evaluation make it difficult to compare most studies on ECT. In addition, most ECT research compares right-sided ECT to bitemporal ECT, rather than the therapeutic effect of shock to the left and right hemisphere.

Galin (1974) cites six studies (McAndrew et al., 1967; Halliday et al., 1968; Sutherland et al., 1969; Costello et al., 1970; Cronin et al., 1970; Fleminger et al., 1970) which compare treatment outcome of left, right and bilateral ECT. Of these, three of the studies (Halliday et al., 1968;

Cronin *et al.*, 1970; Fleminger *et al.*, 1970) restricted the population to depressives, and had adequate blind followups. Two of these three studies (Halliday *et al.*, 1968, Cronin *et al.*, 1970) found ECT to the left hemisphere to be significantly less effective in remitting depression than ECT to the right. The Fleminger study found no difference.

The remaining three studies also found no difference in treatment approaches but are not comparable because of different methodology. Their treatment evaluations lacked followup and were based entirely on the number of treatments given and the patient's self report while in the hospital. These studies also included mixed diagnostic groups of schizophrenics and depressives. A further problem which may diminish the therapeutic differences between left and right ECT is that unilateral seizures often eventuate in bilateral fits, which would make the effects more similar to bilateral ECT. Conversely, what are often referred to as bilateral seizures may have begun unilaterally and spread to the other hemisphere and therefore may not be symmetrical in their effects.

Despite methodological problems which make certain comparisons dangerous the research literature on ECT and therapeutic outcome does reveal differences in the response of each hemisphere to ECT. Assuming bilateral and unilateral non-dominant seizures to be equivalent, as the clinical research seems to indicate, unilateral seizures to the dominant hemisphere are therapeutically less effective. From this one might assume that the non-dominant hemisphere is critically involved in depression. Research on unilateral ECT suggests the differential response of each hemisphere to treatment. The results of Halliday's and Cronin's studies also corroborate the observations of depressive reactions following unilateral lesions of the left hemisphere and sodium amobarbital injections of the left hemisphere, and the report that pathologically depressed patients show less than usual left dominance.

Deglin (1973) also offers some intriguing evidence as to the effects of ECT on emotion recognition and expression. He reports that patients were less able to recognize vocal intonations representing emotional expressions of happiness, sadness or anger following shock administered to the right hemisphere. Deglin also noticed changes in the patient's affective expressions following left and right unilateral shock. After ECT to the right hemisphere the patient's vocalization, posture, gestures and facial expression was like that of a happy person. Following left hemisphere shock, however, the patient's physical and affective presentation was distressed and fearful.

10 Cortical representation of emotion

One striking difference exists between the clinical studies and the experiments on normal subjects that have been reviewed. In the studies of unilateral brain damage and sodium amytal injection, characteristic emotional responses follow the invasion of either hemisphere. Patients show indifference reactions and euphoria following damage to or suppression of the right hemisphere, while they manifest catastrophic responses and depression when the left hemisphere is involved. Such findings would suggest that both hemispheres are involved, albeit in different ways, in emotional reactivity. In contrast, the studies of normal subjects consistently indicate that it is the right hemisphere that is specifically involved in the recognition of emotional state, and that the left hemisphere plays a relatively minor role in this process.

Two interpretations of these data are possible. First, it may well be that lateralization is different for the perceptual and expressive components of emotion. It this were the case, it might be that the right hemisphere is primarily involved in the *recognition/reception* of emotional stimuli, while each hemisphere has a role in the *expression* of affect. Tucker (1978) has articulated an interactional model of hemispheric functioning which is somewhat similar to the above. He suggests that the right hemisphere is responsible for the initial elaboration of emotional arousal, while the left hemisphere has a regulatory function, through the inhibition and control of the right hemisphere's emotional responsivity. Alternatively, the change in emotional expression following left hemisphere invasion may be only a by-product of the language disturbances that also exist. By this argument, it is the right hemisphere that is primarily involved in emotional processes, while left hemispheric effects are essentially artifactual.

If one takes this latter view, two further questions arise. Why is there a right hemispheric superiority for evaluating emotional stimuli? Why does this effect seem greatest for extremely negative stimuli?

There are a number of characteristics of right hemispheric functioning that might uniquely bias it for processing affective information. Semmes (1968) proposed that elementary functions are focally represented in the left hemisphere and more diffusely represented in the right hemisphere. Such an organization would confer a left hemispheric advantage for integrating similar units, and a consequent superiority for abilities involving fine motor control, such as speech and manual skills. The diffuse organization of the right hemisphere would lead to a proficiency in integrating dissimilar units and a consequent specialization for "behaviors requiring multimodal coordination, such as the various spatial abilities" (p. 11).

The right hemispheric organization suggested by Semmes would be especially well suited for processing emotional stimuli. If one believes that recognizing an emotion entails an integration of stimulus information from a variety of sources (both sensory and motor units) and across space and time, such a synthesis would most likely occur in the right hemisphere.

The right hemispheric superiority for synthesizing diverse units of information is closely allied to its oft described "holistic" or gestalt processing capacity (Levy, 1972; Ornstein, 1972; Safer and Leventhal, 1977). Ornstein describes this processing "style":

> If the left hemisphere is specialized for analysis, the right hemisphere. . .seems specialized for holistic mentation. It processes information more diffusely than does the left hemisphere, and its responsibilities demand a ready integration of many inputs at once. If the left hemisphere can be termed predominantly analytic and sequential in its operation, then the right hemisphere is more holistic and relational, and more simultaneous in its mode of operation. (p. 51)

Cross-cultural research on emotions has revealed that all facial expressions can be categorized into nine discriminable, universally recognizable patterns (Izard, 1971; Ekman and Friesen, 1971). Again the ability to recognize such gestalten can be attributed to the right hemispheric holistic processing capacity.

A third characteristic of emotional processing can possibly be associated with right hemispheric functioning. Tompkins (1962) and Safer and Leventhal (1977) have made the point that emotions are often accompanied by or associated with imagery. The right hemisphere is more involved than the left in processing or "generating" imagic material (Davidson and Schwartz, 1976). For example, in the Ley and Bryden studies, the cartoon face stimuli were perhaps too benign to evoke any imagery. However, it is easy to imagine that more lifelike stimuli such as screams, laughter, or gruesome faces, could result in the subjects' imaging. This is a factor which should be controlled in future research on laterality and emotions. Such a danger is exemplified in a paper by Schwartz *et al.* (1975).

These researchers recorded subjects' lateral eye movements (LEMS) to emotional or neutral questions and also varied the verbal and spatial dimensions of the questions. They found significantly greater left LEMS to emotional than non-emotional questions. Because of the contralateral asymmetry of the human body, it is presumed that this result represents a greater activation of the right hemisphere in processing emotional questions. Although this result provides further support for the main argument of this review, one cannot evaluate the

extent to which imaging accompanied affective processing (i.e. reflective answers to emotional questions).

In a similar study, Tucker *et al*. (1977) investigated the effects of the
subjects' emotional state on LEMS. They employed the same set of
verbal/spatial and emotional/non-emotional questions as Schwartz *et
al*. (1975). However, subjects were required to respond to questions
under stressful and non-stressful conditions. Tucker *et al*. replicated the
findings of Schwartz *et al*., namely, that significantly more left LEMS
accompanied emotional as opposed to non-emotional questions. More
importantly, they found a significant increase in left LEMS under the
stress condition, suggesting perhaps that stress, or emotional arousal,
increases the probability of right hemisphere activation.

In summary then, synthetic and integrative characteristics, a holistic
and gestalten nature and imagic associations are three features of
processing affective material that would differentially favour right
hemispheric mediation of the task. The characteristics of right
hemispheric function which uniquely predispose it for evaluating
emotional stimuli have also been described (Semmes, 1968; Levy, 1972;
Ornstein, 1972), thereby lending empirical support to the above
explanations.

More speculative explanations can be mustered for the right
hemispheric involvement in processing emotional information. Some
evidence suggests that physiologically the right hemisphere develops
more rapidly than the left hemisphere (Giannitripani, 1967) until about
18–24 months, when left hemispheric differentiation for language
begins (Lenneberg, 1967). Because of these cerebral maturational
differences, it is assumed that the right hemisphere has a possibly
greater involvement in learning during infancy. Much of the pre-
linguistic child's learning consists of visual spatial relations, patterns,
environmental sounds and rhythms. These are also the same functions
which are better established in the right hemisphere. It is perhaps then
not fanciful to speculate that emotional experiences of the infant,
sounds, pictures, images, and "feelings", which constitute much of an
infant's early learning experiences, are disproportionately stored and/
or processed by the right hemisphere during the formative stages of the
brain. In this regard, it is interesting to note that sad and happy facial
expressions are among the earliest to be discriminated by young
children (Ekman and Friesen, 1971).

Deikman (1971) has also formulated a model of consciousness that
incorporates the possibility of predominant right hemispheric coding
and storage of infantile experience. He has argued that two primary
modes of organization, an active mode and a receptive mode,
characterize consciousness. This dichotomy also corresponds with
hemispheric modes of functioning, so that the receptive mode is the

province of the right hemisphere, and the active mode is better suited to left hemispheric processes. Deikman believes that the receptive mode, which maximizes stimulation from the environment, evolves and functions preponderantly during infancy. As mentioned above, emotion communications prevail in the prelingual child's environmental interactions.

A hypothesis about differential storage of infantile or childhood emotional experiences might also explain the greater effects with extremely negative stimuli, as it is established that negative experiences are more salient and potent than positive ones (Kanouse and Hanson, 1971). These authors' review of the literature indicates that, generally, negative information has greater value than positive information in impression formation, risk taking, performance and situational attributions. It seems that people have a negative bias and disproportionately weigh negative characteristics and information. If we are more attuned to negative stimuli at a sociological and motivational level, it is not unreasonable to speculate that we are perhaps more attuned to a structural level.

Gazzaniga and his associates' case study of a split brain patient (P.S.) offers idiographic support for this assertion (Gazzaniga *et al.*, 1977; Ledoux *et al.*, 1977). Recent reviews have concluded that each hemisphere can, in a limited way, participate in those functions traditionally considered the "exclusive" domain of the other. For example, Searleman (1977) has stated that the right hemisphere does possess basic language skills. This capacity, however, has been difficult to access experimentally. The split brain patient (P.S.) had extensive bilateral linguistic representation, thereby creating a unique experience in nature. The patient's right hemisphere could comprehend nouns and verbs, and was able to perform verbal and pictorial commands, but had no expressive speech. Of the many dramatic results yielded by this research, one is particularly germane to this chapter. When words were unilaterally presented and rated on a Good/Bad scale, the right hemisphere ratings were consistently more negative than the left hemisphere. As the authors explain, "It is as if the right hemisphere was in a 'bad mood' relative to the left" (p.420). Beaumont's (this volume, p.189) and Kinsbourne's (1974) caveats concerning split brain research withstanding, this one case does further support the association between the right hemisphere and negativity that was emerging from the dichotic and tachistoscopic experiments reviewed earlier. Dimond and Farrington (1977) also found greater negative affective judgement with right hemisphere presentation of motion picture material. Also, when one interprets the depressive/catastrophic reaction following left brain lesions and left-sided amytal injections, it would seem to indicate that the right hemisphere is biased towards negative affect.

A possible problem with this argument is that negative stimuli are more "negative" than positive stimuli are "positive". For example, life outcomes are not symmetrical. The worst outcomes in life are more frequent and more distant from neutrality than the best. As Kanouse and Hanson (1971) deftly point out, "ultimate negatives such as death and lifelong suffering do not seem to be balanced by ultimate positives such as immortality and perpetual nirvana" (p.60). In this sense, one can see the evolutionary importance of heightened perception and consideration of negative stimuli and information. It is adaptive to value costs more highly than gains. Perhaps the evolution of the human brain has reflected this simple Darwinian observation on the human condition, and offers a partial explanation of why extremely negative stimuli were more salient in the above experiments. It may be that extreme emotional stimuli are more easily identifiable and as a result, more readily engage some emotional component in the right hemispheric processing system.

11 Conclusions and a crude model

In the preceding pages, we have emphasized the role of the right hemisphere in emotion, and the concurrent effect of the right hemisphere in providing an emotional overtone to ordinary conscious narratization. In doing so, however, we must not forget that disturbance of the left hemisphere also has an effect on emotional reactivity. While we have suggested that some of this effect is an artifact of the language disturbance associated with left hemispheric damage or disruption, the catastrophic or depressive response to left hemispheric invasion is so pervasive that it is difficult to dismiss. How then can a unitary model recognize both the special involvement of the right hemisphere in emotion and at the same time incorporate the bilateral effects of brain damage?

Let us consider first the normal brain. We have suggested that the right hemisphere is more sensitive to emotional information, and in particular to negative information. Such affective information, while not necessarily reaching a level of conscious awareness, can have an influence on normal consciousness by modulating the emotional tone of the narratization. Perhaps the sensitivity of the right hemisphere to negative emotional content is responsible for our tendency to remember the unpleasant events that have occurred in our lives.

If we accept this general view, then disruption of the activity of the right hemisphere leads to a euphoric response by disturbing or damaging that part of the brain that is most sensitive to negative affect. This reduced sensitivity to negative information produces an apparent euphoria.

In contrast, damage to the left hemisphere normally leads to some disturbance of normal language processes. Verbal processes thus become relatively more dependent upon the linguistic mechanisms of the right hemisphere (Searleman, 1977). This greater involvement of the right hemisphere in ongoing language processes implies that the emotional processes of the right hemisphere, and especially their negative components, are able to exert a greater influence on the process of narratization. Thus, left hemispheric damage leads to a more negative emotional content of current consciousness, and to the observation of depression.

This very crude model also provides a framework for thinking about a wide range of clinical behaviours and observations. For example, Flor-Henry (1976), having reviewed experimental and empirical evidence from studies of post-traumatic psychoses, temporal lobe epilepsy, power spectral EEG analysis, electrodermal responses, evoked potentials and cerebral blood flow studies, concludes that the schizophrenic syndrome and psychopathy are manifestations of neuronal disorganization in the dominant hemisphere, while affective disorders such as depression and mania reflect disorganization of the non-dominant, right hemisphere. He notes that the association between schizophrenia and the left hemisphere is more powerfully established than that of lateralization to the right hemisphere of the affective syndromes.

Horton (1976) has asserted that the incapacity for transitional relatedness, the ability to make external objects internally meaningful, is the "cornerstone" of clinical personality disorders. He believes that the locus of transitional relatedness is the right hemisphere and concludes that personality disorder is related to right hemispheric disturbance. Although this argument is contrary to Flor-Henry's association between psychopathy and the dominant left hemisphere, it may reflect differences in the clinical groups observed. Flor-Henry's study involved "primary and neurotic criminals" while Horton's conclusions seem primarily based on the observations of non-delinquent children. It is interesting that a lack of awareness of emotional disturbance is a primary feature of the personality disordered individual, just as it is in anosognosia, which is a result of right hemispheric parietal lobe dysfunction.

It is tempting to relate other evidence which also implies lateral asymmetries associated with emotional states or responses. For example, studies of pain threshold and tolerance, have produced evidence that the left extremities are more sensitive to pain than the right (Murray and Safferstone, 1970; Murray and Hagan, 1973), again implicating the right hemisphere. The fact that this result has been found with feet, as well as hands, would seem to provide more support for an interpretation involving bilateral asymmetry of the brain, rather than the previously accepted one involving hand calluses of the preferred side.

Further, more diverse studies on dreaming, biofeedback and alpha training, hypnotic susceptibility, meditation, altered states of consciousness and lateral gaze phenomena also differentially implicate the cerebral hemispheres (especially the right) and lead one to speculate on the emotional states accompanying these phenomena.

Hemispheric specialization for different cognitive modes now seems well documented, while hemispheric specialization for emotional modes has been largely ignored. The present review is a start at redressing this imbalance. In principle, there was no reason for not believing that the cerebral hemispheres could not be differentially specialized for emotions. In practice, there is now some evidence which suggests that this may be the case. The evidence possibly highlights the prescience of Wigan's (1844) assertion that each hemisphere may make different contributions to "the emotions, sentiments and faculties which we call in the aggregate — mind".

How does this information relate to the issue of consciousness? In effect, we have argued that normal consciousness is largely verbal and narrative, but that the contents of consciousness can be modified by emotional information from the right hemisphere. To a large extent, the present chapter accepts Underwood's (1979) dichotomy between conscious, attended material and unconscious, unattended material. We are adding to Underwood's argument by postulating that the emotional content of unattended material is often registered by the right hemisphere. This affect can then enter consciousness by transmission to the left hemisphere, and serves to modulate the emotional tone of ongoing conscious thought.

References

Alema, G., Rosadini, A. and Rossi, G. F. (1961). Psychic reactions associated with intracarotid amytal injection and relation to brain damage. *Exerpta Medica*, **37**, 154–155.

Alford, L. B. (1933). Localization of consciousness and emotion. *American Journal of Psychiatry*, **89**, 789–799.

Babinski, J. (1914). Contribution a l'etude des troubles mentaux dans l'hemisplegie cerebrale (anosognosie), *Revue Neurologie*, **27**, 845–847.

Bogen, J. E. (1969). The other side of the brain: An oppositional mind. *Bulletin of the Los Angeles Neurological Society*, **34**(3), 135–162.

Bradshaw, J., Geffen, G. and Nettleton, N. (1972). Our two brains. *New Scientist*, 628–631.

Briquet, P. (1859). "Traite Clinique et Therapeutic de l'Hysterie". J. B. Balliere, Paris.

Bryden, M. P. (1978). Strategy effects in the assessment of hemispheric asymmetry. *In* "Strategies of Information Processing" (Ed. G. Underwood). Academic Press, London and New York.

Carmon, A. and Nachshon, I. (1973). Ear asymmetry in perception of emotional non-verbal stimuli. *Acta Psychologica*, **37**, 351–357.

Cohen, B. D., Berent, S. and Silverman, A. J. (1973). Field dependence and lateralization of function in the human brain. *Archives of General Psychiatry*, **28**, 165–167.

Corballis, M. and Beale, I. (1976). "The Psychology of Left and Right". Lawrence Erlbaum, Hillsdale, New Jersey.

Costello, C. G., Belton, G. P. and Abra, J. C. (1970). The amnesic and therapeutic effects of bilateral and unilateral ECT. *British Journal of Psychiatry*, **116**, 69–78.

Critchley, M. (1953). "The Parietal Lobes". Edward Arnold, London.

Cronin, D., Bodley, P. and Potts, L. (1970). Unilateral and bilateral ECT: A study of memory disturbance and relief from depression. *Journal of Neurology, Neurosurgery, and Psychiatry*, **3**, 705–713.

Davidson, R., and Schwartz, G. (1976). Patterns of cerebral lateralization during cardiac biofeedback versus the self-regulation of emotion: Sex differences. *Psychophysiology*, **13**, 62–74.

Deglin, V. L. (1973). Clinical-experimental studies of unilateral electroconvulsive shock. *Journal of Neuropathology and Psychiatry*, **11**, 1609–1621.

Deikman, A. (1971). Bimodal consciousness. *Archives of General Psychiatry*, **45**, 481–489.

Dimond, S. J. and Farrington, L. (1977). Emotional response to films shown to the right or left hemisphere of the brain measured by heart rate. *Acta Psychologica*, **41**, 255–260.

Dubois, P. (1909) "The Psychic Treatment of Nervous Disorders". Funk & Wagnalls, New York.

Eckman, P. and Friesen, W. (1971). Constants across cultures in the face and emotion. *Journal of Personality and Social Psychology*, **17**, 124–129.

Engel, G. (1970). Conversion symptoms. *In* "Signs and Symptoms: Applied Pathologic Physiology and Clinical Interpretation" (Eds C. M. Macbryde, and R. S. Blacklow). Lippincott, Philadelphia.

Fenichel, O. (1945). "The Psychoanalytic Theory of Neurosis". Norton, New York.

Ferenczi, S. (1926). An attempted explanation of some hysterical stigmata. *In* "Further Contributions to the Theory and Technique of Psychoanalysis". Hogarth Press, London.

Fleminger, J. J., Del Horne, D. J. and Nair, N. P. (1970). Differential effect of unilateral and bilateral ECT. *American Journal of Psychiatry*, **127**, 430–436.

Flor-Henry, P. (1976). Lateralized temporal-limbic dysfunction and psychopathology. *Annals of the New York Academy of Sciences*, **280**, 777–795.

Gainotti, G. (1969). Reactions "catastrophiques" et manifestations c'indifference au cours des atteintes cerebrales. *Neuropsychologia*, **7**, 195–204.

Gainotti, G. (1972). Emotional behavior and hemispheric side of the lesion.
Cortex, **8**, 41–55.

Galin, D. (1974). Implications for psychiatry of left and right cerebral specialization. *Archives of General Psychiatry*, **31**, 572–583.

Galin, D., Diamond, R. and Braff, D. (1977). Lateralization of conversion symptoms: More frequent on the left. *American Journal of Psychiatry*,
134, no 5, 578–580.

Gazzaniga, M. S., Ledoux, J. E. and Wilson, D. H. (1977). Language, praxis,
and the right hemisphere: Clues to some mechanisms of consciousness.
Neurology, **27**, 1144–1147.

Geffen, G., Bradshaw, J. and Wallace, G. (1971). Interhemispheric effects on
reaction time to verbal and nonverbal visual stimuli. *Journal of Experimental
Psychology*, **87** (3), 415–422.

Giannitrapani, D. (1967). Developing concepts of lateralization of cerebral
functions. *Cortex*, **3**, 353–370.

Goldstein, K. (1939). "The Organism: A Holistic Approach to Biology
Derived from Pathological Data in Man". American Books, New York.

Gray, W. (1973). Emotional–Cognitive Structuring: A New Theory of Mind.
Forum for Correspondence and Contact, **5**, 1–6.

Haggard, M. P. and Parkinson, A. M. (1971). Stimulus and task factors as
determinants of ear advantages. *Quarterly Journal of Experimental Psychology*,
23, 168–177.

Halliday, A. M., Davison, K. and Brown, M. W. (1968). Comparison of
effects on depression and memory of bilateral ECT and unilateral ECT to
the dominant and nondominant hemisphere. *British Journal of Psychiatry*,
114, 997–1012.

Harnad, S., Doty, R. W., Goldstein, L., Jaynes, J. and Krauthamer, G.
(Eds) (1977). "Lateralization of the Nervous System". Academic Press,
New York and London.

Hecaen, H. (1962). Clinical symptomatology in right and left hemispheric
lesions. *In* "Interhemispheric Relations and Cerebral Dominance" (Ed. V.
B. Mountcastle). John Hopkins Press, Baltimore.

Hilliard, R. D. (1973). Hemispheric laterality effects on a facial recognition
task in normal subjects. *Cortex*, **9**, 246–258.

Hommes, O. R. and Panhuysen, L. H. (1971). Depression and cerebral
dominance. *Psychiatria, Neurologia, Neurochirurgia*, **74**, 259–270.

Horton, P. C. (1976). Personality disorder and parietal lobe dysfunction.
American Journal of Psychiatry, **133**, no 7, 782–785.

Izard, C. E. (1971). "The Face of Emotion". Appleton-Century-Crofts, New
York.

Izard, C. E. (1977). "Human Emotions". Plenum Press, New York.

James, W. (1890). "The Principles of Psychology". Holt. (Reprinted 1950:
Dover, New York.)

Janet, P. (1901). "The Mental State of Hystericals". Putnam's Sons, New
York.

Jaynes, J. (1976). "The Origins of Consciousness in the Breakdown of the Bicameral Mind". Houghton Mifflin, Boston.

Jean, P. and Reynolds, D. (1974). Perceptual defence as a function of repression-sensitization and hemispheric asymmetry. Paper presented at the meeting of the Canadian Psychological Association, Windsor, Ontario, June 1974.

Kanouse, D. and Hanson, R. (1971). Negativity in evaluations. *In* "Attribution" (Ed. E. Jones). General Learning Press, Morristown, New Jersey.

Kimura, D. (1961). Cerebral dominance and the perception of verbal stimuli. *Canadian Journal of Psychology*, **15**, 166–171.

Kimura, D. (1966). Dual fuctional asymmetry of the brain in visual perception. *Neuropsychologia*, **4**, 275–285.

Kimura, D. (1967). Functional asymmetry of the brain in dichotic listening. *Cortex*, **3**, 163–178.

King, F. L. and Kimura, D. (1971). Left ear superiority in dichotic perception of vocal nonverbal sounds. Research Bulletin 188, Department of Psychology, University of Western Ontario.

Kinsbourne, M. (1974). Lateral interactions in the brain: Cerebral control and mental evolution. *In* "Hemispheric Disconnection and Cerebral Function" (Eds M. Kinsbourne and W. L. Smith). Charles C. Thomas, Springfield, Illinois.

Kinsbourne, M. (1976). The neuropsychological analysis of cognitive deficit. *In* "Biological Foundation of Psychiatry" (Eds R. G. Grenell and S. Gabay). Raven Press, New York.

Ledoux, J. E., Wilson, D. H. and Gazzaniga, M. S. (1977). A divided mind: Observations on the conscious properties of the separated hemispheres. *Annals of Neurology*, **2**, 417–421.

Lenneberg, E. (1967). "Biological Foundations of Language". Wiley, New York.

Levy, J. (1972). Lateral specialization of the human brain: Behavioral manifestations and possible evolutionary basis. *In* "The Biology of Behavior" (Ed. J. A. Kiger). Oregon State University Press, Corvallis.

Ley, R. G. (1978). Asymmetry of hysterical conversion symptoms. Paper presented at the annual meeting of the Canadian Psychological Association, Ottawa, Ontario, June 1978.

Ley, R. G. and Bryden, M. P. (1979). Hemispheric differences in recognizing faces and emotions. *Brain and Language*, **7**, 127–138.

McAndrew, J., Berkey, B. and Mathews, C. (1967). Effects of dominant and nondominant unilateral ECT as compared to bilateral ECT. *American Journal of Psychiatry*, **124**, 483–490.

Murray, F. S. and Hagan, B. C. (1973). Pain threshold and tolerance of hands and feet. *Journal of Comparative and Physiological Psychology*, **84**(3), 639–643.

Murray, F. S. and Safferstone, J. F. (1970). Pain threshold and tolerance of right and left hands. *Journal of Comparative and Physiological Psychology*, **71**, 83–86.

Nemiah, J. C. (1976). Hysterical neurosis, conversion type. *In* "Comprehensive Textbook of Psychiatry/II" (Eds A. Freedman, H. Kaplan and B. Sadock), vol. 1. Williams & Wilkins, Baltimore.

Ornstein, R. (1972). "The Psychology of Consciousness". W. H. Freeman & Co., San Francisco.

Paivio, A. (1971). "Imagery and Verbal Processes". Holt, Rhinehart & Winston, New York.

Robertson, A. D. and Inglis, J. (1977). The effects of electroconvulsive therapy on human learning and memory. *Canadian Psychological Review*, **18**, 285–307.

Rossi, G. F. and Rosadini, G. R. (1967). Experimental analysis of cerebral dominance in man. *In* "Brain Mechanisms Underlying Speech and Language" (Ed. F. L. Darley), pp. 167–184, Grune & Stratton, New York.

Safer, M. and Leventhal, H. (1977). Ear differences in evaluating emotional tones of voice and verbal content. *Journal of Experimental Psychology: Human Perception and Performance*, **3**(1), 75–82.

Schwartz, G., Davidson, R. and Maer, F. (1975). Right hemispheric lateralization for emotion in the human brain: interactions with cognition. *Science*, **190**(17), 286–288.

Searleman, A. (1977). A review of right hemisphere linguistic capabilities. *Psychological Bulletin*, **84**, 503–528.

Semmes, J. (1968). Hemispheric specialization, a possible clue to mechanism. *Neuropsychologia*, **6**, 11–26.

Sperry, R. W. (1974). Lateral specialization in the surgically separated hemispheres. *In* 'The Neurosciences: Third Study Program" (Eds F. O. Schmitt and F. G. Worden). MIT Press, Cambridge, Massachusetts.

Stern, D. (1977). Handedness and the lateral distribution of conversion reactions. *Journal of Nervous and Mental Disease*, **164**, 122–128.

Suberi, M. and McKeever, W. F. (1977). Differential right hemispheric memory storage of emotional and non-emotional faces. *Neuropsychologia*, **15**, 757–768.

Sutherland, E. M., Oliver, J. and Knight, D. (1969). EEG memory and confusion in dominant and non-dominant and bitemporal ECT. *British Journal of Psychiatry*, **115**, 1059–1064.

Terzian H. (1964). Behavioral and EEG effects of intracarotid sodium amytal injections. *Acta Neurochirugia*, **12**, 230–240.

Tompkins, S. S. (1962). "Affect, Imagery, Consciousness". vol. 1. Springer, New York.

Tucker, D. M. (1978). Dialectical processes in emotion and hemispheric function. Paper presented to the International Neuropsychological Society, February 1978.

Tucker, D. M., Roth, R. S., Arneson, B. A. and Buckingham, V. (1977). Right hemisphere activation during stress. *Neuropsychologia*, **15**, 697–700.

Underwood, G. (1979). Memory systems and conscious processes. *In* "Aspects of Consciousness" (Eds G. Underwood and R. Stevens), vol. 1. Academic Press, London and New York.

Weinstein, E. A. and Kahn, R. L. (1955). "Denial of Illness: Symbolic and Physiological Aspects". Charles C. Thomas, Springfield, Illinois.

Wigan, A. L. (1844). "The Duality of the Mind". Longman, London.

Subject Index